Shree Krishna
and
Bhagvat Gita on Man's Dharma

Shree Krishna
and
Bhagvat Gita on Man's Dharma

A commentary on the Bhagavat Gita from the view point of Science and Secularism

SHANABHAI KHUSALBHAI PATEL
B.Sc., LL.B.

G. RANGARAJAN
Ph.D

SHARADA

Sharada Publishing House
Delhi-110 035
2003

First Published : 2003

ISBN : 81-85616-45-0

Published by :
B.L. Bansal
SHARADA PUBLISHING HOUSE
(Publishers on India's Past & Present)
40, Anand Nagar, Inderlok,
Delhi - 110035. Tel. : 23657538

Laser Typesetting by :
Elegant Printographics
319, IIIrd Floor, R.G. Complex,
Sector-14, Rohini, Delhi-85

Printed at :
Santosh Offset, Delhi-110 035

Dedicated

to

Shree Shirdi Sai Baba

&

Sri Muktaanand Swami

HINDU MANDIR

(201) 478-9886

The Hindu Community Center

1 Gaston Ave
Post Box # 116
Garfield, N. J. 07026

The version of Bhagvad-Gita written by Mr. S.K. Patel and G. Rangarajan is a collection of deeply sympathetic emotions, intelligent thoughts and literary expressions of undoubted integrity.

The scripture will provide enough courage and consolation to a modern man in order to face any circumstances of the contemporary time.

This book will enlighten any person with its messages, which originate in true India, ancient India and eternal India.

With Blessings,

Dinesh Shastri
Priest
Hindu Community Centre,
Garfield and Kearny

Contents

Note : Normal effect of the sermons heard once or twice.

Introduction

I

We are making a beginning to study, understand and grasp the Dharma practiced by Shree Krishna and taught by him in Gita. Its importance in every aspect of life from birth to salvation has never been doubted by any Hindu. Sire of the universe himself has sung this divine song. It is a treatise teaching you the ways and means to reach the pinnacle of perfection. To attempt to write even few words about such a master scripture for a worldly man like me is almost an ego toppling into arrogance and yet as a devout devotee I am unable to refrain from offering one more lily with love in addition to many already offered by Saints, Sages and Savants.

Age of Gita: Gita forms Chapters XXIII to XL of Bhishma Parva of Mahaabhaarat. The experts have tentatively fixed the time of Mahaabhaarat to be some where about 3300 BC. So Gita must be of equal age if not earlier.

Officially Gita is an Upanishad. Its validity is equal to Upanishads and Brahma Sutra: Three are collectively called Prasthaan Trayi.

Aim and object of Krishna and Gita

In Gita Krishna speaks 620 Shlokas: Arjuna 75 and Dhritraashtra only one. Till the end of 11th couplet of 2nd chapter Gita poses the questions of life one faces while living and the rest is an answer how and in what spirit and frame of mind an individual and society should act and react with each other in consonance with the constitution of beings, Ishvar, universe and their source and how to reach the source. Krishna and Gita favor full freedom of action for the individual in all matters of living life as is consistent with the constitution of his Being and with the peace, prosperity and stability of society.

Treating it to be a purely religious treatise and equating religion with Dharma, youths and house holders dismiss it for study and its practice after retirement. Is it really meant for an old age? Can an old age allow any one to do any thing with zest and zeal of a youth till the onset of an old age? The difficulties and disabilities of the old age are too well known needing no enumeration. So it cannot be for an old age only: Incarnate Bhagawaan Krishna who bustled with activity would not advise Gita for the fag end of life when body functions with pain and sufferings. No, It is not. Reasons are many. Most important is that it is a treatise teaching you to dance on the world stage for lives till emancipation with Joy and laughter. Look at the setting where it is preached. It is sung on a battlefield where two giant armies of India opposed each other in an all out war: where a Paandu army almost half in strength of the opponent but united was engaged in a Dharmic war against a mighty but hired army of wicked and Adhaarmic Kauravas. It should be specially noted that the principal warriors of both the sides were related to one other by blood or marriage and it was also certain that war will not come to end till all warriors of both the sides were killed. It is a dialogue where one of the principal fighter refuses to fight just when the armies were ready to use the wielded weapons: Gita is dialogue between Vishnu- Incarnate Krishna and Arjuna refusing to fight a just war after inviting it and for which he was yearning till then. It is an advice to the ruling and warrior class to fight the criminals of the society even if they be dear and near relatives or persons worthy of respect. It is also an advice to take what is rightfully yours by all means allowed by the society in which you live. It is an advice that Criminals against property, life and women must be rooted out and not prison-celled. This is an absolute necessity to maintain the integrity and peace of the society: No nation can survive for long in peace, health and wealth if criminals against property, life and women are allowed to roam, thrive and live luxuriously within or without the prison walls. It is not a wise state policy to punish the peaceful and law abiding citizens by burdening them with the maintenance of the heinous criminals. Such a nation is bound to perish sooner or later.

It is a message to fight evil and destroy every evil perpetrator even if he be nearest and dearest one if he does not reform himself. Gita's Dharma is a Dharma that is applicable to all persons and societies irrespective of age, sex, place and time as it is based on the constitution of the universe amply vindicated by the modern science.

Conditions leading to Mahaabhaarat War

In order to grasp clearly Dharma including the Social and Spiritual message of Gita it is necessary to know the conditions leading to war and what was said by Shree Krishna and Sanjay in their respective peace missions the failure of which precipitated the epic war. In addition to this we should also take note of how He acts during his life.

Short history of Kuru dynasty ruling India till Gita is sermonized

The section of history of the Kuru dynasty then ruling India till Gita is sermonized is briefly stated below.

We begin with King Shantanu of Surya dynasty ruling over Hastinapur [present Delhi]. Till this time it was a rule that only a fit and proper person would become a king. In absence of peoples' unanimous approval even king's son would not be entitled to the kingdom of his father. Normally heir-apparent to the throne was chosen during the life time of the king to avoid disputes on demise of the king so that he can be crowned immediately.

Bhishma takes two Vows: Shantanu was married to celestial Ganges and had a son by her named Gaangeya Bhishma who was to be the heir-apparent. King Shantanu while on a hunting expedition fell in love at first sight with a fisher woman Matsyagandhaa who already had a son named Vyaas by sage Paraashara. He lost all interest in life and began to live in seclusion. On learning the lovelorn condition of the father Bhishma went to the father of Matsyagandhaa and put the marriage proposal. The Dasyuraja was ready to give his daughter in marriage provided her son was to be the king after Shantanu. Bhishma okayed the proposal without hesitating even for a moment but Dasyuraaj argued that Bhishma had the right to renounce his right to the throne but he had no moral or legal right to bind his son.

To remove all doubts and obstacles to the marriage Bhishma took two vows: [1] He will remain celibate for life and [2] he will protect the king of Hastinapur till his death. It is the second vow that became the heart etching as it did not allow him to fight against the frauds of Kauravas nor allow him to leave them. This vow forced him take the side of Adharma. Shantanu had three sons by Matsyagandhaa viz: Veerya, Vichitravirya and Chitravirya. Bhishma kidnapped three daughters viz: Ambaa, Ambaalikaa and Ambikaa of Kashiraaja for their marriage with the princes. Ambaa was in love with another prince, so Bhishma sent her with all respect to her lover who refused to marry her as he had lost her in the battle after kidnapping and did not want her as a gift under these conditions. Bhishma refused to marry Ambaa because of his vow of celibacy. She vows to kill Bhishma, dies with the desire to kill Bhishma and is reborn as a prince Shikhandi for killing Bhishma. Three sons of Shantanu died without leaving heir to the throne. So as per the custom then prevalent Matsyagandha invited Bhishma to raise the family with Ambikaa, Ambaalica and the maid-servant who had accompanied as an attendant. Bhishma refuses on the ground of his vow of celibacy. So ultimately she invited her son Sage Vyaas to raise the family which he does in obedience to her mother's order as per the custom. The sons born were [1]: blind Dhritraashtra, [2] anemic Paandu and [3] wise Vidur. Anemic Paandu, though younger was declared heir-apparent in preference to elder Dhritraashtra as he was blind. On the death of King Shantanu, Paandu ascended the throne. Dhritraashtra felt aggrieved from the beginning that his right to throne was snatched away on the flimsy ground of his blindness for which reason he harbored a secret hatred for all.

King Paandu decided to expand his kingdom by subjugating the kings and make them his vassals. So Blind Dhritraashtra was seated on the throne as his representative to take the care of the kingdom while he was away on war campaigns. Once on the throne Dhritraashtra decided to stick to it at any cost and the result was Mahaabhaarat war.

Paandu returned after subjugating the kings of Bharat. Instead of handing over the throne, Dhritraashtra contrived to send him to stay in the jungle under the shrewd pretext of rest after the long wars. Unsuspecting Paandu gladly went to forest with his two wives Kuntaa and Maadri. By the powers of the Mantra, Kuntaa gives birth to Yudhisthir, Bheem and Arjuna while Maadri to two sons Sahadeva and Nakul. Unfortunately Paandu dies in the jungle due to curse: Maadri becomes Sati and Kuntaa returns to Hastinaapura with all the five children who are despised by Dhritraashtra and his sons though outwardly treatment fit to a royal family was given. Duryodhan, the eldest son of Dhritraashtra openly showed hatred and challenged the right of Yudhisthir to throne.

Duryodhan in an attempt to kill Bheem poisoned him but was depoisoned by cobra Vaasuki. On coming of age Yudhisthir was declared Heir apparent. Duryodhan and his maternal uncle Shakuni hatched a plan to kill the entire Paandava family by burning them alive. They built a palace of highly inflammable materials in a town Vaarnaavrat where a fair attended by the king of Hastinapur was held every year. Duryodhan contrived through his father king to send Yudhisthir to attend the fair as the representative of the king. Paandu family along with mother Kuntaa go to the fair and reside in the palace. King's policy advisor Vidur comes to know of the plot to burn the Paandavas alive. He sends a tunnel digger to Yudhisthir with a warning of the plot to burn them and advising them to escape via tunnel to be dug by the digger. Tunnel becomes ready one day early. Paandavas set fire to the palace and escape through the tunnel and move incognito keeping all in the dark as to their escape. Only Vidur knew it and he kept mum for the safety of Paandavaas.

Incognito Paandavas come out in the open in the Svayamvara of king Drupad's daughter Draupadi: A tough condition was set by the king for winning the hand of Draupadi. All the assembled Kshatriya kings failed to fulfill the condition and Arjuna in the dress of a Brahmin comes forward to fulfill the condition and successfully pierces the eye of the fish moving in the circles above by looking at its image in the water below. It is here that he had to declare himself that he was Arjuna as Kshatriya alone was eligible to take part.

During this period Duryodhan was declared Heir-apparent and now the question was who is the Heir-apparent, Duryodhan or Yudhisthir? Dhritraashtra did not want to hand over the throne but he did not desire to expose his unwillingness. He put forward Duryodhan as his shield and divided the kingdom. He gave Yudhisthir undeveloped jungle area of Indraprastha. Paandavas accepted with murmur their part of the kingdom and in few years developed it into a flourishing kingdom after successfully burning out the Khaandava Jungle.

On the advice of Krishna and Naarad Yudhisthir begins to perform Raajasuya Yajya: Duryodhan is doing the work of accepting the gifts from kings in the Yajya: Seeing the affluence of the kingdom and the gifts given to Yudhisthir, he begins to burn with the envy and a desire to take it away by any means. So goes to his father Dhritraashtra and says, "Hey, king! Maternal uncle desires to take away the wealth of Paandu-sons by playing Dyuta i.e. Dice-Gambling, Kindly give permission and invite them to play dice game. Sabhaa 45:40.

If we search the history of the earth we will find few rogues who can outwit Dhritraashtra in roguery. Instead of restraining his son from such a game he invites Yudhisthir for the dice gambling with such a desire. In the gambling

Shakuni plays deceitfully and Yudhisthir looses every thing first and then one by one Himself, his brothers and lastly the joint wife Draupadi: Draupadi being in the period is dressed in sari only. In such a physical condition she is dragged by hairs to the open court by Duhshaashan who shouts with pride: Krishna, Arjuna, Hari or Nara call whom you please, here I am dragging you to the court.

Under the conditions she asks the elders in the court, "Tell, whether I am conquered or not if he wagered me after he lost himself in wager?" Bhishma escapes simply by saying who am I to opine in what Yudhishthira does? But Vikarna, the brother of Duryodhan says: Mrugayaa Paanamakshaancha Graamye Chaivaatisaktataam\ Sabhaa 61:20.

Any act done by a person who is under the sway of hunting, drinking, gambling or propelled by Vaasanaa is Adharma. Sabhaa 61:20.

Very same are the words of Krishna when he comes to visit forest-dwelling Paandavas as per the terms of the gambling.

Striyokshaa Mrugayaa Paanametatkaamasamutthitam \\ Aaranyak 14:7.

Attachment to women, Gambling, Hunting and wine-drinking: these four make a man without Shree i.e. wealth and affluence. Aaranyak 14:7. Krishna has considered this whole dice-play as Adharma and destroyer of wealth. Please note that Yudhisthir did not seek advice from Krishna in this matter i.e., whether to accept or not to accept the invitation for gambling.

Even the limits of Adharma are crossed when Duhshaashan begins to make Draupadi naked in the open court. When her husbands and elders fails to protect her honor and decency, she calls upon Shree Krishna with all the love and faith but with distress to protect her honor. Remaining invisible Krishna does the job by supplying saris as they are removed till Duhshaashan faints. Scenario of making her nude ends in fiasco. She rises like a lioness in a limitless rage and raised her hands to curse the entire Dhritraashtra family. At this juncture Gaandhaari the queen-consort and the aunt-in-law of Draupadi enters the court and calls upon her sons to make her naked as they tried with Draupadi. She entreats Draupadi not to curse the family and requests the king to restore Yudhisthir to his former status. The king does with great reluctance.

Duryodhan and Shakuni immediately go in conference to discuss how to take back what was won and given back by the king. They decide to invite Yudhisthir to play only one game with two conditions: [1]: whoever loses will reside in jungle for a period of twelve years and in the thirteenth year remain incognito: and [2] if the condition is fulfilled loser will emerge from the jungle and begin to rule his kingdom but if recognized during the thirteenth year the conditions will repeat. On the insistence of Duryodhan King again invites Yudhisthir to play on the above conditions. Yudhisthir plays and loses.

Krishna says it is Adharma to wage a war without trying for peace.

Paandavas fulfill the conditions of the wager and emerge: All well-wishers of Paandavas meet at the marriage of Arjuna's son Abhimanyu with Uttaraa. All are agreed to wage a war but Krishna refuses to decide in favour of war. He says, "How can we decide for war when we do not know what Duryodhan will do? We do not know his opinion. How can we so decide without knowing the thought of the other side." Udyog 1:23. Krishna does not deny the possibility of change of heart of the other side and think of giving the kingdom. He says it is Adharma to decide to wage a war without even trying for peace.

Saatyaki opines strictly from the legal and moral angle. Can any one of you now find slightest fault with Dharmaraaja? Kauravas have defeated him by fraud and yet Paandavas have fulfilled the conditions of wager. They have stayed for 12 years in jungle and one year in secrecy; Now why should they beg? Shamelessness of Kauravas knows no end. Now they falsely allege that "We have discovered them before the year was over." Saatyaki says in anger, "There is no sin in killing criminal enemies. It is dishonour. It is Adharma to beg from enemies." Udyog 3:21.

At the end of full and heated discussion the opinion of Shree Krishna prevails and it is decided to send the Purohit of King Drupad as an emissary to Dhritraashtra for the return of the kingdom.

Dhritraashtra sends Sanjay on peace mission: His advice to Paandavas

Dhritraashtra and his son Duryodhan refused to hand over the kingdom but king wanted to avoid war without parting a single inch of land and so sends Sanjay as peace emissary: Normally an emissary can and will speak strictly within the limits of his briefing. Sanjay is sent without any briefing: Dhritraashtra tells him, "Remember, Paandavas are extremely shrewd and valiant. Shree Krishna is their ally to help. Remembering this my heart throbs and palpitates with fear. Therefore You as my peace emissary to Paandavas will speak in their court in such a way and manner you deem fit under the circumstances so that they would abandon the idea to wage a war for taking their kingdom.." Mahaabhaarat: Udyog; 31:36-40.

Sanjay is shrewd, Dharma-lover and great statesman. Like Vidur he is a great lover of Paandava and Shree Krishna but even so he was fully devoted and loyal servant to Dhritraashtra. His words supply a fine example of master political intelligence. In fact he had nothing worth to offer or to talk about: Even so what he tells is so impressive that it solidly settles in the mind of Arjuna, though Yudhisthir and Krishna smilingly dismiss it as piece of scripture quoted by Satan. It is what is stated at this mission that is being ruminated by Arjuna and which visualizes before him when he surveys the opposing army and depress him so much that he refuses to fight at a crucial moment. What did Sanjay say?

He told, "Oh, Mahaaraaj Yudhisthir! You are highly Dharmic, even then you have been a victim of great tragedies and calamities so it seems that one cannot understand what tragedies cannot befall?"

"Hey, Ajaatshatro! [enemy of none] you have quietly endured till date all these miseries, tragedies and calamities. With that very same wisdom it will be proper to endure with tranquillity and forgiveness. Looking to your nature You will never be able to discard Dharma for self-interest and therefore you should make a beginning of peace which will result in Kalyaan of all. You Kunti- sons are merciful, Dharmic and straightforward. You know karmic fruits. You have valor and vast army but censurable and evil act like war does not behoove you. What nobleman would be ready and willing to do the Karma which destroys all producing sin and rebirth as an end-result.? You had freed Duryodhan and others defeated by Gandharvas in the times of Gosh-journey. You have proved to be the real brothers of Kauravas and fit to be congratulated for this act. So, now, how have you become ready to kill the same brothers whom you saved once: and with what result? If you people become victorious on killing Kauravas, even then your life will be like dead ones on account of killing kinsmen. You have on your side heroes like Shree Krishna, Saatyaki, Dristadhumna. Who can defeat them in war? Kaurava army has also fighters like Bhishma, Drona, Krupa, Karna and other grand fighters. Is it possible to conquer them without the annihilation of one's own side?. [i.e. your annihilation is certain: this is an indirect threat also]. What is the use and importance whether one looses or wins if extreme annihilation is to take place on both sides. Oh Paartha! I do not see any Kalyaan, or good of any one in this war. This is non-dharmic act and you, Oh Paandavas! how have you become ready to commit it?"

Yudhisthir replies, "Oh, Sanjay! who will wage a war if the fruit can be had without a war? Hand over our kingdom Indraprastha and let Kauravaas rule over Hastinapur. This is the way to calm us."

Devil quotes the Scripture

Sanjay replies: "Hey, Enemy-of-none! It is good for you to maintain by begging in the kingdom of lineal descendants of Andhaka and Vrishni kings but it is not Shreya for you to gain kingdom by war." Udyog 27:2.

"Oh, Yudhisthir! Our life is transitory; knowing that do not destroy it. If Kauravas are not handing over your kingdom, then stay in the kingdom of Krishna and live the remaining life by begging. That is fit and proper but war is not worth. Kingdom obtained by war is not beneficial. Our life is transitory and miserable. Again do not commit a sin destroying your fame. Sense-objects are obstacles in Dharmic behavior: knowledgeable keeps sense objects away: Wealth and thirst bind."

"This thirst for things will destroy your Dharma and non-dharmic persons perish even if he obtains the kingdom of the earth:" "Man without self control loses happiness. This sinful act will reach the other world before you and give you miserable fruits there, You should not go to either anger-generated hell or joy-generated heaven but develop knowledge, yoga, and do selfless Karma for salvation. Knowing the destination of Karma do not discard truth, mercy, organ's control. If you wage a war with envy towards Kauravas, then it will have to be said that it was proper Dhaarmically for you to have suffered pangs of jungle life."

"Why did you go to jungle at all if you wanted to kill the kinsmen? You were strong then and Kauravas weak then but strong now: Victory and defeat are uncertain in war."

"Even ignorant and sinful are victorious in war while knowledgeable and Dharmic persons are defeated becoming devoid of all happiness. You have never committed a sin. Why are you bent on committing this sin now? Do not wage a fame destroying sinful war."

"Obtaining the sovereignty over the earth by killing Bhishma, Drona, Krupa, Ashvatthaamaa, Shalya, etc. is abominable and discardable then what to talk of smaller enjoyments? because by doing so you are going to be miserable. So do not commit this sinful act."

Dharma Raaj replies: At places Adharma takes the form of Dharma. At places Dharma remains in its natural form: Intelligent persons think over it and perceive its real form. Udyog 28:2.

Shree Krishna's reply

Yudhisthir though a dharma-knower, asks for the opinion of Krishna who says to Sanjay:

Sanjay ! I desire non-destruction of Paandavas: I yearn that they get Aishvarya and that their good happens. Along with it and similarly I also desire the welfare and growth of Dhritraashtra, the father of hundred sons. I desire his upgrade: Udyog 29:1. but Krishna clearly tells, "Kauravas have committed one crime: they desire to take away the land of others: Is there any difference between Duryodhan and a thief and a looter of others' money and wealth?

Krishna neither begs nor bugles for war but quietly says Paandavas are ready for peace and are powerful enough for war therefore tell your king what you think best. As against the powerful Duryodhan and his army Yudhisthir says, 'My strength is my Dharma,' Udyog 30:42. And in no uncertain terms send a message that: " Give me my Shakrapura or Oh, Bhaarat hero, Fight." Udyog 30:47.

Krishna finally says, "I am glad you are advising high philosophy but I would only say this much that it is highly desirable that it should begin at the very place from where it has originated."

In nut shell Sanjay tried to entangle Paandavas in the wordy web of happiness-misery, Dharma- Adharma, sin-Punya, mercy, valor, other world, salvation, Knowledge, destiny, obtaining kingdom by killing kinsmen, brother, guru etc. Yudhisthir and Krishna are not charmed and cheated by the sweet words of Sanjay but Arjuna is and remains merged in the delusion till Bhagawaan removes it with Gita-Sermon.

This is Sanjay policy: Let Kauravas do any Adharma, but you do not spoil your other world by doing Adharma: this world of yours is already spoiled, why spoil the other? The Western world and the congress, communists secularist and Muslim of India are advising the Hindus of India in the terms of Sanjay.

After Sanjay leaves Yudhisthir goes to Krishna and says, "We desire neither to renounce the kingdom nor desire to destroy the families. If this condition is acceptable then we are ready and willing to bow down if peace can be achieved." Hearing this Krishna says, "In the interest of both the parties and peace I will go to the assembly of Kurus." Udyog 70:79.

Shree Krishna agrees to go on peace mission though fully aware of the negative result. He tells Arjuna: "I will do whatever is possible with my words and action but I have not the least hope that peace will prevail nor the reconciliation." Udyog 77:18

Shree Krishna goes on peace mission

Rejecting the invitation of Duryodhan Krishna accepts the invitation of Vidur to be his guest. Vidur hiding his surprise at this peace mission asks Krishna, "Howsoever powerful your words be they will prove to be impotent before Kauravas as they, who are followers of anger and passion have already concluded that even Indra cannot defeat their armies." Udyog 90:20.

Shree Krishna replies

"When this entire earth together with horses, chariots and elephants is ready for destruction then any one who tries to save it from the Jaws of death gains best Dharma. Udyog 91:5

Shree Krishna says he has come to try to save the earth from destruction. He knows very well the futility of his efforts. Shree Krishna knows very well what his Dharma-duty is and puts it into practice knowing full well its futility: What happens in the court of Dhritraashtra during peace Mission? Krishna enters the court for his mission and observes that great Rishis were present but they were still standing and no body had prayed them to take their seats. Krishna's vigilance for the values and respect for the traditions manifests here. He quietly tells Bhishma to welcome the Rishis and invite them to take their seats because none can take his seat before they were seated. Udyog 92:42-43. After Rishis take their seats Shree Krishna sits on the seat reserved for him in the middle of the court.

After narrating the various benefits from the peace between the two sides he states what will happen if it does not prevail.

"Hey, Mahaaraaj! great destruction is seen if there is war: Only great annihilation is seen and what Dharma do you perceive in the destruction of both the sides?" Udyog 93:28

Shree Krishna sees the destruction of both the sides. There is truth in the words of Krishna. He utters with extreme compassion and pain. He says, "Hey, Kuru-son! protect these Peoples so that there is no destruction of the entire body of peoples. All people will be saved if you remain stationed in truth." Udyog 93:33

The message sent by Yudhisthir to Dhritraashtra was equally important for the members of the court so Shree Krishna delivers it.

"The members of the assembly should also be considered as murderers where there is murder of Dharma by Adharma and Truth by lies and vain words." Udyog 93:48.

Finally Shree Krishna says: "Hey, Bhaarat! I am desiring Shreya of both yours and Paandavas: Do not deprive the entire subjects of Dharma, wealth and happiness" and finally says, "Choose your path." Udyog 93:49.

Shree Krishna exhibits his omniscient and omnipotent powers.

For some reasons Duryodhan had made preparations to arrest Krishna as soon as the mission was over: Krishna knows this before hand and so he had taken Saatyaki along with him and also his army. When Duryodhan goes out to confer with Shakuni and others Krishna roars: "I have the ability and power to arrest and imprison the entire body of these Kauravas overflowing with anger but I can not commit sin nor any censurable Karma." Udyog 128:25.

Krishna had not uttered these words in vain. He shows his powers and ability. He manifests his universal form as a living being when Duryodhan reenters the court after conferring and says, "Behold, all the Paandavaas are here, hundred valiant of Vrishni genealogy are here, Aadityo, Rudro, Vasus and Maharishis are also here." Udyog 119:3.

Krishna manifests his universal form only thrice during his life-time: here to prove to Kauravaas who he really was and on the battlefield to fulfill the desire of his beloved Arjuna in satisfaction of his yearning for knowing the finality. Shree Krishna shows his cosmos form in his open mouth to Mother Yashodaa when she asks him to open the mouth to test whether he had eaten the earth or not..

Mission fails and war is declared

And exactly at the beginning of the war at the critical juncture all what Sanjay had said vividly comes to Arjuna's memory plunging him into dejection and despair: Arjuna repeats and reiterates what Sanjay had said. Shree Krishna Bhagawaan delivers Gita to dispel the delusion by preaching Man's Dharma vis-a-vis himself, family, society, Ishvar i.e. God and finally Brahma, the source of all.

II
OVERALL DHARMA PREACHED BY SHREE KRISHNA

Central theme of Krishna's words in Mahaabhaarat and Gita is Man and his activity vis-a-vis himself, his family, society in which he lives, the physical universe including Earth of which he is a part, Ishvar i.e. God the creator and finally Brahma the source of all the above and how one should live as a source with all his varied activities. Biologically man is born, lives for a time and dies. Birth conditions of each one differs from the rest: is born with or without physical and mental defects: in rich or poor family: lives happily or miserably: dies due to heart-failure due to disease or in an accident or is murdered straight way or cruelly. We find man against man: society against society: nation against nation: religion against religion. We find every where strife, quarrel, battles and wars with some oasis of peace in between: Question is "Is this all that human life means?' Reply is No: It is beyond this. What is it? It means to live peacefully enjoying life in all its fullness in Jeevan Mukta state becoming Videha-Mukta on death. Life means rolling with laughter and joy followed by salvation from the flesh for ever. It means Mukti, Moksha and Salvation, through laughter and joy. It does not mean grief, misery and bathing in tears. What is the method?

Hindus proclaims it can be achieved through the practice of Sanaatan Dharma only and by no other means. Veda Vyaas tells precisely and concisely in four concluding couplets of Mahaabhaarat the course of correct action for man to achieve money and wealth, to enjoy fullness of life and finally salvation. These four couplets are Known as Bhaarat Saavitree.

In this Samsaara man has experienced, is experiencing and will remain experiencing the joining and separation of thousands of parents, wives and sons. Svargaarohan: 5:60.

This is eternal truth whether you believe in rebirth and emancipation or not.

Stupid person gets hundreds of opportunities of joy day in and day out and also the place of dangers and is deluded: But one who knows, one who is a pundit is not deluded by these. Svarga: 5:61.

With raised hands, I shout but no body hears me: certainly one gets not only emancipation by Dharma but he also gets money and wealth, enjoyments and pleasure: then why do people not behave Dhaarmically? Svarga: 5:62.

Veda Vyaas pointedly draws our attention to the reason

of our Adhaarmic conduct. We talk of Adharma: talk of corruption: we talk of evil things: we perform evil things because the only thing fixed in our mind is that one achieves salvation only by observing Dharma while we want wealth and enjoyments first in life and then emancipation. This is the reason why we take the refuge of Adharma as wealth, power and enjoyments are normally found centered in the hands of liars, rogues, rascals and criminals. So we abandon the path of Dharma and harbor Adharma.

Sage says with confidence that act Dhaarmically and it will roll at your feet not only salvation but money and wealth, power and all the enjoyments of the world too. So he further says:

Do not discard Dharma by Kaama, fear, greed or for saving life. Dharma is eternal. Happiness and misery are transient. Soul is eternal and rest is transient: Svarga: 5:63.

The essence of Mahaabhaarat is: station steadily your intellect in that which is eternal and not the transient.

What is Sanaatan Dharma?

Now arises the question what is Sanaatan Dharma which Veda Vyaas so confidently exhorts us to practice. He mainly talks of Dharma enunciated by Shree Krishna and also practiced by him. Why so much importance is given to the words and actions of Shree Krishna? Because Shree Krishna is the incarnation of Shree Vishnu and has descended on earth to teach Dharma not only by words but by action too. So his life-history must be taken into account in deciding what is the Dharma that is taught in Gita and in Mahaabhaarat. Vyaas refers to Shree Krishna in the following words in the beginning and at the end in Mahaabhaarat:

Majestic Vaasudeva manifested in the human world from a single degree of Shree Naaraayan is the deity of deities and beginningless. Aadi Parva: 167:153.

Mahaabhaarat concludes who is Krishna in the following words:

Vaasudeva-son Shree Krishna is the degreecal part of that deity of deities who is well-known by the name Naaraayan. Svargaarohan 5:24. Bhagawaan Shree Krishna was no ordinary human form: he was Naaraayan in Human form with all the majesty in tact and had taken the human form to reestablish Dharma, to meet his loving devotees and finally to clear the society of evil doers then roaming and ruling some part of the then that part of the earth known as Bhaaratvarsha

Despite being the Vishnu-Incarnate what was his daily routine ? How did Bhagawaan Krishna begin his day?

We find his routine in Shaanti Parva where it is stated that after returning from Bhishma who was lying with the arrows pierced, all went to sleep: Krishna wakes up at Brahma Muhurta i.e. four AM. Yaamamahtraardhasheshaayaam Yaaminyaam Pratyabuddhyata\ Shaanti 53:1

What is the activity of Krishna after waking at this early hour? Krishna sits in meditation. Whose meditation he does? He meditates on his eternal Brahma form. While Rakta-Kanthaa and learned great-minded are praising Prajaapati Vaasudeva. The morning activity in Vaasudeva palace i.e. at Krishna's residence was as under: First Meditation then bathing etc. then Japa of mystic Mantras, then Agnihotra, followed by alms to Brahmins then Veda recitation by Brahmins and blessings. Thereafter to see ones self in clean mirror and then other worldly activities begin.

Thus by his own example he preaches that every one should begin his day with meditation on the self or Bhagawaan. Krishna was an incarnate and Brahma personified: what need had he to meditate on his self? He had no need but to show the way to all he was doing meditation on the self.

On whom should we meditate? We may meditate on Brahma, self, or any God of our choice but it should be done in Brahma Muhurta i.e., at about 4 AM.

Who is Shree Krishna?

In Mahaabhaarat Bhishma advises Yudhisthir to meditate on Krishna. He says, " Devakinandan Krishna is Tapah - form Mahaadeva: By his grace all your miseries will vanish. Krishna alone is the actor and the supreme destiny of Brahma-knowledgeable. And so Bhishma advises: and therefore go to Devakinandan Krishna who is the master of all organs. And in the presence of Krishna declares that Krishna is not only an incarnate but unthinkable Parameshvar. Shaanti 207:46.

Bhakti of Shree Krishna for Mahaadeva

In the presence of Krishna Bhishma sang the glory of the Bhakti of Krishna for Maheshvar Mahaadeva saying, " Krishna has satisfied Maheshvar in every Yuga. Mahaadeva always remains pleased with the Bhakti of Krishna; Anushaashana 14:13.

Shree Krishna Worships Mahaadeva and obtains boons from him. Getting initiated by Upmanyu in the Bhakti of Shiva Shree Krishna worships and pleases Mahaadeva and receives in all 24 boons from Mahaadeva and Mother Paarvati.

Shiva being pleased tells Krishna to ask eight boons: Krishna asks: [1] to be firmly stationed in Dharma: [2]: Ability to destroy enemies in war: [3]: Yashastathaagrayam i.e. best Yasha: [4] Supreme strength and power: [5] Yoga: [6] to be dear to all: [7] To be always in your presence: [8] Ten thousand sons. Anushaashan 15:2.

In turn Umaa tells Shree Krishna to ask for eight more boons and Krishna asks:

[1] Anger should not arise in my mind for Brahmins: [2] My father should always remain pleased with me: [3] Let me gain thousands of sons: [4] Best enjoyments be always available: [5] let there remain always pleasantness in my family: [6] Let My mother always remain pleased with me: [7] peace be with me: [8] success in every work, and undertaking. Anushaashana 15:6.

Of her own accord Mother Umaa gives eight more boons of her choice:

[1] eternal Prabhaava: [2] will never tell a lie: [3] will have 16000 queens: [4] will be dear to all: [5] will acquire inexhaustible wealth and money: [6] will have love of brothers: [7] the beauty of the body will ever remain: [8] will always serve dinner to seven thousand guests. Anushaasan 15:8.

With what materials Shree Krishna did the Aaraadhanaa of Mahaadeva?

This incident in Mahaabhaarat advises that one should worship and please Mahaadeva in the manner Krishna had done and reap the sweet results.

At nearly the end of war Ashvatthaamaa goes to kill the sons of Draupadi. He sees a Ghost guarding the sons. He is unable to kill with all his divine weapons. So he begins the worship of Tripuraari Mahaadeva who being pleased with the praise says with a smile: "Great Karma doer Krishna has done my Aaraadhanaa by Satya, Shauch, Aarjava, Tyaaga, Tapa, Niyam, Kshamaa, Bhakti, Dhairya, Buddhi and Vaani i.e. speech. One who does such an Aaraadhanaa is dear to me. So Krishna is dear to me. There is none Ishta than Krishna to me. Now the life of Paanchaalas is over. It is Krishna's desire." Sauptik 7: 62-63.

Gita does not talk of Vishnu, Brahmaa and Shankar the trinity who rules our world. There are numberless such Trinities. In fact each world is ruled by its own Trinity. Gita talks of the ultimate source of the entire manifestation so it does not talk in terms of Trinities. But this does not mean that Krishna does not believe in them or worship them. He did worship Mahaadeva as stated above.

Shree Krishna says in Gita that other gods and goddesses are his manifestations only and their worship gives the results soon but the same are temporary. He had immense faith in Shaktis and so before the war begins Krishna asks Arjuna to get down the chariot and recite Durgaa Stotra which one will find in Bhishma 23:4-16. On completion of the recital Durgaa manifests and tells Arjuna, "Hey, Paandava! you will conquer the enemies in no time because firstly you are difficult and secondly Naaraayan is your helper." Bhishma 23:18.]

Sanjay sees the future of war and in conclusion says to Dhritraashtra respecting Shree Krishna and Dharma:

Dhruti and Kaanti are there only where there is Dharma: Shree and intellect are there only where there is Lajjaa. Krishna is there where there is Dharma. Victory is there where there is Krishna. Bhishma Parva: 23:28

This statement by Sanjay is the most important and the basis to judge and evaluate the actions of Shree Krishna. It says Krishna will not touch even the shadow of Adharma: Krishna will be found only where Dharma is and so victory will be there where Krishna is.

Shree Krishna proves the Dhaarmicness of all his actions

Many actions of Shree Krishna are considered controversial from the point of Dhaarmicness in modern society. We forget that Shree Krishna has put to acid test all the actions of his life and proved beyond doubt the truth, power and the efficacy of their Dhaarmicness by bringing back to life the dead child of Abhimanyu, the son of Arjuna. Here is what happened:

At nearly the end of epic war, Ashvatthaamaa kills the Paanchaalas [sons of Draupadi]. Bheem comes to know of these ghastly murders and sets out to kill Ashvatthaamaa. Krishna comes to know of this. So he and Arjuna go to assist Bheem because Bheem alone was incapable to finish the job. Seated within the assembly of sages and seeing Bhima, Arjuna and Krishna coming, Ashvatthaamaa darts Brahmaastra in anger. Arjuna though Kshatriya waits for the consent of Krishna to dart Brahmaastra. Brahmaastra is the same but both use it with different motives. Ashvatthaamaa darts it with the Sankalpa, 'Let there be destruction of Paandavaas'. Arjuna darts with the desire of the Kalyaan of Teacher's son Ashvatthaamaa and also the welfare of his wife and brothers and with the further Sankalpa, 'By this let the Brahmaastra of the enemy be rendered quiet.'

The entire world trembles

Veda Vyaas hurriedly comes and demands the reason for darting. It cannot be used against the humanity. Arjuna calls it back but Ashvatthaamaa is adamant. He desires to root out the dynasty of Paandavas i.e. the child in the womb of Uttaraa and he concentrates the energy of Brahmaastra on the child in the womb. It is one of the rare occasions where Krishna manifest his glory and power. He says, "Seeing Uttaraa, one Vratmaana Brahmin of Uplavya city had said, "You will have a son when Kaurava dynasty will end and the name of that son will be Parikshit. The words of this Brahmin will prove true. The son of Uttaraa will carry on the line of Paandavas". Ashvatthaamaa reiterates that his weapon will destroy that fetish there is no doubt as to that. At this Krishna curses him that he will roam for three thousand years in the jungle devoid of human beings and says further, "I will enliven him who is burnt by the fiery light of your weapon. Hey, wicked Person! behold then, the power of my penance and Satya i.e. , truth." Sauptik 16:16.

Yudhisthir undertakes to perform Ashvamegha Yajna

Krishna comes to attend the ceremony. Uttaraa gives birth to Parikshit but this child became the giver of Joy and sorrow: Joy as he was born but the boy without movements became the cause of sorrow. Embryo had almost died before birth by the effect of Brahmaastra darted by Ashvatthaamaa and died on birth.

Kuntaa runs to Krishna and says, "Hey, Madhusudan! for the benefit of the family, falling at your feet I beg of you to do Kalyaan of this Kuru family by making the child alive." Aashvameghick: 66:26.

Subhadraa also prays this child must come to life and reminds Krishna of his words, "Aham Sanjeevayi shyaami Kirititanayaatmajam// Aash: 67:11. I will bring back to life the grandson of Arjuna by my Prabhaava i.e. power", uttered at the time when the weapon was darted and she tells her brother that time had come to prove his words to be true. Krishna drowning the crying of women thundered, "So it shall happen." and immediately goes in the delivery room. Draupadi at the juncture goes to Uttaraa and says, "Bhadre, See! Madhusudan, like your father-in-law is coming here, Unthinkable Aatmaa, invincible and Puraanarishi. Such a Krishna is coming." Ashvamegha Parva: 68:9-10.

Uttaraa cries and with bursting heart and raising her hands request Krishna to give life to her child and swoons away. Recovering from unconsciousness she takes the dead child in her lap and says, "son! You are the son of a Dhaarmic father! Don't you understand that your are behaving Adhaarmically? Best heroic Krishna of Vrishni dynasty is standing before you and you are not bowing to him?"

Krishna sees all this with composure

Taking Aachaman he freezes the Brahmaastra of Ashvatthaamaa and thunders these Six couplets of 192 alphabets which are the keys to understand the personality Krishna: to understand the efficacy of the Dharma practiced by him.

Krishna begins with his vow

"Uttaraa! I do not speak Mithyaa [in vain], whatever I have said shall happen: Behold, Uttaraa! In the view of all the embodied beings present I am bringing back your son to life." Ashva: 69:18.

He proceeds

"If I have not uttered Mithyaa [in vain] at any time even in play or a joke and if I have never retired from war at any time, let this child come to life!" Aashva: 69:19. Shree Krishna may have retreated from war but never retired from war. He exterminated all enemies of peace and Dharma in the end.

"If Dharma and Brahmins are specially dear to me let this

child of Abhimanyu who died immediately after birth, come to life." Aashva: 69:20.

One can not remain without wondering at these word of Krishna. Just the other day in a fight between Bhima and Duryodhan Krishna says, "Duryodhan cannot be killed with Dharma." It is Krishna who inspires to kill Duryodhan by Adharma and here Krishna with vow of Dharma tries to bring back to life a dead child ? Where is Dharma here? In his view it is not Dharma to keep alive Adharma through Dharma. Krishna advises do not follow that Dharma which keeps Adharma alive. Under such condition Dharma looses its Dhaarmicness and must not followed. It is Adharma to follow such a Dharma.

"I do not know if I have ever opposed Arjuna. On the strength of this truth [fact] let this dead child come to life." Aashva: 69:21.

In the next couplet Krishna makes even a greater claim: He says, "If I have been always stationed in Truth and Dharma then let this child of Abhimanyu come to life." Aashva 69:22.

The Satya is relative and absolute: Krishna is talking of absolute truth here and not the relative one: He was always stationed in Brahma, the absolute truth.

And lastly Krishna says, "If I have killed Kansa and Keshi in accordance with Dharma then by the power of this truth let this child come to life." Aaash 69:23.

Kansa was Krishna's maternal uncle: He ascended the throne by deposing his king-father and put him in Jail. He oppressed his subjects. Krishna's parents were also Jailed by him and Krishna was brought as a foster child according to modern standard. He made several attempts to kill Krishna in childhood but who can kill an incarnate? Krishna made the beginning to destroy Adharma by killing Child-killers sent by Maternal uncle Kansa and finally Kansa and showed that one must destroy Adhaarmic person even if he be one's near relative. It is the paramount Dharma of persons entrusted with the maintenance of Dharma to destroy Adhaarmic persons irrespective of caste, creed, sex and relations.

Keshi assuming the form of a horse had come to kill Krishna and Krishna had killed him by stopping him from breathing by thrusting his hand in his mouth. These killings by Krishna were with Dharma, by Dharma for Dharma.

By the power of the acts enumerated by Krishna the dead child comes to life: Being at Brahma stage he could have brought back to life by mere desire or words but no, he does not do that. Krishna has not muttered any mantra nor any blessings. He has put to test each and every action of his entire life and has proved their Dhaarmic efficacy. He tells us to act in the spirit as he has done and have all the powers of the Brahma.

Saints, Sages and Yogis have interpreted Gita from purely religious and spiritual angle. We will try to interpret Gita also in the light of the life-history of Shree Krishna and see also how far its message is relevant in life under the confusing conditions of modern space age.

Major stress of Shree Krishna is on the human activity vis-a-vis himself and society consistent with his journey to Brahmahood and on attaining Brahmahood to act for the benefit of the society. He shows how each one in society should act so that he remains happy in life and in slow stages attain salvation and society remains peaceful and prosperous. He says man is always active mentally and most of the time physically together with some continuous automatic activity like breathing etc. normally beyond his control. Life cannot be sustained without activity. Abandoning activity is impossible for a human being. What should be done? What is the way out? He gives a royal method. He says that close observation will reveal that all activities except automatic ones are directed by mind but you are alleging them in you. So he says either discard them mentally or dedicate them to Almighty. He says go in his refuge and asylum or believe that It is He who acts and not you. He say free yourself from the ego that you are acting and you have won half the battle.

Some how or the other mentally detach yourself from the activity without discarding the physical activity: Various methods are suggested but surrender is the royal one because you cease to be the doer. In your place Almighty becomes the doer though your body acts. He becomes responsible for acts and you have nothing to worry.

Over-all position of Truth and Dharma

In matter of truth and Dharma, Krishna sums up the overall position in advising Arjuna during an incident when Arjuna becomes angry and takes up his sword to chop off the head of his elder brother Yudhisthir though he was under the vow that he would kill any person who will spill the blood of Yudhisthir. Read the incident and the exposition.

During the Epic war, on one occasion Arjuna was defeated by Karna and Yudhisthir chides him in these words, "Hey, Arjuna! There be repeated hates to your Gaandiva bow, your valor, your flag with the sign of Harumaan, and your Fire-deity-gifted chariot. Hand over your Gaandiva to one who claims to be more powerful than you." Arjuna had taken a vow that he would kill any one who asks him with hate to hand over his bow to the one stronger than him. To fulfill his vow he took up a sword to chop off the head of Yudhisthir. At this juncture Shree Krishna tells Arjuna, "Why have you taken the sword?" Arjuna immediately comes to his senses and tell, "What should I do under the circumstances." At this juncture Krishna explains the real form of truth and Dharma like this, " Hey, Arjuna! ignorant looks only to the literal and gross meaning of the words but the knowledgeable looks to the subtle meaning and the intention behind the words and act accordingly. Your vow was to kill one who hates your bow in contempt and envy. Yudhishthir never told these words of hate in contempt and envy but has uttered these words with love to augment the praise and honor of your Gaandiv by enraging you to kill Karna. Even so if you want to kill in the manner of an ignorant one then killing is not done purely by weapons or of the gross body. Yudhishthir is knowledgeable. For him body is like a pair of clothes, to be separate from the body is not the death for him. The words are more piercing than weapons. They are like death. So kill him by words." Keeping the entire body of circumstances in mind Shree Krishna advises Arjuna the arrangements of Truth and Dharma as under in 69th chapter of Karna Parva of Mahaabhaarat:

"Hey, Paandu-son Arjuna! Knower of the Dharma divisions does not do such acts as you are doing in the manner of a Dharma-timid and ignorant." 17

"Hey, Paartha! one who becomes active in doing the deeds not proper to be done and becomes inactive for doing the deeds the deeds worth doing is Adharma. [lit: or: One who joins the deeds not worth doing with activity and joins deeds worth doing with inactivity is Adharma.] One is wicked who does not do deeds worth doing and does deeds not worth doing." 18.

"The staunch followers of Dharma have firmly laid down the rules of Dharma: You do not know their decisions and conclusions either briefly or in detail." 19

"Stupid person, Hey, Paartha! not knowing the duties and non-duties is bound to commit the mistake like you." 20.

"It is not easy to come to know the duties and non-duties, all these can come to be known by the study and hearing of Vedas and scriptures: you do not know this." 21.

"Hey, Dharmavit Arjuna! You are desiring to protect Dharma without knowing the Tattva and essence of Dharma: even with Dhaarmic inclinations, you do not know this that when should the creatures be killed?" 22.

"Oh, Son! 'It is best of all not to kill any creature.' this is my opinion. You may speak the lie but never commit Hinsaa i.e. injury." 23

"Bestman! so like other ignorant persons how do you kill your elder brother, the knower of Dharma essence and a king?" 24.

"Good people do not approve the killing of one who is not fighting, who is retreating in a fight, who has come in your refuge, who has come with folded hands, whose intellect is lost. All these things are present in your reverend Yudhisthir." 27.

"Hey, Paartha! the vow you have taken is childish. Because of that foolishness you are taking the decision of doing non-dharmic act. Without deciding and concluding the subtle and far-reaching movement and consequences of Dharma, Hey, Paartha! why are you running to kill your elder brother?" 28.

"The speaker of truth is a Saadhu. Nothing is better than truth: you see, Practical truth is unknowable in essence: Where lie becomes the truth and truth becomes the lie there to utter the truth is non-duteous [ceases to be the duty] and lie and falsehood becomes the duty." 31-32.

"It is proper to tell a lie in a condition where every thing will be taken away by wicked killer. [here to speak a lie becomes the duty]. One who desires to follow the truth must know this very essence of truth. If it is fit and proper not to tell the truth then one should not tell truth as it is. Thinking thus about the essence of truth and lie one becomes the Dharmavit i.e. Dharma knower." 33-34.

"One who does not remove his doubts by asking the knowledge-old persons remains in the ignorance- ditch. For this reason I am telling you some characteristics, signs and objects of Dharma. The knowledge is very difficult. You can decide about it by logic only." 54.

"Many people say one acquires the knowledge of Dharma from Shrutis only. I do not desire to refute this but everything of Dharma cannot be decided by Shruti only." 55. [one has to decide as per the conditions of place and time.] "The Dharma is proclaimed for the protection of creatures. That which is united with non-injury is alone the Dharma. Understand this decisively. Dharma is also proclaimed for not killing the killers even." 57.

Dharma upholds the peoples i.e. keeps them in order.

Because of keeping them in order it is called Dharma. The actions which keeps the people in proper order is Dharma. This is the conclusion of scriptures." 58.

"The opinion of those who believe the action as per the justice, equity and good conscience and logic to be the characteristic of Dharma is: if one is relieved by keeping silent then keep mum there and if speaking is necessary and a doubt will be created by not speaking then it is beneficial to tell a lie there: This is called truth even without thinking." 59-60.

"If one takes a vow of a certain thing and does it with changes therein: Thinkers say that he does not get the fruit of the action." 61.

"The lie and falsehood spoken in a situation of danger to life, during the time of marriage, the situation of extreme destruction of Gyaati [society, town, nation etc.] or in a joke, is not considered to be lie." 62.

"If one gets released from the hands of the thieves and looters by telling a lie when caught by them, the knowers of the essence of Dharma do not call it Adharma." 63.

"It is better to tell a lie when contacted by thieves etc. it is a truth even without thinking: Wealth should not be given to them so long as is possible by strength." 64.

"Wealth given to a sinner gives misery even to the giver: therefore person is not a liar even though speaking a lie for Dharma." 65.

"Arjuna! I am your well-wisher, Today I have given you the characteristics and the objects of Dharma intelligently and in accordance with Dharma. Hearing this tell, whether Yudhisthir is fit for killing?" 66.

Bhagawaan Krishna is of clear opinion that Scriptures are for protecting man and his society. Dharma is that which maintains the freedom of man consistent with the maintenance of the peace and prosperity of society. Dharma is that which keeps the society safe from the internal strife and from criminals against life and property and from the outside aggression in any form. Krishna's lifelong war had been against criminals whether he was a king or a subject in all societies of Bharat of his time which was far more extensive than the present mutilated one handed over as a parting kick by the Britishers.

Do not raise a controversy over his actions as to their Dhaarmicness but try to judge the same in the light of the his above exposition of truth and Dharma keeping in mind that he has proved the correctness of his view by enlivening the dead child of Abhimanyu. Apart from other actions of his life after preaching Gita he himself does many acts and advises others during the war to do acts which would be appear to many to day as blatantly Adhaarmic but judge them what he said in enlivening the dead child.. Consider his following acts:

[1]: He discards twice his own vow not to take arms during the war when he finds that Arjuna does not fight with all his heart. This is described in the note at the end of Chapter 18.

[2]: In a fight with Bhagadatta Krishna catches on his chest the Vaishnavaastra darted by Bhagadatta and that terrible weapon become Vaijayanti garland. Drona Parva 29:22. Arjuna tells Krishna, "How do you forget you have vowed to remain weaponless and only control the horses? It is all right if you do it when I am weak but not when I am stable in my work." Krishna says, "I have not taken any weapon in hand. I have only come in the way of the weapon and it struck my chest and you know the result". Bhagadatta's elephant goes out of his control and Arjuna kills him.

[3]: Bhishma had already discarded his weapons when Arjuna killed him from remaining behind Shikhandi.

[4]: Drona was without weapons when Drishtadhumna killed him. Krishna advises Yudhisthir to utter a lie so that Drona discards his weapons.

[5]: Wheel of Karna's chariot was stuck in the ground when Arjuna killed him. It was Krishna who chided Arjuna for waiting to strike when Karna was engaged in removing the wheel. Arjuna takes the heed and strikes.

[6]: In the presence of all Bhima killed Duryodhan in

flagrant breach of all the rules of Gadaa-fighting at the behest of Krishna.

As against this Kauravas had killed many by Adharma

As an Eternal Dharma-Protector Krishna had preplanned to destroy the remaining evil doers to protect Dharma.

Vishnu incarnated as Krishna in Bhaaratvarsha at a time when the Adharma prevailed at its height. His maternal uncle Kansa, King Jaraasangh, and many other Yavana and Mlechcha kings were ruling their kingdoms ruthlessly and cruelly. Krishna himself was the victim of the cruelty of Kansa and was raised as foster child. It was the Dharma of Krishna as an eternal Dharma-protector to destroy the evil and evil-doers both. He begins to clean the society of its criminals from childhood. He kills Putanaa and other child-killers and molesters: he drives away Kaaliya Cobra from the river Yamuna and kills Kansa before he was 12 years old and afterwards contrived to kill others one by one and finally all the evil doers are finished in the all out war fought on Kurukshetra.

Yaadavas were the victims of repeated attacks by King Jaraasangh. Krishna retreats and builds well fortified Dwaarikaa city on the island.. He retreats but does not retire from the fight. As an eternal Dharma protector his aim was to destroy the Adharma and their perpetrators. On the establishment of Shakrapur Indraprastha peace had prevailed but Krishna was not satisfied with the conditions. Krishna wanted that either Jaraasangh and Duryodhan accept the invincibility of Paandavas and become quiet, meaning they should understand that Dharma is invincible and stop their dharma-destroying activities or go to the extreme of evil and wickedness so that time becomes ripe to destroy them. If Paandavas had remained quiet after inhabiting Indraprastha in Khaandavaprasta, war would not have taken place but the Adharma practiced by Duryodhan, Duhshaashan, Shakuni, Karna, Jaraasangh and other Yavana kings would have gone on spreading which Krishna did not want as an eternal protector of Dharma.

He asks Maya Daanava to construct Maya Sabhaa and advises Dharma Raaj to perform Raajasuya Yajna.

So He plans: He asks Maya Daanava to construct a Sabhaa which will be incomparable in the mortal world. He was one of the six persons who were saved from the Khaandava - fire. He harbored revenge for Krishna and Fire-deity but he tells Arjuna to ask for a boon. Arjuna says, 'Do as Krishna tells' and Krishna bids to construct the Sabhaa. Sanskrit word Sabhaa has many meanings. It means an assembly, courthouse, assembly hall, or a public house and includes even a Casino. This Sabhaa was partly responsible for the war. He establishes Paandavas as the owners of incomparable Maya Sabhaa and advises Paandavas to perform Raajasuya Yajna and goes to Dwaarikaa. Devarishi Naarad comes after Krishna leaves and also advises Yudhisthir to perform Raajasuya Yajna. Once Yudhishthira understood the glory and power of the Raajasuya Yajna, his sleep abandoned him. In his worry for the Yajna he lost happiness though he was the owner of Maya Sabhaa, the kingdom of Indraprastha, comrade like Krishna, Father-in-law like Drupad. You name it and he had it; But the idea of majestic Raajasuya Yajna kidnapped all happiness. Though Yudhisthir is well known for his Dharma he calls Krishna for advice. Krishna tells in clear words that Raajasuya cannot be completed so long as the emperor like Jaraasangh is alive on the surface of the Earth. Raajasuya is the personal ambition of Yudhisthir and Arjuna is ready to fulfill it: He says, "It is easy to get ochre-colored clothes for the sages desiring peace from the beginning. It is not difficult to get ochre clothes for peace but war must be fought if one wants an Empire and we are ready for war." Krishna does not allow to slip away the opportunity and encourages Arjuna for war and says, "We do not know the time whether the death will come during day or night. It is never heard that the death does not come by not fighting. Death is going to come at its predecided time. It is useless to believe that death will not come if fighting is postponed." It seems here he inspires Arjuna to become active in a Dhaarmic war.

He says that he also does not say that it is easy to have victory over Jaraasangh. This is, "Praanyuddhena Jetavyah/" Sabhaa 18:2 It is putting life in jeopardy. It is a battle of life for victory as it will end with the death of one of the combatants. Paandavas are convinced that victory is there where Krishna is. Krishna advises to send Bhima and Arjuna with him to Giriraaj the kingdom of Jaraasangh and 'We will conquer Jaraasangh through battle for life.' Yudhisthir obeys and says, "Hey, Krishna! we are bound by your orders and so we have already killed Jaraasangh: We have freed the enslaved kings and have also performed the Raajasuya Yajna." What a confidence in Krishna?

When the three are going to Giriraaj, poet gives a fine simile: they proceed towards the house of Jaraasangh as if three lions of the jungles were going to the compound of çows.

Jaraasangh is Adhaarmic but Dhaarmic in his own way. He has his own individual Dharma. The trio had gone in the garb of Brahmins and seeing them behaving in non-Brahmin way Jaraasangh does not beat them nor arrest them but on the contrary says, "Tell the truth you are not Brahmins. You seem to be royal personages and it behooves the royals to speak the truth." Sabhaa 19:40. Truth was the strength so Krishna refers to the kings imprisoned by Jaraasangh. He does not hesitate but confidently says, "Yes, I have conquered them in war and have imprisoned them, Is it possible for any one to become an inmate of prison without being vanquished?"

He is invited for the dual of life. Even there he does not act unjustly. He chooses seemingly strong Bhima. Even at this stage he is proud. He does not deny the possibility of his death. He says, "Bhima! I will fight with you because there is greatness even in loosing with the superiors." Sabhaa 21:7. Bhima kills Jaraasangh as Yudhisthir had imagined. Interpolated stories of fraud in killing Jaraasangh are not found in original Mahaabhaarat: On the fifteenth day of the dual between Jaraasangh and Bhima, Krishna inspires Bhima and tells him not to torture Jaraasangh any further. So Bhima kills Jaraasangh and frees the kings. The slaying of Jaraasangh is one of the controversial topic of Krishna's actions; No doubt, Krishna had old accounts to settle with Jaraasangh and so Krishna utilized this opportunity to settle it: On the face of it this seems to be so. But think also that if Raajasuya Yajna begins Jaraasangh titling himself to be an emperor will not remain without becoming an impediment. The main prank of Krishna's action was that Jaraasangh was a living evil: Krishna calls upon Jaraasangh to stop the sacrifice of kings or fight a dual of life with Bhima with these words: "We [Bhim, Arjuna and Krishna] are Dharmaachaaris i.e. followers of Dharma and we are capable of protecting Dharma. It is not fit and proper to sacrifice human beings as oblations in the sacrifice. We desire emancipation of kings from your prison. Sabhaa 20:23. Thus Krishna is not actuated for this duel due to personal vengeance but in the larger interest of protecting Dharma. If Jaraasangh had released the kings Krishna and party would have returned without a duel with him.

Krishna takes great care in keeping the promise he gives in maintaining truth. He bears the insults flung by king Shishupaal just to keep the promise he had given to his aunt. See how he bears it at the Raajasuya Yajna. It was the custom before initiating the sacrifice to give Ardhya of worship to the Aachaarya, Ritvija, Relatives, Snaatak, Friend and kings who are present. Question arose to whom should it be given first. Bhishma opines, "There is light here due to Krishna and there is fragrance here due to Krishna alone: This area appears to be illuminated and joy-giving due to the presence of Krishna: The place which the Sun has amongst luminous objects the same is the place of Krishna here amongst valiant persons." Sabhaa: 29.

King Shishupaal raises an objection with rage flinging insults at Krishna: here is one sample: "You believe yourself to be great by acquiring the part of Pujaa first though unfit and enjoy it like a dog eating the oblation of sacrifice in lonely place." Sabhaa 43:19.

Krishna hears these words quietly without loosing composure while Bhishma says ,"Let the dogs bark till the Vrishni-lion is asleep." Krishna does not enter into the war of words. He chops off the head of Shishupaal without least hesitation when hundredth abuse was flung. He had promised his aunt who was the mother of Shishupaal that he will not kill till he completes hundred faults against him.

Krishna does not preach about the rights of man in society. He preaches what are his duties and responsibilities to himself, his family, the society in which he lives and finally to the maker. He talks of one right only and i.e. right to act without expecting any fruits thereof.

One has no right to the fruits of his actions. The domain to give fruits belongs to the Maker and it is his sweet will to give or not but he does says that he gives the fruits commensurate with the efforts put in but it is not obligatory on him. He has proclaimed the bundle of duties and obligations circumscribing Man's course of actions and that too without being obliged to give the fruits. He has laid the great stress on Bhakti specially Prem.-Bhakti i.e. Love devotion after selfless Karma. Great celestial Rishi Naarad says Bhakti Prem.-Swarupaa i.e. Bhakti is love-form and devotes chapter 12 to state what kind of devotee is dear to him.

Krishna could have avoided the war but he did not want to because He desired Adharma to perish: He was the master of the world he could have destroyed Adharma by his power but that would make people dependent on the master to act. Neither results were desirable. Krishna's view was that Adharma must perish. Krishna knew very well that Duryodhan, Shakuni and many other kings were rogues and rascals requiring death and it is a fact that once a rascal and a rogue always a rascal and rogue. You can never improve them.

Keeping this purposes in view in Gita Shree Krishna synthesizes the major trends of Hindu thought on 'existence' then in vogue into one unitary whole view of existence. By applying occum's razor Shree Krishna has harmoniously unified Vedic view of Brahma, Chit-energy, Maya and sacrifices for benefits, AUM of Tantras, the Upanishadic interpretation of Vedas and their own views, Purusha and Prakruti with her three Gunas of Saamkhya philosophy of sage Kapil, Yoga methods and Bhakti based on Bhaagavat Theism. He has synthesized a comprehensive view of existence vindicated by various branches of science. These doctrines and their terminology is discussed in brief in the Introduction Chapter 2. and also in their proper places in the dealing with the Gita text.

Before ending this Introduction, chapter I would say only this that Krishna's words in Mahaabhaarat and Gita translated into his life-long actions give you correct understanding of Dharma based on absolute knowledge, relative knowledge and ignorance the practice of which will make you happy and blessed in life and salvation at the end of life or lives. It gifts you the art of doing unbinding Karma and abiding Bhakti with yoga method to control the mind, all based on the constitution and working of Brahma, chit-energy, God, man and universe. It is a message of God Vishnu incarnated as Krishna with all the qualities of Brahma in tact advising you to lead the life of a lively living dead for merging in the maker or live in His presence till His emancipation.

III
THE DOCTRINES WITH THEIR TERMINOLOGIES USED IN GITA

[A]: Terminology used and the Scheme of Gita:

One is very likely to misunderstand Gita's social and spiritual message unless the basic doctrines and terminology of the systems used in Gita are understood in their proper perspective. Let us begin with the terminology used in it.

Chapter:1 Casting aside his Kshatriya dharma Arjuna refuses to fight a righteous war on the ground that by killing specially relatives and friends though they were criminals he would incur sin and portrays the pathetic scene on the destruction of the family and society.

Chapter:2 Dehi i.e. body dweller. Arjuna is afraid of incurring sin by killing. Krishna categorically states that death or slaying merely separates the Dehi i.e. the body dweller from the physical body but there is neither killing nor the death of Dehi. The body dweller is immortal and merely changes the physical bodies to suit his needs in his onward march to emancipation and goes on so changing the bodies till he metamorphoses into Aatmaa who then realizes that He is Brahma, the eternal and highest state of bliss. 2/11-14:17-30. Dehi as a soul is referred to in 13/27.

When man dies the Dehi leaves the body with mind complex and Praan and enters the other body at proper time.

In 2/45 Shree introduces Prakarti and her three gunas: advises Arjuna that Vedas sing the glory of three gunas of Prakruti: that fruits acquired by rites and rituals are temporary and producers of happiness and miseries which come and go. Therefore be without three gunas i.e. become gunaless. Realize that You are Aatmaa and beyond the effects of three Gunas of Prakruti.

In 2/49 Param is introduced saying that your subtle interest in physical pleasures will vanish on seeing Param i.e. on realizing Param. Param means supreme Brahma.

In the last stanza 2/72 Shree introduces Braahmi state and Brahma Nirvana i.e. emancipation into Brahma.

Man cannot acquire the Naishkarmya state by not doing actions or renouncing actions. Man can not remain without activity even for a moment. Goaded by the gunas of Prakruti creatures act ceaselessly. If it is so, Krishna says why not act in consonance with scripture and your inborn nature nurtured by education discarding all desires for fruits? Krishna reiterates the postulate that the only right man has is right to act and not to its fruits: To give fruits or not is the sweet choice of Ishvar: it is his job. Therefore act discarding all desires for the fruits. Chapters 3-4-5 deal with this aspect. The only way to escape the effects of karma is to detach from the desire for the fruits of the one's karmas. This is selfless Karma Yoga also called Buddhi yoga.

Chapter:3 Refers to :

[1]:The three gunas born of Prakruti.3/5; 3/27;
[2]:Prajaapati Brahmaa 3\10.
[3]:Brahmaa: yajya: Akshara: Brahma: 3/15.
[4]:Aatmaa:3/17
[5]:Gunas act and react with each other and not Aatmaa: 3/28
[6]:Purusha; 3/36.
[7]:Knowledge and relative knowledge:3/38-39-40-41.

Chapter:4 Introduces:

[1]: Karmas of individuals are as per the gunas composing his physical body and on this basis four Varnas are created. 4/13
[2]: Everything is Brahma:4/24

Chapter:5

[1]: Bhagawaan does not create anything but it is Prakruti that creates. 5/14.

Chapter:6

After telling various Yogas Krishna finally defines who is a real yogi or a Sanyaasi: He is one who does duteous acts as per Svadharma without having the refuge or recourse to the fruits of actions.

He states tells to control the mind by practice of meditation and explains how to do it and introduces Aatmaa: Paramaatmaa 6/7.

Chapter:7 Explains Jyaana and Vijyaana i.e. knowledge and relative knowledge that is Brahma and universe. Krishna tells that out of millions who try to know Me rarely one knows Me by Tattvas. Explaining the Tattvas He expounds that his physical inert prakruti is proliferated into eight kinds and active soul prakruti is the ninth one. All living beings are the products of these two Prakrutis. He is in every things like a thread through the gems in a necklace. All are fascinated by the feelings composed of three gunas and so do not know Me who am beyond three gunas. Krishna tells worship any form for fruits but He is there in that form and that form gives you results as prescribed by Him. But the results are temporary as that form is temporary. Chapter introduces the following terms.

[1]:Jyaana-vigyaana.7/2.

[2]:Eight inanimate physical Prakrutis 7/4

[2]:Animate Jeeva Prakruti.7/5.

[3]:World is fascinated by three gunas and so do not know Him who is within. 7/13.

[4]: All deities are his forms only and give the fruits as empowered by Him. 20-24.

[5]: Refers to Brahma, Adhyaatma, Karma, Adhibhoota, Adhidaiva and Adhiyajya. 7/29-30.

Chapter:8 Explains various terms introduced in the last chapter.

[1]: Brahma; Adhyaatma and Karma. 8/3.

[2]: Adhibhoota, Purusha and Adhidaiva, Adhiyajya. 8/4.

[3]: Paramam Purusha 8/8, 10.

[4]: Akshara, One word AUM Brahma 8/13.

[5]: Brahmaa, creation and destruction of the worlds and their time scale. 8/16-19.

[6]:But Brahma is superior to both and is not destroyed when Brahmaa and his worlds are destroyed. 8/20-22.

Chapter:9 States:

[1]:He pervades and permeates the entire worlds and their contents.9/3-6

[2]:Creation is through Prakruti.9/8-10.
[3]:What are the results of worships of different deities and what is the result of worshipping Him?

Chapter:10 States: Bhagawaan has manifested as universe and describes his chief forms and says the entire manifestation is from his very minute part.

Chapter:11 Krishna manifests his universal form as a living Being.

Chapter:12 Krishna tells that it is more difficult for the embodied beings to worship and meditate on the formless form of Bhagawaan than the formful one and shows alternative methods to achieve the goal and describes what kind of devotees are dear to Him.

Chapter:13 states:
[1]: Human body is the Kshetra i.e. field and its knower is Kshetragya i.e. field knower: Ishvar is the Kshetrajya in all bodies.13/3
[2]: composition of the field: 13/ 6-11.
[3]: Brahma is neither SAT nor ASAT. 13/13.
[4]: Brahma though being every thing is without the gunas 13/15.
[5]: Prakruti and Purusha of Saamkhya explained and 16 Vicaars are produced from Prakruti. Prakruti is the cause of acts and Purusha is the cause of enjoyments and is Maheshvar and Paramaatmaa. One who know thus Purusha and Prakruti is emancipated. 13/20-24.
[6]: Animate world is created by the union of Kshetra and Kshetragya. 13/27.
[7]: Paramaatmaa is located evenly in all 13/28.
[8]: All action are done by Prakruti only.13/29-30.
[9]: Aatmaa is unsoiled.13/33.

Chapter:14 states:

[1]:Mahat Brahma is the uterus where Bhagawaan deposits the fetus.14/3-4.

[2]: How three gunas bind the body dweller:

[3]: Who attains to Brahma.

Chapter:15 states:

[1]:Param Dhaama i.e. supreme residence is without elemental lights; 15/6. His minute part is Jeeva i.e. soul.15/7.

[2]: Kshara Purusha and Akshara Purusha 15/16.

[3]: Uttam Purusha i.e. Best Purusha.15/17,18,19.

Chapter:16 describes:

[1]:What are the divine and demonic wealth i.e. virtues and vices and for actions and karmas Scriptures are the authorities. None should discard them in deciding what actions are proper and which ones are not.

Chapter:17 states how three gunas of Prakruti composing the body affect the faith, mind and actions:

Chapter:18 In summation tells with what intellect one should carry out his duties to avoid the Karmic bondage and attain the Brahmahood.

Gita lays down the scheme of the working of the universe and man's place in it but has not detailed what is Brahma and the process by which Brahma appears as universe with all its animate and inanimate contents. Thus we should know the following four things to put Krishna's word and Gita into practice..

[B]: Doctrines: -

[1]: Brahma, Aatmaa-Paramaatmaa, Param, Param Dhaama i.e., supreme residence and Shakti i.e. Energy as stated in Vedas and Upanishads:

[2]: Purusha-Purushottama, Prakruti and her Three gunas, Mahat Brahma, eight inanimate Prakrutis, sixteen

altered products of Prakruti of Saamkhya system.

[3]: AUM written as -

[4] Brahmaa the creator and time cycles of creation and destruction of the worlds.

[5]:Rebirth and Incarnation are dealt with in the body of the Text clearly and needs no further explanation.

World view of Science

Before proceeding to understand the above let us consider the views of the science concerning these topics.

Science views universe in terms of waves and their interrelatedness. Albert Einstein writes, "We may therefore regard matter as being constituted by the regions of space in which the field is extremely intense... There is no place in this new kind of physics both for the field and matter, for the field is the only reality." quoted in M. Capek, The Philosophical Impact Of Contemporary Physics., p. 319. Hermann Weyl writes, "According to the field theory of matter a material particle such as an electron is merely a small domain of the electrical field within which the field strength assumes enormously high values, indicating that a comparatively huge field energy is concentrated in a very small space. Such an energy knot, which by no means is clearly delineated against the remaining field, propagates through empty space like a water wave across the surface of a lake; there is no such thing as one and the same substance of which the electron consists at all times." Philosophy of Mathematics and Natural Science, p. 171. Thus science has rubbed out the very existence of atoms and replaced it with wave fields.

Virtual particles are essential part of all particle interactions and the properties of the particles and are created and destroyed by vacuum which means the void takes active part in cosmic dance of creating and destroying energy patterns endlessly.

What are the true elementary particles as no particle is indivisible? Quantum mechanics tell us that all particles are factually waves and higher the energy of a particle, the smaller the wave-length of the corresponding wave. With the use of wave/ particle duality every thing in the universe can be described in terms of either particles or waves or both or partly in one and partly in another.

All energies and forces propagate in the form of short, medium and long waves in various ranges through empty space.

Einstein's famous equation E=MC2 simply means that how matter is equal to energy and that both are convertible in each other. Devi Bhaagawat [referred to little later on] has said the same thing in simpler terms 6000 or more years ago but did not give in the hands of scientist and politicians the power to destroy the earth.

The above picture of the universe with its parts from particles to galaxies to physical bodies of living beings and the working of energies and forces makes it clear that this whole inanimate universe consists of vibrations i.e. waves only and that the play and interplay of waves and wave packets in strings and strips produce what we experience as universe. So every object is nothing but a complex combination of waves. Waves combine to produce forms and shapes of every object which is given a name. Thus the whole universe is nothing but shapes formed by waves carrying the names given by us.

Science talks of all sorts of waves e.g. radio waves, X rays, gamma rays, light waves, and so on and so forth but does not tell us what is it that vibrates producing these waves within itself. Hinduism stoutly declares that the forms and shapes consist of kinetic Brahma and its energy: Waves are nothing but Vibrating Brahma: each and every thing is Brahma in its original constitution and composition.

With all the progress Science boasts of It has as yet not touched the constitution or composition of the sky. They simply view it as a void or vacuum. Science deals with diseases and their propagation through genes, foods and chemicals that affect the physical structures but has conspicuously failed to deal with that part of the living being called soul and correlate it to mental faculties and various energies of the body which are utilized in running the body for the purpose to sufferenjoy the previous actions or fresh actions resulting in pleasures and pains. It has also failed to correlate the waves of various energies to the faculties that run the human machine. Hinduism does it with remarkable success. Doctrinal base of Gita will explain all this.

As we will be discussing the eight Prakrutis of Bhagawaan in the formation of the universe it is necessary to briefly note the scientific view in the progressive formation of the universe from Big Bang onwards.

In nut shell the present conclusions of science regarding creation of the physical universe are:-

[1]: Some 15-20 billion years ago an infinitely small knot of infinite amount of energy at an incredibly high temperature burst with a big bang and began to expand at an incredibly high speed.

[2]: Time began to run from the point of explosion. It does not say which system of time began to run? It is important to know because our system of time is based on our sensory experience and measurements. There are many star-systems and many universes.

[3]: Exploding point is supposed to have zero size and consequently limitlessly hot. During the first 0 to1/10second the universe expanded from less than the size of an atom to about the size of a grape fruit.

[4]: With the expansion of the universe the temperature of the radiation progressively fell to about ten thousand million degrees during the first second of its existence and universe mostly consisted of photons, electrons and neutrons and their anti-particles and with a possibility of some protons and neutrons.

[5]:At the end of about hundred seconds after the explosion the temperature fell to one thousand million degrees which is the temperature within the very hot stars. At this temperature nearly 25% of the protons and neutrons combined to form helium nuclei together with minor quantity of heavy hydrogen and other elements. Uncombined neutrons degenerated into

protons, the nuclei of the normal hydrogen atoms.

[6]:The formation of helium and other elements must have stopped within few hours after the explosion. From three minutes on wards when the temperature of the expanding cosmos fell to about few thousand degrees the electrons and nuclei had lost enough energy for overcoming the electromagnetic attraction between them thus forcing them to combine forming atoms.

[7]: It is silent as to from what source the point of knotted energy arose? or why ? It simply says it exploded and is the seed of the universe.

[8]: Science assumes the apriori existence of space wherein the point of knotted energy was. Hinduism says elemental space arose on explosion within Chid-space of Brahma.

[9]:All laws of physics came into existence simultaneously with the big bang eventuality. Hinduism goes beyond this and says the formation of the knotted energy and its explosion took place following the innate nature of Brahma which is the seed of all laws that governs all that is produced from it.

[10]: These discoveries of science does not teach us how to live happy, wealthy and wise life. After explaining the composition of the universe and us, Gita tells how to enjoy the fullness of life followed by emancipation.

Now let us see whether the doctrines on which Gita is based are vindicated by the above scientific views so far as they are formulated.

Arjuna refuses to fight because killings will mulct him in sins. Krishna counters where is the killing and death? Soul only leaves the dilapidated body to take another body of his choice. It is the body that is subject to decay and death and not the soul: He tells detach mentally from everything and every activity and soul will be metamorphosed into Aatmaa who will emancipate into Brahma. All actions at this state will not create conditions for rebirth. To tell this much only He has summonized Gita: Shree Krishna does not enter into the cosmological creation of the universe but merely states what are the Prakruties that constitute the living Beings and what are their effects in the behavior of beings. Not that Bhagawaan could not tell but it was useless for common man to know. Knowing complex composition of wave-structure of animate and inanimate universe will not help common man in attaining happiness or avoiding misery or attaining Brahmahood. What are three gunas, how they arise and how universe construction begins etc. are important aspects for the scientific minds and yogis who are following the yoga path of meditation. For the rest it will not make a jot of a difference whether they know it or not. They are interested in the enjoyments of the worldly pleasures: Gita is for them because it gives them an unsurpassable method to enjoy the pleasures of the world and at the same time to reach the pinnacle of perfection. But even for them it is imperative that they should know in nut shell the spiritual and cosmological base of Krishna's selfless action yoga. This chapter supplies that need along with other terms..

[B][1] Brahma and Paramaatmaa.

Now let see what Brahma is? It is the source and the end of every thing. How?

From nothing only nothing can be produced. Nothing cannot produce anything. Beginning, evolution, or creation from absolute nothing is an impossibility. Why? Your spiritual progress will never begin unless you ask this question.

Reasoning of the observed facts reveal that there is no true cause but each phenomenon is either a cause or an effect in the chain of causation. It is always in the between, but neither a beginning nor an end. It is only a link in the cause-effect chain.

Origin of the original cause defies detection or discovery. Most highly trained intellect and ripened reason would retire in dismay, disgust and defeat on facing this problem. The law of causation demolishes the origin of the first cause.

It is amusing to muse on this law of causation leading us to causeless universe experienced by us through senses despite this irrefutable law. We are facing an almost insoluble conundrum. Don't worry. The very same law defeats the conundrum. Sage Vashishta argues, "Whatever SAT i.e. 'IS' remains after great dissolution is not zero-void-vacuum whether this universe is fact or a fiction or a product of magic or miracle even then how can that in which it exist and from which and in which it is created, formed or evolved be a void-vacuum-zero." We exist and therefore it must have a cause that exists in timeless time and spaceless space or capable of arising out of absolute nothing or that it is there in existence since prior to inception of time or space or irrespective of time and space. Inexorable force of logic leaves no alternative but to assume the apriori existence of a First Cause whose source defies every prying and probing.

None of the religions of the world, their scriptures, Prophets, Avataars, Masters or the scientists have as yet postulated much less proved the origin, evolution or the creation of the first primary Paramount Cause of the universe and us from an absolute non-existence, absolute nothing. All simply declare that It exists.

Hinduism and Gita terms this eternal world stuff Param Brahma or Brahma, Chidaakaasha, Paramaatmaa, Aatmaa, Rit, Parameshvar, Purushottam and Param-Shiva or Shiva.

Hindu scriptures describe this world-stuff as under

"Creation, dissolution, other states and relativities are in the categories of phenomenon but not in Aatmaa[Brahma]: He remains same as he is since beginning. Just as a dream dissolves in slumber so does this moveable-immovable, animate-inanimate world disappears during dissolution. At that time, steady-stable, deep and profound, thoughtful, considerate, abysmal, different from darkness and light, extensive, nameless, formless, Some SAD= is-substance remains. Learned have named it for the convenience of understanding and talking to each other Rit, Aatmaa, Paramaatmaa Brahma etc." [f].YMR: 3:1:9-2.

"During great dissolution every thing having become extremely infinitesimal and subtle it had become unable to do any activity, and when as yet beginning of the next universe of scenic- sub-stances had not begun, then at that time obstructionless, gapless, continuous, deathless, birthless, luminous, harmless, eternally capable of doing every thing, all form Maheshvar, only and quiet Paramaatmaa had remained; Senses cannot cognize its form and return. Freed and emancipated people experience it directly. Names are not its natural adjuncts but are alleged in it. Saamkhya call it Puroosha (pure state), Vedaantist call it Brahma, Vijnanika i.e., scientist call it temporary Vijnaana. i.e.. temporary matter and Shoonyavaadis call it zero-void." [g].YMR :3:5:3-6.

This passage makes it abundantly clear that the creation and dissolution of universes go on in ever repeating cycles and that the stuff has no natural name but man has named it for the convenience of communication.

"When universe dissolves then such-as cannot-be-called pervasive, without name-form, movementless and grave some SAT-substance remains. that 'SAT' is not light-form, darkness form, is not zero-void-form, is not formful, is not scene, is not sight-form and is not the group of created substances. He stays as infiniteness, the description of its own-form cannot be done in any way. Is more complete than completeness, cannot called SAT nor can it be called ASAT, is not creative nor creation-form. He is Chaitanya-only, is separate from the intellect-Tattva, is endless, oldageless and is happiness-form. He is without beginning, end and middle. He is causeless i.e., uncaused is without pain,....... He is universe-form and not-universe-form, he is Paramaatmaa staying in the manifested and unmanifested state of the universe." [h].YMR:3:7:47-51.

"During great dissolution this whole universe vanishes, nothing of the universe remains and at this time some Sat i.e., IS remains which is nameless and formless, stable and gravely commanding. That Sat i.e., 'IS' is neither light-form nor darkness-form: is neither zero-void nor formful: Is neither scene-scenery nor a collective form of created things: It stays in infiniteness. Its form cannot be described by any means. It is more complete than completeness and fuller than full. It can not be called either Sat or Asat i.e., IS or IS NOT. It is neither created nor creation form. It is Chaitanya only different from intellect-essence: is infinite, ageless, happiness-form, bliss-form: is without beginning, middle or end: is without cause: Is universe-form as well as non-universe form." [i]. YMR 3:9:46-47.

"Brahma is birthless, without old age, without beginning or end, immovable, immutable, eternal, bliss form, stainless and untainted, is not lost after knowing, is extremely pure, extremely venerable, is without all constructions and arrangements, is causa-causans, experience-form, knowledge-form, all form and stays secretly through every thing." [j].YMR: 3:9:76.

"Brahma is the cause of sub-atomic particles, is subtler than the subtlest, smaller than the smallest, thinner than the thinnest, bigger and grosser than the biggest and the grossest, is purer, Para i.e. beyond and quieter than mother of space and is infinitely extensive: is without beginning or end." [k].YMR: 3:10:32-33.

Whatever SAT i.e. IS remains after great dissolution is not zero-void-vacuum whether this universe is fact or a fiction: or a product of magic or miracle even then how can that in which it exist and from which and in which it is created, formed or evolved be a void-vacuum-zero.

Let us see what is its relation to Space and Time: Brahma is boundless and endless in extension. It exists in spaceless space. One cannot say it to be in space because itself is an illusion in Brahma. Brahma is not within space but space is within Brahma. Our notion of space is vacancy i.e., noting exists therein, according to the notion of science space can be created only by removing something to another place i.e. shifting a thing to a different place when the place occupied by the thing previously would become vacant and called space. On this reasoning space would become unlimited and Brahma-inscrutable matter would become limited and circumscribed. This leads us to presume many causes and not one axiomatic base which is the basis of all religions. Assumption is that

Brahma exist and is not surrounded by space which is an illusion within Brahma and therefore we state that it is all pervasive. Each and every part of Brahma from smallest to biggest has Shakti-energy-power-ability to arise or modify in any form and shape it desires to assume. Certain part of it is our universe. It has no form and shape and so can assume any shape and form. Throughout the length, breadth and height of Brahma, whatever Brahma be, there is not a slightest possible gap in its continuity and entireness. It never snaps. It will stretch indefinitely without breaking or snapping creating even a slightest gap.

Reasons for describing Brahma-Stuff in such terms is logically obvious: It is birthless and deathless because its origin is not knowable neither its end is knowable: It is formless because its very unlimited vastness defies comparison with any forms and shapes of things that are within it: It is neither light nor darkness because both evolve from it at later stage: It is nameless because names belong to forms: It occupies spaceless space because space is formed in it: It is ageless because time begins and ends along with the evolution and dissolution of the universe in it" Time and space evolve and dissolve in Brahma-stuff along with universe but not vice-versa. It does not move because movement is within space which itself exists in Brahma. It is thinnest and subtlest because every thing springs from it and is grosser and thicker than it. Space, time and universe began and appeared together simultaneously and will disappear and end together simultaneously.

Thus far Brahma-stuff is described in negative terms i.e., it is said to have no attributes and no qualities because it has no attributes and qualities as found in physical matter and forces which are its products. But it certainly has non-material spiritual property and quality i.e., It does possess a property which is the parent of all other properties and all other attributes. A Substance, a stuff which is a source of such an infinitely variegated and diversified universe can not be without some inherent nature. This innate nature is its ability to appear as anything it proposes and desires including our animate and inanimate universe.

The extremely pure form of this Chetan Brahma is described in simpler terms for common man in Vedas and various Upanishads: some of them are quoted below.

[a] "Whose eyes are every where, whose faces are every where, whose hands are working every where, who activates through his hands every soul according to their karmas; that very Deva creates deities paradise and earth.:[l]Rig Veda:10:81:3.

[b] Who ever is holding Praan, whoever sees with eyes and whatever luminous divine substances are in divine regions all come from Uchchhishta i.e., Paramaatmaa." [m].Atharva Veda:11:7:23.

[c] Ancient extensive Tattva is secretly pervading everywhere; hiddenly present. Even becoming manifested remains hidden in every way; Who holds Praan, who moves and who remains stationary, all of them are surrendered in one Tattva only." [n].Atharva Veda:10:8:6.

[d] That Parameshvar who is pervading-permeating in sky etc. the bhootas as well as in sun and all other regions, who is filling fully all directions and dimensions, from whose permeation not even an Paramaanu is excepted, vacant, who is Aatma of his own powers, who is the creator of the world, The Aatma who knows by himself that joy-form Paramaatmaa; he alone enjoys salvation by obtaining." [o].Yajur Veda:32:11;

[e] That Deva is one, hidden in all bhootas, is omnipresent, omnipervasive, is inner Aatmaa of all bhootas, is the president of all karmas, is the basis of all bhootas is witness, chetan lonely and only and qualitiless." [p].Shvetaashavar 6:11.

[f] "That omni-permeating pervasive Aatmaa is present in the universe like butter in milk: Aatmic knowledge and penance are the root means to obtain it. That is the supreme Tattva of Brahmo-upanishad." [q].Shvetaashvar :1:16.

[g] "The unmanifested pure form of that Brahma transcends manifested and unmanifested." [r].Vedanta:3:2:23.

[h] "That pure Brahma is truth, knowledge and infinite."

[s].Taitariya:2:1:1. This means that Brahma is not possessed of knowledge but knowledge itself. And so Brahma is not a subject of knowledge as it is knowledge itself.

[i] "Oh, Gaargi! Brahmins call this AKSHARA, he is neither big nor thin nor small nor long nor red (it has no color): is without shadow: is without darkness: He is not Vaayu, He is not Space, He is without attachment and contacts: is without juice: is without smell. He has neither eyes nor ears nor speech nor mind nor Tej i.e. heat nor Praan i.e. life-currents nor face nor resultants nor anything within: nothing is outside him: He does not enjoy anything nor is He enjoyed by anything."[t].Bruhadaaranyka:3:8:8.

[j] "Wise seers see Him Who cannot be seen by the eyes: who cannot be caught by the hands; who has no family ancestor; who has no form nor color; who has no eyes nor ears nor hands nor legs; who always is; is Vibhu, omnipresent, smaller than the smallest, who is imperishable, who is the birthplace of all bhootas." [u]. Mundakadaka: 1:1:6.

[k] "There is neither day nor night; there is neither Is nor Is-not; there is only Shiva when the light of Braahmic knowledge dawns and arises." [v].Shetaashwara:4:18.

[l] The peace prayer of the followers of Upanishads of the Shukla-Yajurveda branch tells volumes about the nature of Brahma. It says, " That Brahma is complete; This universe is complete; This complete universe gets created from this complete Brahma; The complete Brahma remains even after deducting and removing this complete universe from this complete Brahma. AUM SHAANTIH SHAANTIH SHAANTIH." [w].Brahadaaranyka:1:5:1.

Pure monism, the finest experienced philosophical flower of Hinduism declares that nothing exist save and except Brahma-stuff in its unaltered-unchanged-nascent-original form and the universe never existed and does not exist. Whatever Solidity comes to be seen is nothing but an illusion, merely an appearance without substance depending only on senses. Even science admits that in ultimate analysis the smallest known particles are nothing but waves.

Krishna accepts Brahma as an axiomatic fact beyond proof and description. Who and what can prove the proof of all proofs. Universe is accepted as a relative truth.

Shakti i.e., Energy works in Waves

Now let us turn to what Hinduism says in the matter of Shakti-Spandans i.e., Energy waves and how it has expressed it. Surprise is in store for the science.

Brahma and Its Shakti i.e., Energy. Prakruti and her three Gunas

Brahma is everything and yet he is nothing. Brahma appears as animate and inanimate universe by Vivart. Vivart means alteration in shape or form but not in substance. Constitution and composition remains the same. Only change that takes place is a change in shape: e.g. Gold and its ornaments: here the shape of gold changes but not the composition. How can this happen? consider water and its waves: thus It is possible by vibrating. Vibrations produces wavy structure of the substance which vibrates: Wave has a shape and therefore combination of waves also will have a shape. We do not see and experience the waves because our gross body is not programmed to experience this but with practice it can be. Thus Brahma appears as universe with out changing its constitution by merely vibrating and is fully illustrated by Gold and its ornaments: and vibrations and waves by waves in water. The wave length of these waves cannot be grasped by ordinary person. It is in the range of one billionth of a millimeter or less. Gita accepts this position when it talks in terms of Prakruti and her three gunas.

Brahma has no properties as found in our universe but is it without any nature? Being the cause of such a vast variegated universe It can not be without any innate nature: It is spiritual. This innate nature is its unlimited capacity and ability to appear as universe and life or any other thing at its sweet will and pleasure. This ability to appear as other than what it is, is due to his Chid Shakti or Maya Shakti. How does it do it? It does this by throbbing, by vibrating, by Spandan, by Sfuran. Sanskrit words Sfuran and Spandan means and includes to throb, to vibrate. Brahma is also referred to as Chetan: Chaitanya.

Hindu scriptures describe this throbbing or vibrating in various ways some of which are quoted below with comments where necessary:-

"To make or not to make Sfuran are both the nature of Chaitanya, (Brahma): It is joyous and active when it is in saurian and remains quiet when there is no sfuran, is not in Sfuran. When there is Sfuran of Avidly i.e. ignorance, then it is called Spandan by which universe appears. By the Spandan of pure Chaitanya there is Sfuran of universe i.e. universe springs, and by Aspandan i.e. non-Spandan there is Sfuran (springing) of eternal Brahma. Soul, cause, and karma are different names of Spandans of Chaitanya." YMR 3:67:6-7-8.

The English equivalents of the word Sfuran is to spring and to inspire and of the word Spand is to quiver, to throb, to vibrate. Thus couplets rendered with the above equivalents reads as under, "To throb or not to throb, both are the nature of Chaitanya i.e. Brahma-stuff. When it is throbbing it is joyous and active and when not throbbing it remains quiet. When there is throbbing of natural Avidyaa in Brahma then it is called Spandan i.e. vibration by which this universe appears. By the vibration of pure Chaitanya there is inspiration and the springing of the universe and by non-vibration there is springing of eternal Brahma: Souls, cause and karmas are different names of vibrations of Chaitanya."

Above is a clear statement that energy in the form of waves constitute every thing from particles to galaxies and virus to man. To throb and to vibrate (Sfuran and Spandan) means undulations and pulsations creating and producing waves and this wave formation is explicitly made more clear by the following couplets from YMR:-

"Just as waves, ripples and bubbles arise in quiet ocean waters, similarly in Chaitanya-form water of Brahma-form ocean there arise soul-form circles, Chitta-form waves, and world-form bubbles by reason of vibrations (Spandans) of Shiva-form cause." YMR: 3:67: 18-19.

"Kalpanaa-form kalaa suo-moto i.e. of its own accord arises from Brahma-Tattva i.e. Brahma- essence or stuff. That kalaa is thought to be of three kinds: first as Sukshma i.e. subtle, then Madhyam i.e. medium and lastly as Sthool i.e. gross. After being Kalpanaafied as subtle that kalaa is Kalpanaafied as mind-form when it stays as medium kalaa called HiranyaGarbha: There after it is Kalpanaafied as Viraat-form when that kalaa stays as Sthool i.e. gross. In this way the very same kalaa exist in all three states, "that kalaa itself is said to be Prakruti and Satva, Raja, and Tama are her gunas i.e. properties. Consider that three-Guna-possessed Prakruti as Avidyaa." YMR:6P:9:3-8.

For understanding the above passage in its proper perspective the meaning and the explanation of the Sanskrit words used is a must and now read them.

One of the meaning of Kalaa is an arc of the moon. Moon has seventeen Kalaas, the curved rims of the moon seen during the Bright-half or dark half of the month. The shape of the kalaa is a quarter circle to full one and is alluded to show that the energy that arises in Brahma-stuff is in the form of waves. Initially the energy arises in the form of subtle kalaa then it becomes medium kalaa called Mind and HiranyaGarbha: Hiranya means gold at great heat and Garbha means an embryo: Thus the word means gold-colored embryo or golden egg at great heat and is used as symbol to represent the state of Brahmaa at a stage of exploding to viartify as universe. Viraat means inconceivably big and vast and is used to mean and represent cosmos. Sukshma, Madhyam and Sthool means subtle, medium and gross representing short, medium and long waves in Brahma- stuff. The very same energy creates all these waves and runs through them. Size, length and combination of waves bestow the properties and qualities to the substances formed from them. And the properties and the qualities of the waves and the substances formed are Satvic, Rajasic and Tamasic depending on the waves composing them.

This kalaa i.e. wave is said to be Prakruti and Satva, Rajas and Tamas are her three properties or three qualities. Prakruti is also called Avidyaa. There is no substance in our universe which is not composed of these three properties i.e., waves in combination. Every substance is a compound of these three properties i.e., waves. The word Kalpanaa means thought and imagination and suggests that every thing is the thought of universal chitta merely, which is nothing but a wave, if we take factually it all amounts to nothing but that Shakti or energy when active is in a wave form.

Now let is refer to Devi Bhaagvat, a treatise on Goddess who is personified and deified energy.

Goddess Ambaa says, "In this universe there is no substance without three gunas of mine. In this universe every thing, visible or invisible, is always by virtue of three gunas. Whatever is in this universe is never without three gunas and will never be. Nirguna i.e. qualitiless i.e., waveless is only one and that is Brahma and Paramaatmaa and he will never be visible. I am with qualities and the attributes at the time from creation till dissolution of the universe. I am always cause form and never effect-form. I am saguna as a cause but Nirguna near Purusha: Brahma i.e. I am propertied as a cause but propertiless near Brahma. You should always remember me and Brahma together: not Brahma alone or me alone because there is always Abhed i.e. non-difference between me and Brahma; Shakti and the Shaktimaan: energy and the energy-holder. There fore nothing can be accomplished except by remembering us together."

The above passage is nothing but E=MC2 in simpler terms and fully intelligible to common man.

Devas while praising Goddess Ambikaa and Chandikaa after killing demon Mahishaasura [buffalo-demon] say, "You in fact art root prakruti; you being composed of three gunas: Satva, Raja and Tama i.e., short, medium and long waves are the root cause of creation, continuance and destruction of the entire universe. Maarkandeya Puraan: Devi Mahaatmya.

Once we accept Prakruti and gunas means waves the base

of Gita is vindicated by quantum physics with the only difference that in Vivartavaada Brahma vibrates while in science the medium of vibration is missing. Science has yet not thought of the medium of vibrations. Science will be amply rewarded if they accept that Goddess and Prakruti are personified energies and gunas means waves and that vibrating Brahma is Prakruti. It is difficult for common man to understand mathematical formulas of quantum physics while this personification is easy to follow.

[B][2]: Purusha, Prakruti and Five Mahaabhootas of Saamkhya.

We have seen that universe is constituted by the combination of waves of the vibrating Prakruti or Brahma: But how do they combine to form the universe? This is ably done by Saamkhya system developed by Sage Kapil.

Its premises are three basic Tattvas on the following reasoning:- [1]: Chetan Tattva: Aatmaa: Purusha [acting as Ishvar and Soul] Who feels pleasures and pains? If misery is its nature or natural adjunct then It would never try to save itself from it. So it must be some such Tattva whose natural property, quality or nature is not misery and unhappiness: It is Brahma circumscribed in living creatures called Aatmaa and Purusha that acts as soul under the alleged influence of Chitta.

This Tattva is inactive, immutable, unaltering and eternal. Soul is Aatmaa in contact with inanimate Tattva: Ishvar is Paramaatmaa in contact with inanimate matter. Look at the fun! inert is active while Chetan is inactive and knowledge form. The theory is that the seeming knowledge and the orderly activity of the inert Tattva is the result of mere presence of the Chetan Tattva: Chetan Purusha is the catalytic cause while inert Prakruti is concomitant material cause.

[2]: Inert Tattva: Prakruti: Nature: Who produces pleasures and Pains? It must be some element which is separate, different and of nature opposite to that of chetan Aatmaa and from where pleasures and pains emerge. This is the inert Tattva which is variously called Prakruti, Maya etc.

[3]: Paramaatmaa, Brahma, Special Purusha Purushottam.

Supreme Chetan Tattva: With the assumption and belief of Chetan and inert i.e. Purusha and Prakruti it becomes necessary to assume and believe in a third Tattva which is not only like Chetan in all respects but is also omniscient, omnipresent and omnipotent, is completely opposite to Prakruti and wherein there is total absence of miseries and unhappiness and is the final aim and object of Aatmaa to reach and identify.

Let us consider how the universe and creatures come to be from the contact of these two Tattvas viz. Purusha and Prakruti and what are their characteristic and properties:-

Kapil Muni describes Prakruti as under:- "Ashtau Prakrutayah \\2\\ and Shodashah Vikaaraah \\3\\. Tattva Samaasa:2-3. He initially divides Prakruti in two broad divisions:-

[1]: eight Prakrutis: Pradhaan i.e. root prakruti, Mahattattva, Ego, and five Tanmaatraa viz. Shabda =word, touch, form, Rasa, and smell [these are subtle elements]:

[2]: sixteen alterations: Five gross elements viz. space or sky, Vaayu, Agni, Jal and earth: and eleven organs viz. five sense organs, five action organs including their energies and eleventh Mind.

Prakruti is not the product of any previous thing but is the cause of a product. In this sense Pradhaan is the only prakruti, rest seven are prakruti-Vikruti both because they are the products of Pradhaan and by altering produce sixteen alternations which do not further alter to produce products but they do so by merely combing without altering them selves.

Prakruti: She is assumed to be inert and inanimate, Chinmaatra i.e. chit only, formless and shapeless, effect-producing and composed of three gunas, qualities, properties which are satva, rajas, and tamas. As explained the Gunas are nothing but short, medium and long waves.

Pradhaan or the root Prakruti is the homogenous and equilibrium state of three gunas and is purely a matter of deductive presumption. By the mere presence of Purusha the Prakruti becomes active and three gunas exhibit individually and begin their work of universe construction. Descent or creation proceeds as under:-

Prakrutermahaanstato A hamkaarastasmaad Ganashcha Shodashakah \ Tasmaadapi Shodashakaat Panchabhyah Panchabhootaani \\ Saamkhya Kaarikaa :22.

From root prakruti Mahattattva, Ego from Mahattattva, a group of sixteen from Ego i.e. five Tanmaatraa [subtle elements] and eleven organs, and of the sixteen, five Tanmaatraa produce five Bhootas [elements] viz. space or sky, Vaayu, Teja, Jal and Prithvi.

[1]: Mahattattva: It is the first product of modifying Prakruti. It is composed of satva guna admixed with just a necessary quantity of Rajo to make it active and just marginally enough quantity of Tamo guna to maintain and /or stop the activity and stabilize the product. This extremely pure satva-guna-composed-Mahat is called Satva-constituted-chitta of Ishvar and contains universal ego in seed form. When this purity of Ishvar-chitta is abandoned with the increase of Rajo and/ or Tamo guna it is called individual Sattva chitta and contains individual ego in seed form. These chittas are innumerable and so do the souls.

This just-a-chit form Mahattattva is the seed of all laws and rules of world formation and world regulation. It is the parent substance of the universe. In Yoga Darshan it is termed universal- Ishvar chitta and individual chittas while in Saamkhya system these are termed universal Ishvar- intellect and individual soul intellect. In Vedic lore Chetan Tattva in contact with Mahat is termed Hiranya Garbha: This is the point or Bindu in the lap of the moon in AUM written as ॐ. This is the energy-condensed point of Big Bang.

[2]: Ego: Ego stays in seed form in Chitta i.e. intellect i.e. Mahat. Mahat modifies as Ego and depending on the proportion of the gunas composing it. Ego is of three kinds: Saatvic, Raajasic and Taamasic ego.

[A]: Saatvic Ego: Satva guna is predominant over the remaining two: It modifies into:-

[a]:Chitta, Mind, Intellect, and ego; it is a complex and is collectively termed Antahkaran or inner-organs.

[b]:Five senses or five Tanmaatraas [subtle elements] termed Shabda i.e. Word, Touch, form-sight, Rasa, and Gandha i.e. smell.

[B]: Raajasic Ego: Rajo guna is predominant over the remaining two: it modifies into:-

[a]: five sense organs which are merely energies of the outer physical organs which are ears, skin, tongue, eyes and nose; sense organs here means energies which bring out these results i.e. make us to cognize these senses from sense objects.

[b]: five action organs: energies of Hand, feet, excretory and procreative organs and the tongue.

[c]:the fourteen deities controlling the fourteen organs.

[C]: Taamasic Ego: Tamo guna dominates over the remaining two and produces:-

Five Mahaa Bhootas. The word Bhoota has no English equivalent in the sense in which it is used here and we shall continue to use the word Bhoota. These are five in number: [1]: Aakaash or Avakaash, [2]:Vaayu or Pavana, [3]:Tej or Agni, [4]: Jal or Aapa, [5]: Prithvi or Avani, which are translated as [1]: Sky, [2]:Air, [3]: light or fire, [4]: water, and [5]: earth. These gross elements compose our physical bodies.

In Sarvavedaanta-Siddhaanta Saarsangraha Aadi Shankaraachaarya says regarding subtle Bhootas as under:- "Aakaash i.e. space or sky arose from Paramaatmaa united with Prakruti predominated by Tamo guna. Vaạyu is said to be from Aakaash and Agni from Vaayu, Aap = i.e. jala i.e. water from Agni and Prithvi from Jal or Aap i.e. water. The bhootas arose in this chronology. The product exhibits the gunas of the cause and therefore these bhootas are inert because ego prakruti was dominated by tamo guna. These bhootas are also termed subtle bhootas or the Tanmaatraas of the bhootas. Sarvavedaanta-Siddhaanta Saarsangraha:335-336-337. Subtle bhootas combine to produce the gross bhootas by the process termed `Panchikarana'. Aadi Shankaraachaarya in his Sarva Vedanta Siddhanta Saar Sangraha describes it as under:-

Now I tell about gross Prapanch i.e. the gross material world.

Those very space etc. the subtle Bhootas combining with each other become Gross bhootas, hear how it happens:-

Divide space etc. each one of them into two equal parts; Leaving aside the first half divide the other half of each Bhoota into four equal parts: Add and combine the one part from these equally divided parts of each Bhoota with the half of the each Bhoota other than itself. By adding this way each Bhoota is converted into five Bhootas. Thus by combining it self with the one fourth of the one half of the remaining Bhootas The space etc. the Bhootas attain to grossness: become dense: become the gross elements of science. This process of combining and compounding is Termed 'Panchikarana'. We may term it Pentication i.e. compounding in the fives. Sv S S :396-401.

On simplification the law is: the proportion in which these subtle bhootas are combined to form the gross Bhootas is one half of Each subtle Bhoota combines with one eighth of each of the other Subtle bhootas to form one whole Bhoota. Thus twenty gross bhootas are formed. Let us term them twenty master elements and the five subtle great bhootas as super elements.

Let us recapitulate the chronology of creation unto this point in nut-shell. Brahma desires to become many as one alone cannot play in lonliness and onliness. Desire means vibration is already stated. The Brahma, the world-stuff began to vibrate setting in motion series of waves varying in wavelengths from almost zero to immeasurable lengths increasing in an imperceptible slope and not like a staircase. Difference in the wavelengths of the two adjacent waves is almost immeasurable. Till the creation of the intellect or Mahat these waves go on manufacturing shapes and forms haphazardly whereafter the creation proceeds in the most orderly manner. These waves are of three kinds Satva, Raja and Tama and no product is formed unless all the three are present in combination. There is some difference of opinion regarding the formation of Prakruti but after the stage of Purusha and Prakruti all the sects of Hinduism agree on the further stages of development. The first product of Prakruti is Mahattattva, Chitta or Intellect from which three types egos arise viz. Saatvic, Raajasic and Taamsic. Taamasic ego is the raw material for the creation of the physical gross universe which goes to compose the physical bodies of all living beings including man.

Hindu sages and Rishies broadly outlined the evolution of elements, their compounds and the formation of living beings from them which was enough for yoga and religious practices for emancipation from the worldly cycle of rebirth, for Moksha and Niravaana. This broad base of universe construction and the place of every great element and the part played by them in the making of the man is tacitly accepted by all Hindus irrespective of their caste and the creeds though they may differ in their religious practices based on monism to dualism and monotheism to polytheism and even to naturalistic polytheism.

In nut shell Vibrating Brahma acting as Prakruti successively modifies as sky, Taamsic ego, Penticated sky, Vaayus i.e., all the forces and gases, light and heat, as the temperature lowers gases pass in to liquid phase and at still lower temperature into solids. Light and heat produce liquids and solids means gases by phase transition become liquids and solids. These subtle and gross elements combine to form the various components of gross matter and living creatures including human body which Gita expounds in a language every man understands.

Let us consider from slightly different angle. We are told by the big bang theory that an indeterminate mass of neutrinos [predecessor of gases] exploded with a big bang and many of the elements were formed within first three and half minutes after the explosion. In the first minute all most the entire mass of the neutrinos was converted into hydrogen and helium and few others were formed in the next two and half minutes and all the elements were in the gaseous state at the temperature at which they were formed.

Leaving aside what has been said let us consider from the angle of temperature only. Sky is a vast field of active energy from which forty nine Vaayus evolved out of which gases and all the forces including the electromagnetic forces are some. By fission and fusion gases produce light and heat which radiate out in waves. All the elements formed are in the gaseous state and the formation of liquids and the solids is but the play of temperature. Each element has its own phase transition temperature. Except for carbon all elements pass through gas to liquid to solid as the temperature falls through their respective phase transition temperatures and vice versa. This is what scriptures meant when they said that gases to light to liquid to solids. Initially everything produced is in gaseous state: gases combine to form further elements in gaseous form producing light and heat. Gases on cooling become liquids i.e., Jal or Aap; liquids are produced from light. Liquids on cooling produce solids i.e. earth. They describe phase transition in very simple words for the common man.

Scheme of Five great gross elements widely differs from that of Physics. Hinduism considers sky and light also amongst the physical elements. Bhagawaan Krishna refers to earth, water, fire, air, sky as well as mind, intellect and ego as his Eight inert Prakruties: And soul Prakruti is the 9th. He does not go into the details of the formation and composition of these elements because it will serve no useful purpose for the common man who will not be able to grasp it: He asks you to put faith in his words because the practice of dharma will slowly lead through all the stages and finally emancipate the practitioner in Brahma. He simply states that Brahma vibrates as Prakruti manifesting three gunas which produce all his nine Prakrutis composing animate and inanimate universe. He elaborates how the three gunas i.e., three waves of prakruti affect the human psyche and behavior specially in Chapters 13,14,16,17.

We have differing terminology of Vedas, Bhaagavat, Saamkhyas and the Tantras in matter of creation: let us try to harmonize.

Prakruti is an energy state wherein three qualities or gunas lie in a homogenous or equilibrium state. The state of Naada-Maatraa is called Maayaa Shakti or point mistress or the wife of Bindu State Ishvar; The united homogenous state of Shakti of Bindu Maatraa is the modified chit energy of Brahma. On the disturbance of the Prakruti energy twenty four elements arise: [1]: Five great elements from the Tamo Guna i.e., long waves: [2]: Ten organs from the Rajo Guna i.e., medium waves. [3]:Five Tanmaatraa [subtle elements], ego, chitta and intellect from Sattva guna i.e., short waves. These twenty four Tattvas are within the Prakruti womb located in the body of Maayaa Shakti who is the twenty-fifth and the Parameshvar is the twenty-sixth Tattva who remains unchanged. He is the lord of all. Bhaagawat has tried to harmoniously unify the Vedaant and the Saamkhya views of the cosmos. Bhaagavat: Skandh 2 and Skandh:11: These twenty four Tattvas, the affluence of Prakruti Shakti are the opulences of the Maayaa-powered Brahma called Ishvar who is signified and symbolized by Pranava AUM written as united with Naada the half syllable and Apara-point; Paramaatmaa with the Chid-Shakti located as inner knower is the 26th Tattva and constitutionally unchanging remains as he always was.

Let us understand Maya little more in detail. Avyaakrut i.e. unaltered i.e. undisturbed Maayaa is sheltered in Kaivalya-Brahma-Chaitanya or we can say the Maya is the potential energy i.e. Shakti located in Brahma-Chaitanya. Unaltered Maya harbors and hides in herself the seeds of name, form and karma or action. This Maya keeps holding on the Abhaas i.e. the illusion of Chaitanya. Pure Brahma Chaitanya tries to alter the unaltered Maya i.e. tries to convert the potential energy into kinetic energy. That chetan which activates and manifests the unmanifest Maya is Ishvar. Pure Brahma is beyond speech while Guna clad Brahma i.e. powered and empowered Brahma can be worded: Thus that which is consciousness or awareness of Kaivalya in unaltered Maya is Ishvar. Pure Brahma Chaitanya tries to alter the unaltered Maya simply means Brahma with desire to become many vibrates forming waves.

That Chaitanya which becomes circumscribed and limited in Maya form Upaadhi is called Maya clad Chaitanya and in three states of slumber, dream, and waking is respectively called Ishvar, Hiranya Garbha and Viraat or cosmos. Chaitanya Aabhaas falling in Vidyaa is Ishvar and so he is omnipresent and when the Chetan Aabhaas falls in Avidyaa, it is called soul. Avidyaa clad Chaitanya is called Praajnya, Taijas and Vishva i.e. universe respectively in slumber, dream and waking states. Just as universe is Maayaa clad Chetan, so Avidyaa i.e. ignorance clad Chetan is every creature.

Beyond the three states is the fourth state called Turiya wherein Ishvar Chetan and Soul Chetan separating from the three states enjoy the form of Witness chetan: Chetan becomes a witness and ceases to be an enjoyer; an actor in the play and individual experiences Monism. Birthless Master cause is not knowable; is not the subject of knowledge because it is knowledge itself and knowledge cannot become the subject of knowledge; It is the subject of experience and on experience the knowledge alone remains.

From the forgoing it is fairly clear that Brahma and Chiti or Chid Shakti of Vedas, Param-Shiva and Kaali-Shakti also called Kaalraatri, Kaali, Bhagvati or Tripura Sundari of Tantras, AUM written as symbolizing Brahma, Param-Shiva, Ishvar and Maayaa Shakti of Bhaagavat are synonyms and they modify or transform into Purusha and Prakruti who further transform or modify into animate and inanimate worlds where human beings rule at least on this planet. It is further clear that the Shakti is a term used for energy and are personified and deified as Goddesses.

From the above it can be deduced that Aatmaa and Purusha are synonyms for the same thing: Paramaatmaa and Purushottam are the synonyms for the same being. Aatma and Purusha when in the body are Akshara Purusha: but they are indivisible part and parcel of Brahma, Paramaatmaa and Purushottama. Aatmaa and Purusha are that part of Brahma, Paramaatmaa and Purushottam which occupy the living being but remember that they are undivided and indivisible from them. Paramaatmaa, Purushottam, Param Brahma and Param Shiva are used for the root substance of the universe. It is controversial whether vibrating Brahma is prakruti or Prakruti is separate from Brahma and vibrates in the presence of Brahma: We may not enter into the controversy because it makes no difference except at one stage lower than the highest state of existence. One may solve it when at that stage.

On the theory of Spandan postulated by Veda, Saamkhya, Shaaktaa and Shaivites It follows that the entire universe is constituted by nothing but waves: When we say that gunas act and react it means waves produced in Brahma or Prakruti are acting and reacting with each other and that Aatmaa or Pure Purusha is not affected by it but It believes that It is affected. This is the stand taken by Krishna in Gita. For common man it is not useful to consider whether Brahma and Prakruti are one or separate? It will not make any difference whether you believe one way or the other. [B][3].

AUM written as

AUM is the all pervasive Mantra in Hinduism and is complete Mantra by self. No other Mantra is complete unless preceded by AUM. Why? Because the doctrine of AUM written as describes one of the very important and generally accepted view of creative modification of some part of Brahma into the universe. Let see how?

Some portion of Kinetic Brahma becoming extrovert contracts, congeals and solidifies forming a zero i.e. a hollow sphere called 'Bindu'. This Bindu is shown as a point in the hollow of the crescent moon of the AUM written as - and is the fifth syllable of AUM. Though Zero like, as if nothing, it possess the combined and unified power and strength of knowledge-energy, action- energy and desire-energy wonderfully secreted and hidden within it. This Bindu i.e. point called Sad-Brahma, Sadaashiva and Kaarana-Bindu i.e. cause-point by reason of these hidden energies and because this Bindu i.e. point is the immediate starting cause of the universe.

Prapanch Sara Tantra strikes a slightly differently note in the matter. According to it Maayaa is just a chit and when she is impregnated with a desire to create in the presence of Jyoti i.e. a flame, she congeals forming a Bindu-point-a hollow sphere. In due course of time this Bindu i.e. point divides within herself into two distinct sections and finally explodes into two parts. Right side is a single point called Bindu and the left side consists of two points vertically placed called Visarg. Bindu i.e. point is called Puroosha and the Visarg is called Prakruti. Union of the two Hamsa; eagle; a dove. This is only a different way of putting the explosion of the Bindu. Tantra Doctrine states with full confidence on the authority of experience that, slowly in due course of time Homogenous Sadaashiva begins to form and divide into Shiva and Shakti till they fully separate and are known as Shiva and Shakti; or Puroosha and Prakruti still they maintain that the division is illusory.

This Kaaran Bindu i.e., cause point arises, floats and plays as universe on explosion and finally gathers as a point and subsides in the unmanifested state of Chidaakaasha from which it arose. This Bindu is Hiranya Garbha of Veda, Upanishads and Mahaabhaarat. This Bindu is called Ishvar when it becomes ready to create and modifies further. In due course of time this cause Bindu explodes setting forth vibrations producing waves having wave lengths varying in a continuous slope with no end cutoff at either end. The word used in the text is Shot which means explosion. The explosion of this Bindu can be compared to the explosion of the hot mass of neutrinos of the hot model of Big Bang theory because this Bindu like the knotted point of energy of science is the parent substance of all that exist as universe.

Cause Bindu on point of explosion becomes the Action Bindu and finally explodes: Causal state passes into action state. SadaaShiva is also called Paraa Bindu i.e. Supra point. Action Bindu is termed Shabda Brahma or 'Word-Brahma' meaning Brahma in the shape of energy spectrum or producing it.

This exploded Bindu forms the three divisions of AUM from which are developed the Upsargas i.e. sub-Tattvas or sub-creations. These are the three Maatraas i.e. Alphabets A, U, M manifesting in the following Trinities:-

[1]: Gunas viz. Sattva, Raja and Tama i.e. short, medium and long waves of the energy spectrum.

[2]: Vedas: Rig, Yaju and Saam.

[3]: Bhogya i.e. enjoyables viz; Bhooh, Bhoovah and Swaha.

[4]: Bhoktru i.e. Enjoyers viz. Vishva, Teijas and Praajnya.

[5]: States viz. waking, dream and slumber.

[6] Bhoga i.e. Enjoyment viz. Gross, subtle and causal.

[7]: Deity viz. Vishnu, Brahmaa and Rudra.

Shabda Brahma i.e. Word-Brahma is called 'Pranava' and also AUM written as. It is a natural symbol of Ishvar and fully represents the entire universe in its evolution and devolution states rising, floating and dissolving within Brahma substance.

From the above it will be seen that AUM is the symbol of Purusha and Prakruti; Purusha playing in various forms in the variously formed Prakruti.

The equilibrium Unmanifested state of root Prakruti is purely inferential and Aagam-known and for this reason, causal universe is nothing but chitta composed of almost pure Sattva guna and causal body is almost pure Sattva-chitta.

Tattva Chintaamani:6:6:36 and other Tantras state that a

yogi in meditation sees that Aum is surrounded on all sides by luminous fiery particles and above this sees a brilliant light like flame of a wick-candle stretching from earth to sky.

Bindu and AUM surrounded by particles and light suggest either a state after the explosion of the Bindu or the formation of the Bindu from the particles; We have no way to tell which one.

Pantanjal Yoga Sutras tells why and how one should chant AUM. [B][4]. Time and Time Scales Employed.

Gita repeats that all the worlds including the universe are created, maintained and destroyed in the due course of time, and has told us the time scale of one world in ch:8:16-17-18. So let us consider the notion of time and time scales of creation and annihilation of universes under Hinduism. What is Time? Is it a Fact or a Fiction?

No concept of modern physics is devoid of Space-time continuum though the same are now accepted to be the constructs of mind. Hinduism slightly differs from this idea. In Hinduism space is the illusion created by the initial vibrations of Brahma. On the basis of Panchikarana Theory it is the second degree product. Space has an illusory or relative existence as the rest of the universe but time has not even that illusory existence. Time is purely a ratio invented by man to describe the chronology of events and it has acquired a very important place in describing the working of our universe.

Hindus were well conscious that prior to the coming into being of the universe there was neither time nor space. Vashishta says: "Hey mighty-armed! what you say is true. Space, time etc. there was nothing in the beginning of the srushti of great dissolution." YMR Vasistha says, "The time interval between the dissolution period and the beginning of another creation cannot be calculated in absence of suns etc. and remains quiet as if in a dream or slumber state. This quiet dissolution period continues for a very long time but incalculable in absence of sun. Thereafter Mahaa Chidaakaasha remains in samkalpaless-form like slumber-state within Maya-form covering immeasurable in time and space and located within initial-form-of-all, experience-form and quiet Chidaakaasha-form that supreme Tattva, as if experiencing the dream state.". YMR. 6 U: 73: 9-10. Thus they were not only aware but conscious of the fact that in the absence of sun, moon and earth calculation of time would not come into existence neither would have the time calculation devisors.

What is the basis of our calculations? Earth spins on its own axis thus causing our day and night which is divided into twenty four sections called hours. Hours are divided into minutes and minutes into seconds. Earth moves round the sun and the time taken to complete the circle round the sun is divided into twelve months on the movement of the moon round the earth. Again all these are based on the seeing apparatus of man. If the eye lens had different focal length all our calculations of time and space would have been different. Thus present time calculations are based on the conditions of our sensory organs and the planetary system we live in. Each planet will have its own time system provided intelligent beings are there.

Hindu theory of creation and dissolution of individual worlds within a galaxy and galaxies within the universe and finally the universe itself are calculated in terms of the days in the life time of Brahmaa and Mahaa Vishnu all of whom are subject to death and rebirth repeatedly.

Three kinds of dissolution is described in the scriptures:

[1]: Instrumental dissolution which takes place at the close of Brahmaa's day and contintues till he wakes up in the morning.

[2]: Praakruta Dissolution i.e. the dissolution of galaxy which takes place on the death of Brahmaa the life span being 100 celestial years.

[3]: Extreme end dissolution when Mahaa Vishnu along with the entire universe consisting of all the galaxies merges in the Brahma.

[1] Instrumental Dissolution or Daily dissolution: The time

required for this dissolution is described in Gita:8:16-19. i.e. At the close of Brahmaa's day but exact calculations are not given but certainly it is very long time compared to human years. Lord Krishna's purpose in making this exposition is mainly to bring home that every thing is subject to birth and death and nothing is permanent save and except Brahma which vibrates only creating the illusion of the universe and never alters in its constitution. The life span of Brahmaa in terms of human years is given in other scriptures. The day of Brahmaa consist of one thousand units each unit consisting of four Yugas. That fourteen Manvantars come into being and destroyed during the day of this Ishavar and the night is of equal duration. That fourteen Indras have their rule in succession in one day of Brahmaa. The three worlds [i.e. paradise, mortal and Paataala] are destroyed at the end of the day. It is called nimitta Prarlaya i.e. instrumental dissolution. Equally long is the night i.e. the resting period of Brahmaa. This may be taken to be dissolution of individual solar system.

[2]:Praakruta Dissolution: The dissolution of the galaxy takes place on the death of Brahmaa: He lives for one hundred celestial years.

[3]: Aantyantic i.e. Extreme-end dissolution or dissolution of the universe with all its galaxies. This takes place on the death of Mahaa Vishnu whose life span is Two Paraardha human years. The entire universe is dissolved into Brahma. The position which was before the beginning of the formation of point in the lap of moon in AUM is restored. All quiet and deep.

Day of Brahmaa = 1000 units each of four Yugas. which is equal to 4,320,000,000 years.

At the end of the day the night of Brahmaa begins and he sleeps: his activity of creation ceases and the world begins to die and dissolve. This is termed daily dissolution. His night is as long as his day and so his day and night lasts 8,64,00,00,000 years. What is created during day dissolves in the night and at the dawn of the next day Brahmaa begins his activity of creation. This is instrumental dissolution described in Gita.. Brahmaa keeps his body for 100 years calculated as above at the end of which the world with all the fourteen regions is destroyed. Every thing born of Prakruti dissolves in the Prakruti. This is said to be the third dissolution of the world i.e. death. Possibly this may have the reference to the death of a galaxy. There is the fourth dissolution known as the great dissolution when the entire universe with countless galaxies dissolve in the light of Chidaakaasha.

A Kalpa is made up 14 Manvantars: One Manvantar is equal 306720000: At present Varaaha Kalpa is running whose time scale is 4320000000 human years. World Dissolution takes place at the end of every Kalpa. The life of the universe is Two Paraardha years which is equal to 31105-00000000000000 human years; At this time universe totally dissolves including Vishnu.

Hindus have clear conception that there are many time scales and there cannot be an end of absolute time though relative time begins and ends. To them life is deathless and continuous with change in forms and names only.

Always remember that Prakruti and her three gunas Satva, Rajas and Tamas means energy spectrum with three kinds of waves i.e., short, medium and long in every range. Keep these terminology in mind and you will be reading Gita Dharma based on modern science.

CHAPTER : 1

Dejection Yoga

Chapter one begins by telling that Arjuna is afraid to kill even an Aatataayin i.e., a criminal against life, property and women because he thinks he will be committing a sin. Killing of any one whether relative or not and sins are the two prominent factors which hold back Arjuna from fighting. Besides the destruction of the family-gentry, the reasons adduced are spoilage of the family customs and usage, hybridization of the progeny, and consignment of the ancestors to hell for a long time. His love for family and elders does not diminish though he affirms that his Moha had disappeared by the sermon as is evidenced by his behavior during the progress of the war.

Dhritraashtra Spoke: Oh, Sanjay! Assembled on Dharma-field Kurukshetra with a desire to fight what have my sons and Paandu's done? 1.

The first chapter gives a clear idea of the battlefield and the horrifying effects and results of war. It describes the condition and atmosphere then prevailing. Gita has taken its roots from confusion, bewilderment, agony and distress. This is a Moha-dispelling dialogue between grief-stricken, dharma-confused, sin-fearing, dejected and despaired, Arjuna and love-filled Bhagawaan Shree Krishna. Thus Gita is a panacea for all our ills in social and spiritual life.

Dharmakshetre Kurukshetre

Gita begins with Dharmakshetre Kurukshetre. It was a land ploughed and developed by king Kuru. Kshetra means a field: It is a field of Kuru. Thus come to be called Kurukshetra.

Kurukshetra is called Dharmakshetre because it was made

holy by the sixth Vishnu incarnate Parashurama by chopping the heads of Kshatriyas who were arrogant and cruel by reason of wealth and power. He did it twenty one times. Idea in killing was that no king with power who has become cruel and arrogant should remain a ruler. He destroyed them to upkeep Dharma.

Kurukshetra compared to human body. It is also opined that Kurukshetra refers to human body. War goes on right from waking till retirement for sleep and from birth to death. That war is to be fought on the basis of Dharma. It teaches that human life is vain and wasted if it is not lived in the spirit of a roaring lion without doing good karmas and attaining perfection. Abandon all sorrows and arrogance: always remain tranquil under all conditions. Gita teaches why and how.

Dhritraashtra is carefree for the war front as Grandfather Bhishma was commanding his army. Bhishma was a vowed to protect the Hastinapur dynasty. That he was invincible: any body cannot kill that he had the boon of choosing the time of his death and so unless he decides to die. Yet king is not at ease because elders were not pleased with his actions. He does not ask televisioned Sanjay to describe what was taking place on the war-front but puts questions as to life generally. Days are passing. On the tenth day of the war, on being asked Sanjay describes the evolution of earth and thirteenth chapter begins when Sanjay abruptly exclaims: "Hato Bhishmah Shaantanavo Bharataanaam Pitaamahah Bhishma. Shantanu's son grandfather Bhishma is killed." Bhishma 13:3. Sanjay thus abruptly exclaims what happened in the evening of the tenth day. On being asked he relates the scenario of the war-front during the last ten days by way of flashback.

Gita begins with the dejection of Arjuna under dangerous conditions of war. One is likely to turn towards Paramaatmaa under the pressure of the trying conditions but not always. One may take to alcohol and drugs.

Gita vividly presents to our view the evil-minded and blinded father worrying for the welfare and safeties of his gang of one hundred wicked and arrogant sons ready to fight an all out war to keep an ill-gotten empire. The language and mood of the question beautifully express the worry of Dhritraashtra. Sanjay begins to tell from the very the beginning.

Immediately after observing the Paandu-army in battle-array, king Duryodhan went to Aachaarya [Drona] and spoke these words. 2.

Warriors in Paandu Army

Oh, Aachaarya! Behold the great army of Pandavas strategically arrayed by your intelligent pupil [Drushtadhumna] the son of king Drupad. 3. Here is the heroic and great master archers like Bhima and Arjuna and charioteers like Yuyudhaan [Saatyaki] and Drupad. 4. And there are valorous men like Dhrishtaketu, Chekitan, powerful Kaashiraaja, Purujit, Kuntibhoja and Shaibya. 5. And heroic Yudhaamanyu, powerful Uttamanja, Sons of Draupadi, All of them are mighty charioteers. 6.

Warriors in Duryodhana's Army

OH, best Brahmin! Also know them who are important ones on our side. I name the chief ones of our army for your information. 7.

You and Bhishma, Karna and battle-victor Kripaachaarya as well as Ashvatthaamaa, Vikarna and Somadatta's son Bhurishravaa.8. And many other brave ones ready to lay down their lives for me. They are experts of different weapons and well-versed in military art of war. 9. Protected and guarded by Bhishma our army is Aparyaapta: but theirs protected and guarded by Bhima is Paryaapta. 10

After surveying the armies of both the sides King Duryodhan goes to his guru and describes the battle-arrayed armies with chief commanders and concludes that, "Our army is Aparyapta and theirs is Paryaapta." Each of the two words Paryaapta and Aparyaapta has double meaning. Aparyaapta means immeasurable, incomplete and not united: Paryaapta means small but united. He in effect says Pandava army is complete because they were on the battlefield with all their heart and our army is incomplete because it was hired and will act on orders only. This is why he is afraid within. This is the reason he indirectly censures Drona guru by addressing him, 'Dvijottam' i.e., best of the Brahmin. Brahmin is not a warrior and a fighter. Drona was a guru of a warrior class but not a warrior. In couplet seven he is addressed not only as 'best of the Brahmin' but is taunted by statement 'your intelligent pupil whom you have taught, that very pupil Drushtadhumna is standing on the other side to kill you.' All this points to the fear settled within. He has not only realized the weakness of his army but also the strength of the opponent. Duryodhan has realized that under the conditions his chances for success were not great. Duryodhan was also aware that many in his army were feeling that they were on the evil side especially after Krishna's mediation and were secretly wishing for the victory of the Pandavas. Duryodhan appears confused and alarmed.

All were not in favor of war: even Gaandhaari and Dhritraashtra tried to dissuade but in vain. Except Duryodhan and Shakuni none had fought this war wholeheartedly. Bhishma says, "What can be the greater misery than be forced to fight with Paartha who serves, has faith in Brahma, truth-speaker and without envy." Udyoga 137:3. From the beginning Bhishma says to Duryodhan that he will not fight with Shikahandi and will not kill the sons of Kunti. He said to Duryodhan, "Hey, Duryodhan! You must have heard that Shikhandi was initially a woman, then he became a man: I will not fight with him. In the war I will kill all the kings except the sons of Kuntaa." Udyoga 169:20-21.

Drona, the weapon-guru of Kurus says, "Arjuna in dearer to me than my son. How should I fight with him? Hate to the life of these Kshatriyas who have to fight with Arjuna who is immutably fixed in execution of Kshaatra Dharma i.e. the duties of a warrior. Udyog: 137:5. He says to Duryodhan, "You will not be able to conquer Yudhisthir whose adviser is Krishna and whose brother is Arjuna. Udyog: 137:19

Forget about Bhishma and Drona, did Karna, the most dear and trusted friend, fight with his whole heart? Except few each one fights with dejection at heart.

The order of blowing the conches described in the following couplets tells in no uncertain terms that the army of Duryodhan though lacking the luster of devotion to purpose and unity was none- the less very well disciplined because of Bhishma. So also is the army of Pandavas: Paandu- army was divided into seven divisions each with his commander: all commanders were under Chief Marshall Drushtadhumna: Arjuna was commander-in-chief: And Arjuna was under the control of Shree Krishna. Army was united and satisfied that it was fighting on the side of Dharma.

Feeling of unity, oneness and being on the side of Dharma is absent in Kaurava army. Bhishma did not allow Karna to fight so long as he was the chief of the army. Drona was not ready to fight with all his might so long as Bhishma was present on the battlefield. Karna was not ready till Drona was present. Ashvatthaamaa was not prepared to come to the battlefield till Karna was there. Shalya was not ready to fight till Ashvatthaamaa was on the battlefield. Thus Kaurava army was full of animosity and malice toward each other and full of self-importance while Paandu army personnel is selfless and united.

Therefore all of you stay-fighting from your strategically assigned places protecting Bhishma from all sides. 11.

To delight him [Duryodhan] Majestic old-Kuru grand father [Bhishma] with a lion-roar blew his Conch loudly. 12. There after conches, drums, bugles, trumpets and other war musical instruments sounded simultaneously: The sound was fierce and tumultuous. 13.

Thereafter Maadhava [Shree Krishna] seated in white-horse-yoked chariot and Pandavas blew divine conches. 14. Shree Krishna, Arjuna and Bhima-karma doer Vrikodar Bhima blew their PanchaJanya, Deva-Datta and big Pondra respectively. 15. Kunti-sons king Yudhisthir, Nakul and Sahadeva blew their conches Anant Vijay, Sughosha and Mani-Pushpak respectively. 16. Mighty archer Kaashiraaja, Great charioteer Shikhandi, Dhrishtadhumna and Viraat, invincible Saatyaki, 17. And Oh, king! King Drupad, Draupadi's sons, long-armed Abhimanyu; all of them blew their conches separately. 18.

And that tumultuous noise thundering and resounding through the sky and earth ripped open the hearts of Kauravas, Dhaartaraashtra nationals.19.

And Oh, king! Seeing Duryodhan and his systematically arrayed army ready to use the weapons and arms Kapidhvaja [Arjuna] lifted his bow and spoke thus: 20.

Arjuna asks Shree Krishna to park his chariot in the middle of the armies to know who were the warriors.

Oh, Achyuta! [Krishna], Station my chariot in the middle of both the armies. 21. So that I may observe those present here with a desire to fight and with whom I have to fight in this war. 22.

And I may as well also see those warriors assembled here desiring to do good to the wicked intellected Duryodhana. 23.

Sanjay spoke: Oh, Dhritraashtra! On Arjuna saying thus, Hrishikesha - Krishna parking the best chariot in the center of the two armies in front of all kings specially Bhishma and Drona spoke thus: Oh, Paartha! Behold, these Kurus assembled here. 24-25.

Sanjay tells to Dhritraashtra: Krishna parked the chariot as requested and told Arjuna to observe the assembled Kurus and their allies.

Note the choice of the names Kapidhvaja and Achyut for Arjuna and Shree Krishna respectively out of their many names. The chariot of Arjuna always carried the flag with a picture of Hanumaana the great monkey devotee of Shree Rama. Kapi means monkey who is always restless. The name

Kapidhvaja is used to suggest that some thing unusual is rioting in the Arjuna's mind. It suggests confusion and wavering. Krishna is addressed by his another name Achyut that means unwavering, constant, and steady. Confusion and wavering is now facing the constancy, steadiness and unwavering. Look at the reason Arjuna furnishes for asking to park his chariot in the middle! He wants to see with whom he was to fight and who were the well wishers of the wicked Duryodhan. Did he not know who were opposing him? Is it possible that he did not know? No, it is not possible with the life-long struggle with the enemies. Only few days back he had fought with this very horde of enemies in the outskirts of Viraat City to save the cows. Real reason is that Arjuna is wavering. He has lost his composure. Arjuna was strong in health, heart and mind but it seems, the picture created by Sanjay in his peace mission. had already watered down his war-spirit.

Arjuna sees his friends and relatives as his own at this moment: his desire to fight dries up.

And Arjuna saw uncles, grand fathers, teachers and gurus, maternal uncles, brothers, sons, grandsons, Fathers-in-law friends and well wishers standing in both the armies. 26. Considering all those present as brothers, Arjuna filled with compassion begins to speak thus in despair and dejection. 27.

Arjuna Spoke: Oh, Krishna! Seeing these my own people with a desire to fight my limbs are becoming loose, languid and exhausted: my mouth is parching: my body is trembling with body-hairs raised:. 28-29. Gaandiva Bow is slipping from my hand: my skin is severely burning: my mind is reeling and I am unable to stand steady. Oh, Keshava! I see only hostile omens and unfavorable signs: I do not see any Kalyaana i.e. well in killing these relatives in this war. 30-31.

Oh, Krishna! I desire neither victory nor kingdom nor happiness because Oh, Govinda! what happiness can we derive from kingdom, Bhogas, enjoyments and life? Because, those for whom we desire this kingdom, Bhogas and happiness are standing for war ready to die abandoning their wealth and hope for life. Here are present teachers, Pitaras i.e. in general one generation above, sons i.e. in general one generation below Grand fathers, maternal-uncles, Fathers-in-law, grandsons, brothers-in-law as well as other relatives. 32-34.

Oh, Madhusudan! Let them kill me. I do not desire to kill them even for the empire of the three worlds then what to talk of this earthly kingdom! 35. Hey, Janaardan! What happiness will we have by killing Kauravas? We will earn sin only by killing these Aatataayins i.e. committers of crimes against life and property. 36. Oh, Maadhava! therefore it is not proper for us to kill our Kauravas brothers because how can we become happy by killing relatives? 37.

Even though, those whose intellect is killed by greed do not see any fault in family-destruction nor see the sin in treachery to a friend: 38. But Oh, Janaardan! why should we, the knowers of the faults and consequences arising from destroying a family, not think of saving ourselves from the sin? 39.

Ancient family Dharma perishes with the destruction of family and Adharma pervades the entire family on the destruction of Family Dharma. 40. Oh, Krishna! with the increase of Adharma, family women become licentious and Oh, Yadunandan! hybrids are born with such women. 41. Crossbred progeny is for consigning the family killers and the family to hell and the ancestors of those who have stopped Pinda-water-obsequies also fall. 42. Ancient family Dharma and Jaati Dharma perish by the faults of the crossbreeding of these family-killers. 43. We have heard that those whose family Dharma have perished certainly come to stay for undetermined time in hell. 44.

Oh! how strange and pitiable it is that we are willing and prepared to commit a great sin because we have become ready to kill our own people with the greed for kingdom and happiness. [45]. It will be more beneficial for me if the armed Kauravas kill me, weaponless and unopposing. 46.

From couplet 28 to 46 Sanjay describes to Dhritraashtra

how Arjuna was talking in confusion and compassion, despair, dejection and gloom and refusing to fight. From here on the gloom begins and hangs on Arjuna till his ignorance and suspicion are dispelled as stated in couplet 73 of chapter 18. Once gloom and despair occupy man's mind, his body exhibits various symptoms of weakness and worry superbly described in the four couplets 28-31.

But remember Arjuna is not gloomy out of fear of defeat. No. He never had fear. On the contrary he talks with full confidence in his victory but shudders at the result of his victory. He is cock-sure of his victory which will have to be out-right which meant total annihilation of both the armies including elders, relatives, guru and others who were now considered by him as his own people. His gloom is the result of pondering on the pathetic scene that would prevail on total destruction of the armies.

After stating his body conditions he says he sees no good in killing relatives and revered people. He does not desire kingdom or happiness in absence of relatives killed by him: He would not like to kill them for all the three worlds. He further states that the annihilation will destroy family and social customs, family traditions and usage, woman would become licentious and progeny would be hybridized who would stop rituals consigning the ancestors to hell. He refuses to be a party to this result, puts aside his bow with arrows and sits in the back part of his chariot.

The root of this delusion lies in the shrewdness of Sanjay's peace mission described in the introduction. Arjuna was still ruminating the philosophical message of Dhritraashtra sent through Sanjay. No doubt Bhagawaan Krishna had watered it down but its vigor was not fully exhausted.

Seeing the relatives Arjuna falters to fight. Mercy and love of relatives are the hidden causes sprouting into dejection with overflowing compassion confusing Arjuna's mind. He justifies his refusal on various grounds. He is prepared to live by begging.

Sanjay spoke: Arjuna with his grief-bewildered Chitta spoke thus, and casting aside his bow with arrows sat down in the back part of the chariot. 47.

Before we proceed to 2nd chapter let us recapitulate the reasons for the dejection and despair of Arjuna on the basis of which he refused to kill even habitually heinous Criminals and Shree Krishna had to sermon Gita: [a] Killing even criminals for the sake of kingdom etc. would earn him sins and blood drenched enjoyments: He would not like to enjoy even good enjoyments much less blood drenched in absence of friends and relations [b] All families including his own kinsmen who were on the battlefield would be destroyed and in absence of Males Family Females would become licentious giving rise to hybrid progeny: Family Dharma would be destroyed. [c] Hybrids will stop obsequy ceremonies and ancestors would be consigned to hell for uncertain times. Arjuna is mortally afraid of earning sin and destruction of families and Dharma and consignment into hell for uncertain time. He shudders at this pathetic condition after the war and refuses to fight.

He forgets his Kshatriya Dharma to fight and eradicate every criminal against life, property and women from the society: and Shree Krishna brings him on the correct path of Kshaatra Dharma. let us see, how?

Thus it is the first chapter, named Arjuna-despair-yoga in Shree Krishna-Arjuna dialogue on Brahma-knowledge yoga-scripture Shreemad-Bhagavad Gita Upanishad.

CHAPTER : 2

Saamkhya Yoga

What did Krishna do when Arjuna put down his bow-Arrow and sat in the back part of the chariot?

On Arjuna's refusal to fight, any other chariot-driver would have told, "All right, it is your choice, let us go home." But Krishna did not do that. Neither did he retire nor allowed Arjuna to retire. What stakes Krishna had in the war? He was a chariot-driver at the request of Arjuna. No doubt he was a family friend and near relative. Paandavas loved him very much and he too was their lover. In addition he had: 'Pritim Parthena Shashvatim' eternal love for Arjuna. But was that good enough for the interest Bhagawaan was taking in that war? No, there were stronger reasons. Shree Krishna was and is eternal Dharma-Protector and Kauravas were Aatataayin i.e. criminals to the core. They had to be destroyed at all costs.

Who is an Aatataayin? i.e. criminal. Scripture says, 'Persons who burn houses and other immovable properties, kills by poison, wields of weapons to kill people, loots wealth and money, usurps others lands and farms, kidnaps and abducts others wives and women are called Aatataayins.' What is the penalty for these crimes? Smruti says, 'Without thinking kill a coming Aatataayin because killer incurs no sin in killing him.' This was a duty cast on a Kshatriya by socio-economic laws for the purpose of maintaining order and peace in a peace-loving stable society. No society can prosper if an Aatataayin i.e. a criminal against life, property and women flourishes and freely roams in a society. And it is the duty of the Government not to burden the society for the maintenance of such heinous criminals.

Kauravas were criminals to the core: They were fully

covered by the definition. They tried to burn Paandavas in a palace constructed of highly inflammable material, poisoned Bhima, in dice-play cheated Paandavas of their kingdom and sent them to jungle, tried to make Draupadi naked in the open court, wielded weapons for doing only evil things, in short no criminal activity was left undone. So Shree Krishna was steadfast in his purpose. He knew full well that Arjuna was not refusing to fight out of fear but because of his misplaced compassion. Arjuna was showering his compassion on wicked criminal horde of Kauravas and his equally guilty allies. Bhagawaan was sure that intelligent, Dhaarmic and heroic Arjuna was amenable to reason and self-respect. He also knew that Arjuna had immutable faith in him. So Bhagawaan had hopes that with correct under-standing Arjuna would follow his real Dharma. But he wanted to test the type and the intensity of the malady Arjuna suffered. So initially He met Arjuna on his own socio-economic grounds and says. Sanjay further relates to king what Bhagawaan spoke.

Sanjay spoke to Dhritraashtra: Madhusudan spoke these words to grief-stricken and tear-filled Arjuna full of compassion: 1.

Bhagawaan spoke: [to arouse the self-respect.] Oh, Arjuna! from whence has arisen in you this unglorifying Moha i.e. disgraceful fascination unaccepted by Aryans and non-giver of paradise under these trying conditions. 2.

Oh, Arjuna! Don't be impotent. It does not behoove you, Oh, Parantap! discard your trifling weakness of the heart and get up [to fight] 3:

In couplets 2 and 3 Shree Krishna tries to arouse the self respect in Arjuna but these words has no effect on Arjuna: they failed to pierce the mark. They proved to be blunt. On the contrary Arjuna maintained his stance and the real reason for his refusal buried within shoots forth. His malady was different and deep-rooted. Couplets 4-9 are resounding with this disease. His Dharma based on socio-economic principles was in direct conflict with his Dharmic duty touching the very foundation of social respectability, reverence and obedience as prescribed by Smruti: " Aachaarya cha Pravatkaarqam Maataram Pitaram Gurum/Na Hinsyaat Brahmanaangaanshcha sarvaash-chaiva Tapasvinah:" 'meaning do not injure [much less kill] teacher, mother, father, guru, Brahmin, cows and of all one who is a Tapsvi.' Apart from Shruti his love for Bhishma was so deep that he did not fight with all his heart and might against Bhishma and Shree Krishna had to often remind him of his Kshaatra Dharma and had to jump twice from the chariot and run to kill Bhishma much against his wish and vow.

Look! how he expresses his agony in couplet four. Arjuna spoke

Oh, Madhusudan! Oh, Arisudan! How can I fight worship-worthy Grandfather Bhishma and Drona with arrows in the battlefield? 4.

How can I shoot arrows at Bhishma and Drona who are worthy of worship with flowers. Arjuna brings out the sharpness of his situation in contradiction to Bhagawaan by addressing Krishna as the killer of foes and demon Madhu who were not his relatives while he was facing the criminals who were his relatives and his guru. He chides Krishna when he says it was easy to kill enemies who were neither relatives nor gurus. How can he receive his relatives and guru with arrows instead of flowers? It is against Dharma to kill guru and elders. In the same vein he continues and says:

It is Kalyaan - producing [Shreya] to live on begged food without killing Guru and great persons in this world because by killing the Guru people I will enjoy blood-drenched wealth and passion form enjoyments.5.

Again I do not know which is better of the two? [war or begging] or who wins, they or we? because those very Kauravas killing whom we do not desire to live are standing before us. 6.

With greed-killed nature [i.e., not knowing Aatmaa] and dull intellect in matter of Dharma I ask you, tell me decisively what is Shreya for me. I am your Pupil and therefore sermon me who has come in your refuge and asylum 7.

Because I do not see any means, which will remove this sorrow parching, my organs even after acquiring foeless wealthy kingdom on this earth or sovereignty over deities. 8.

Sanjay relates to Dhritraashtra: After saying so sleep-conqueror Arjuna emphatically said further to inner-knower Krishna, 'I shall not fight' and became silent. 9.

At the end of the first chapter Arjuna casts aside his bow-arrow and sits in the back part of his chariot. Here at the end of couplet 9 he emphatically refuses to fight and becomes silent.

If we analyze the reasons for this gloom, dejection and despair of Arjuna we will find that at the base is the fear that by killing the relatives family will be destroyed together with customs and traditions resulting into promiscuous family women producing hybrid progeny who will not per-form obsequious ceremonies consigning the ancestors to hell: secondly by killing relatives and elders worthy of worship he would be earning only sin and have only blood-stained enjoyments which he will not do even at the cost of his life or for three worlds. Arjuna makes blood relation and Guru relation his main plank of support. In nutshell he was obsessed with killing the relatives and earning sin thereby.

In addition to the reasons he adduced Arjuna's mind is torn asunder between two duties: [1] Socio-economic duty to kill at sight an Aatataayin i.e. a criminal committing or about to commit a crime against life, women and property and

[2] Dharmic duty not to kill Aachaarya, teacher, mother, father, Brahmins, Guru, cows and Tapsvins. It is under the shelter of this conflict of duties that Arjuna refuses to fight. It is under this paradoxical situation that Arjuna looses his composure and admits, "My mental states is ravaged by Kaarpanya fault. i.e. Miser-fault. With my intellect confounded in matter of Dharma I ask you, tell me in unequivocal terms, which is better. I am your pupil. Guide me. I am your refugee. I see nothing that can dispel this anguishing dejection which

shrivels up my sinews even if I am to acquire thriving empire on earth or sovereignty over deities."

What is the Kaarpanya Dosh i.e. Miser-fault that confuses the mind of Arjuna?

It means ignorance as to what Aatmaa is? It means greed-form fault of a miser. Miser is one who cannot tolerate the loss of even a cent. The nature of the ignorant is like a worldly miser. They are unable to discard attachment to body etc. and make effort for emancipation. Yaajnavalkya says to Gaargi, "Yo Vaa Etadkshara Gaargyaviditvaa Asmaallpkaatpraiti SA Kripanah/ meaning that person who leaves this world without knowing this Akshara, this indestructible is a miser." Brihadaaranyak.

Again it is said in Smruti 'Kripano Ajitendriyah' i.e. one who has not conquered organs is a miser. Arjuna says he is ignorant of Aatmaa. Arjuna knows that he will not be enlightened on Aatmaa without becoming a pupil. Shvetaashvar Upanishad says 'Naa Putraayaa Shishyaaya Vai Punah' Top secrets can not be opened to one who is neither a son nor a pupil.' and Aatmic knowledge is certainly a top secret. Arjuna declares that he is ignorant, completely confused in the matter of Dharma and says, 'I am your pupil. I am your refugee, tell me unequivocally what is my Shreya. What is best for me.' Remember Arjuna asks to be enlightened in the matter of Dharma though his desire for conquering back his kingdom has died. In nutshell Arjuna asks of Shree Krishna to tell him , 'Why should he fight, if he must?'

Couplets five and six make it clear that Arjuna has lost very inspiration to act. Man acts for happiness, affluence and position. Arjuna wants nothing. His self-interest is gone. It is good. It is proper for self-interest to retire but it is equally true that the inspiration to act must not die. But what can be the inspiration to act once the self-interest is gone? Self interest is the guiding force for all most all-human activities. Rest of the Gita is an answer: be prepared and ready to receive it. Gita lifted Arjuna from the wrong path and put him on the right one. There is no reason why Gita would not do the same to any one who reads and acts on it

When worldly considerations failed to banish the dejection Bhagawaan concluded that he was ready for the Aatmic knowledge and it became necessary to explain the following questions: [1]: What is death? Who are we? [2]: What is universe apart from us? [3]: What is within us and without us? [4]: What is within and without universe? [5]: Are the Tattvas within and without the universe and us same or different? [6]: Who is the director-controller of all these? [7]: What is our role vis-a-vis family, society, Universe, God and the source of all and how best to play our role.

This is a perfect set up, an unavoidable situation for a Master to reveal top secrets of Dharma and Aatmic knowledge. Rest of the Gita is in part the fulfillment of this request from an uncanny pupil.

Bhagawaan does this in a unique manner. Bhagawaan accepts the pupilness of Arjuna. He becomes his Sad Guru, a responsibility that even great persons do not accept easily but Arjuna is fit. He is detached. He does not desire worldly goods. His only desire is to know Dharma for attaining his Shreya i.e. emancipation. This was the most appropriate condition why Bhagawaan becomes his guru and imparts the entire knowledge of all the scriptures by harmonizing them. Arjuna is not an ordinary questioner. He does not request merely replies. He says, "I am your pupil, now direct me, now regulate and reconstruct my propensities, my psyche. I am putting in your hands my destiny regarding my mental and intellectual development from now on through births till Moksha. You are the only person who can do it." Now, Bhagawaan is not in a position to get away by worldly replies. He has to spell out philosophy of life. He has got to see that his pupil Arjuna is Jeevan-Mukta i.e. life-free. From here on Krishna is busy making Arjuna to get up and fight a righteous war not by brow-beating but by soaking him in the knowledge of the Reality running through and through the life and universe and how to play his role evenly and joyfully in it as a Jeevan-Mukta till Videha - Mukti.

Shree Krishna has, it seems, changed his stance or is he naturally smiling at the falsely wise words of Arjuna. He smiled possibly in a taunt. It seems he chided Arjuna in mildly taunting words. It seems taunting was to jolt and alert Arjuna to what Krishna was going to say in reply to his supposed wise words. From couplet 11 of the second chapter till couplet 66 of the 18th chapter Shree Krishna advises Arjuna [and indirectly to all who desire to live joyful life], 'How to become and live the life as a Jeevan-mukta.' From here on the message of Gita on social and spiritual Dharma of Man begins.

Sanjay further spoke: Oh, Dhritraashtra! Hrishikesha i.e. Krishna spoke smilingly [as if in a rebuke] to grieving Arjuna in the middle of the two armies [thus]. 10.

Shree Krishna says to Arjuna: You are lamenting for things not fit to be grieved and yet talk in the language of the knowledgeable. Pundits grieve neither for the living nor for the dead. 11.

You are grieving for them for whom you should not and yet speak words of wisdom: This chapter is titled Saamkhya-yoga and therefore it should be considered as based on Saamkhya system of universe construction postulated by sage Kapil. It is necessary to remember this point as it has important bearing in the interpretation of Gita, specially this chapter. For Saamkhya system see Introduction II. Let us proceed.

Arjuna is afraid of killing kinsmen in the fear of earning sin. Bhagawaan begins with the assurance that there is no killing at all. He stresses that not we but the physical bodies are subject to decay and death. We leave the body and enter the fresh body. Soul does not die but is metamorphosed into Aatmaa and then emancipated into Brahma. Couplets 12-30 deal with this aspect.

There never was a time when I was not nor you were not nor these kings were not and it is not that hereafter we all shall cease to be. 12.

Shree Krishna assures Arjuna that all of them were existing from eternity and will continue to exist in future till the end of eternity. Commentators have differently interpreted this couplet. In all commentaries except Raamaanunja this and the following couplets are taken to mean as referring to Aatmaa. Swami Shankar considers plurality you kings] and [I because conventional plural is used to refer to bodies that are different and not to universal self. Shree Raamaanunja stresses the distinction between Krishna, Arjuna and kings as finalities and views each individual soul to be imperishable and coeval with the entire universe. Lokamaanya Tilak writes," 'I' means Parmeshvar, while you and other kings mean other Aatmaas, though both were in the past and will come into existence in future. Raamaanunja says this proves that Parmeshvar and Aatmaa are distinctly separate from each other, independent and eternal."

With due respect to all, these renderings seem to be farfetched and one sided. To what entity does Shree refers to by the use of the words ' I, you and kings' should be gathered also from what is stated in the following couplets. By the use of the words 'I, you and kings' Shree Krishna means the body-dweller in them and what is meant by body-dweller is made amply clear in the couplets that follow.

If Krishna had meant Aatmaa he could have easily used the word Aatmaa but he has not used the word Aatmaa. Why?. It would be preposterous to assume that he was ignorant of the word because later on he uses the word Aatmaa in different connection. This chapter is titled Saamkhya yoga. In Saamkhya system the word Aatmaa is no where used. It is not a term of Saamkhya terminology. Aatmaa and Paramaatmaa are the terms of the Vedas and Upanishads. Kapil Muni, the propounder of Saamkhya system uses the word Purusha only for all the three Aatmaa, Purushottam and Soul. His theory is that Purusha does not play in the Prakruti but alleges in himself the activities of the Prakruti. In his view Purusha is at the most a catalytic agent in the play of the Prakruti.

It should be noted that in subsequent sections Krishna purposely and assiduously avoids the use of the words Purusha, Aatmaa, or Soul and instead uses the word 'Dehi' and Sharirinah.' What can be the reason?

Gita is the perfect harmonization of the two major systems of world-views then existing side by side. Both were talking of the same existence in different terminology. Shree Krishna unifies the two system by showing that both were talking about the same thing.

In Saamkhya the word Purusha is used for all the three i.e. Soul, Aatmaa and Paramaatmaa. Saamkhya-Kaarikaa: 18 Saamkhya Darshan 1:149.

To avoid this confusing use of the word Purusha and to distinguish it from Aatmaa Krishna uses the word 'Dehi' i.e. Body-dweller or body resident from the next couplet onwards. Aatmaa is undivided indivisible part of Brahma while Jeeva-soul is not. To pinpoint this distinction he uses the word 'Dehi'.

Does Krishna preach and teach monism, dualism or special monism? It depends upon how you interpret. If the description is taken to mean Aatmaa, monism is the end product because Aatmaa and Paramaatmaa are same in substance and continuous. Aatmaa is very minute undivided fragment of Paramaatmaa occupied by physical body: if you dip a bucket in the sea and take it out you have a bucket of sea water which water is not different from sea though separated. Similarly that part of Paramaatmaa which is occupied by flesh bodies is Aatmaa. If there is any difference between Aatmaa and Paramaatmaa then it is like a difference between seawater in bucket and water in the sea.

Just as the body-dweller has, childhood young-age and old age in this body, similarly he obtains other bodies: wise and patient [one] does not become fascinated and deluded in it. 13.

Body-dwellers obtain different bodies on death as per their Karmas. Wise ones are never perplexed at this phenomena. Body-dweller means soul because soul is subject to changes and migrates from body to body till emancipation and not Aatmaa who is changeless and immutable. Krishna does not directly explain who is Dehi but states what causes pleasures and pains.

Oh, Kaunteya! Contacts of sense organs with their sense-objects producing heat and cold, happiness and misery come and go. Being transitory, oh, Arjuna! endure them with Titikshaa i.e. equipoise. 14.

Titikshva means to endure with Titikshaa. What is Titikshaa? Shree Shankaraachaarya in his Sarve-Vedaant Siddhaanta Saar Sangrah says, "It means whatever pains and pleasures etc. come by the way by the force of destiny, suffer-enjoy them with even mind. Maintain your composure." 137. This is preparatory to what is to be said in couplet 38.

Because, Oh, best Person! these [contacts] do not afflict the patient person who remains equipoised in misery and happiness and such a one is thought fit for salvation i.e. Mukti. 15.

ASAT i.e., Is-not never becomes SAT i.e., Is and SAT i.e. Is never becomes ASAT i.e. Is-not: Tattva-knowers have concluded the fundamental principle thus. [16].

This couplet has evoked conflicting commentaries. Does SAT refer to Ultimate reality and ASAT to transient Universe? or does SAT refer to soul and ASAT to gross bodies.? Swami Shankar says,' Yadvishayaa Buddhir na vyabhicharati tat SAT, yad vishaya vyabhicharati tad ASAT.' meaning 'SAT- real as that regarding which our intellect fails not and ASAT-unreal is opposite. Swami Raamaanunja is of opinion that ASAT means body and SAT means soul. SAT can be interpreted as Aatmaa and soul both. Aatmaa and Paramaatmaa being same are eternal so SAT is not subject to destruction. It can also be interpreted as soul because soul is not subject to death: It is Aatmaa soiled by chitta complex and so subject to death only by destroying chitta-complex i.e. it exists till emancipation and so is 'SAT' in this sense. ASAT means passing panorama of universe. Aatmaa and soul were, are and will not be non-existent while transient universe and bodies will never be existent i.e. permanent. If we consider 'SAT' in contexts of couplets 12 and 13 we can safely conclude that SAT is the nature of Dehino and is eternal while Deha-body is 'ASAT' perishable. Tattva seers have perceived and concluded as above.

Know that by which all these [bodies] are occupied-pervaded-permeated to be imperishable: No one is capable of destroying this undiminishing and non-wasting one. [17].

The words 'Idam Sarvam' here means 'all these' and not 'all this' in light of couplets 12-13. All these means all gross bodies of you the kings and I. This is made amply clear by the couplet 18.

The word Avyayasya has been translated as immutable by almost all commentators. Avyaya means undiminishing, unspending and nonwasting. Kutastha means immutable. A thing can diminish or waste without being altered in nature. Metals and materials can waste and diminish by mere rubbing constantly without any alteration in their constitution. Dehi or body-dweller is Avyaya but not Kutastha, is non-wasting and undiminishing but not immutable. Body dweller changes from moment to moment and vanishes in Aatmaa in Mukti. He is Avyaya but not Kutastha: Aatmaa is both Avyaya and Kutastha: immutable and undiminishing.

All the bodies of these imperishable, empirically unprovable and permanent body dwellers are said to be perishable therefore, oh, Bhaarat! fight. 18.

Both of them, one who understands this one [body-dweller] to be a killer and one who believes that this one is killed, do not know that this one neither slays nor is ever killed. 19.

This one is never born as well as does not die: because it is not that being-never-not will come to be and it is not that he is and going to be not. This one is birthless, always, eternal and beyond ancient times who is not killed on slaying of the body. 20.

Oh, Arjuna! Whom and how can such a person who knows this one [body dweller] to be imperishable, always, birthless and unwasting slay or cause to be killed? 21.

Just as a person discards worn-out clothes and garments and puts on new ones even so body-dweller discards worn out bodies and take to new ones. 22.

Weapons do not pierce it: neither fire burns it, neither water wets it, neither winds dry it because this one is unpierceable; this one is incombustible, unwettable and nonabsorbable or undriable: this one is always, going every where, immovable, stable and Sanaatan i.e. beyond beginning. 23-24.

'Sarva Gatah' does not mean all pervading but going every where i.e. in all bodies migrating from body to body in all species. Pervading means continuity in occupying without a break. There is no break. This is the characteristic of Aatmaa and not soul. Souls are many and separate. In all pervading the question of going every where can not arise. As the verse refers to body-dwellers, going everywhere i.e. migrating in all specie is more appropriate than pervading every where. In Saamkhya system Purushas are many. This means Purusha is a soul also and Purusha as a soul goes every where i.e. in all species.

This one is subtle: this one is unthinkable and is said to be changeless in constitution but not in form .Therefore knowing thus it is not fit to grieve in the matter beyond control. 25.

If you believe this one always to be born [with birth] and die with death, even so Oh, mighty-armed! you should not grieve 26.

[because] Death is certain for a born one and birth is certain for one who dies therefore you are not fit to grieve for what is inevitable and unavoidable i.e. in a matter without remedy. 27.

Creatures are unmanifest in the beginning [before birth] manifest in the middle [during life] and unmanifest again on death. Why lament for that? 28.

Some see this one as a wonder, some speak of this one as a wonder, others hear of this one as a wonder and some do not know this one even on hearing about it. 29.

This body-dweller present in all bodies is always unslayable therefore you are not fit to grieve for all creatures. [30].

From couplets 12-30 Shree Krishna explains and emphasizes the immortality of the body dweller of every creature. Birth and death are merely acts of migration of the body dweller from one dilapidated body to a new fresh one and is normal unavoidable routine in nature till emancipation and therefore not worth grieving and lamenting. At the most you may run away from it by medicines or yoga methods for some years but ultimately death will overtake you. Prolonging life beyond its decreed span is not worth the effort as rebirth is there to carry on what is left undone or unenjoyed.

Now Shree Krishna turns to worldly and social reasons for fighting this war. He appeals to Kshatriya duties and pictures an awful situation that would result from failure to perform those duties. Performance would land him in paradise and failure would consign him to hell on death and infamy on earth.

Shree Krishna proceeds

Considering your Svadharma [i.e. own Kshatriya-Dharma] you are not fit to shiver for there exist nothing more good for a Kshatriya [warrior] than righteous war prescribed by duty. 31.

'You are not fit to shiver' is an answer to what Arjuna has said, 'my limbs shiver and tremble' in 1:29.

What is Kshatriya Dharma i.e. warrior Dharma? Shauryam, Tejo, Dhrutirdaakshyam Yuddhe chaapyapalaayanam Daanam-ishvarabhavashcha kashaatram Dharma svabhaavajam/ Valour, Tejo, Dhruti, Shrewdness, not-to-run-away-from the battle and godly nature are the natural adjuncts of a Kshatriya Dharma..

Oh, Arjuna! Happy and lucky are Kshatriyas who gain by Daiva-desire such a war as a gateway to heaven thrown open. 32.

Loosing your fame, eminence and Svadharma you will earn sin if you do not fight this Dharmic war i.e. war imposed by duty. 33.

Shree Krishna counters Arjuna's fear of earning sin by killing Aatataayin i.e. criminal relatives by reminding Arjuna that running away from the righteous war would surely saddle him with a greater sin as he would be acting in breach of his Kshatriya Dharma. He sandwiches Arjuna between two sins differing in intensity.

[Again] People will endlessly sing your infamy and for an honorable one like you infamy is worse than death. 34.

All these great charioteers will believe that you forsook the battlefield out of fear and you will attain to littleness with them to whom you were great. 35.

Your foes, the slanderer of your valor, power and capability will speak unworthy and unspeakable words. What can be greater misery than that? What can be more painful than that? 36.

You will fall in the esteem of those who adore you and backbiters of your strength will utter unworthy words of you. What can be greater calamity than this?

Having described the ugly scene resulting from not fighting the righteous war now. Bhagawaan holds out before him the charming and lovable result of this righteous war. Shree Krishna promises full benefits whether he wins or looses the war.

He says: [you] will obtain Paradise if killed or enjoy the kingdom if victorious: therefore, oh, Kaunteya [Kunti-son] be resolved to fight and get up. Be resolved to fight and rise. Be decided to fight and rise. 37.

To Arjuna's quest Bhagawaan explains the metaphysical truth that body-resident cannot be injured or killed by any physical means and natural forces while body is subject to decay and death despite all care. He further explains the Dharmic duty to fight out to the finish a duteous war thrown in the lap by Daiva-desire. Arjuna hears only but does not utter a word. Arjuna is well aware of all what Bhagawaan said till now but is unable to realize what his guru is driving at. These arguments are not dispelling his doubts and delusion arising from conflicting duties.

Words fail to soften Arjuna's resolve. Bhagawaan realizes this and quietly administers one milder dose of Saamkhya principle of action.

Join this war treating happiness and misery, profit and loss as well as victory and defeat to be even and equal [i.e. with equipoised mind] Thus you will not incur sins. 38.

In this couplet Krishna gives one more key to act without incurring the sin of which Arjuna is mortally afraid.

After having told the fundamental tenets and practice of Saamkhya system whereby the effects produced by the contacts of the sense-organs with sense-objects are annulled and sins eradicated or not incurred at all and the immortality of soul Shree Krishna begins to expound Buddhi yoga, Nishkaama Karma yoga, the yoga of selfless action.

Oh, Paartha! I have told you this intellect-attitude in relation to Saamkhya [system] but hear the same in Buddhi-yoga, united to which intellect-yoga [you] you will be free from karmic bondage. You will not incur karmic bondage. 39.

Karmic bondage means Karmas leave Vaasanaas because of the Attachment to fruits: These Vaasanaas require their fulfillment and force the soul to take a birth. So Karma-bondage: Binds the soul for next birth.

In this [intellect-joined Karma] actions begun do not perish [though left unfinished] nor there is deleterious reaction i.e. creates no sin. Even a very little [observance] of this Svadharma saves and protects one from great danger. 40.

In this Karma yoga no beginning of action is ever lost neither is there opposite reaction if left undone: observing this yoga-dharma in a small way saves [you] from great fear and danger.

One would wonder why should one aim, prepare and act if he is to remain indifferent and unconcerned to results of his action? This attitude would kill the very inspiration to act. But in this case Arjuna is already in a detached state. He does not want anything in this world or next by killing even usurpers of their kingdom and their aids. So Bhagawaan begins to open the gateway to the secrets of selfless action.

Oh, Arjuna! [Kuru-son] in this yoga intellect is firmly fixed with one resolve. There is single-pointed intellect but the intellect of the wavering, irresolute and undecided ones is many-branched and indefinite. 41.

Bhagawaan continues in the same vein and says that for the lovers of enjoyments and paradise Vedas have described in barren flowery language various activities.

Oh, Arjuna! such non-discerning passionate persons who are believers in the fruits of Vedas and paradise-proned declare that there is nothing else [greater happiness] and utter at length in a language like beautiful but barren flowers describing many specialized rites and rituals to enjoy worldly happiness and paradise producing endless birth-death cycle. 42-43.

The intellect of those, whose mental activity is abducted by these Veda-words and who are devoted to sense-enjoyments and Aishvarya does not become decisive for Samaadhi, fit for Samaadhi. [does not get established in the self by Samaadhi]. 44.

The subject of Veda is three Gunas, therefore, Oh, Arjuna! be devoid of three Gunas, be possessed of non-contradiction, be always stabilized in SAT, be without worry of maintenance [be indifferent to acquisition or preservation], be self-possessed and be stationed in Aatmic-form. 45.

Vedas sing the affluence of three Gunas only and you have to go beyond them: What three Gunas and what mean going beyond Gunas means? See Introduction II.

Be Nirdwanda, be possessed of non-contradiction: Normal meaning taken by commentators is, be without the pairs of opposites i.e. misery-happiness, victory-defeat etc. Pujya

Paanduranga Aathavale interprets differently: 'discard fruit-desire and ego of doing Karma also'. To discard Karma means not physically but Ego of 'I am doing'. This is Nirdvandva: noncontradiction. Fruit and ego are Dvandva.' Does Bhagawaan advises to renounce fruit of action and action also? What does renounce Karma mean? If Karma is to be abandoned then where is the necessity for the advice to abandon the fruit of Karma ? In absence of Karma the question of its fruit cannot arise. Here what is meant is discard the ego of doing the action, ego that 'I am acting'. This is the Nirdvandva i.e. contradictionless state. Shree Krishna who was bustling with activity all his life could not have advised physical inaction. No, He exhorts you to act without ego of doing.

Be Niryogakshemavaana, discard worries from life for life and in life. Take the life as it comes and make the best of it not grudgingly but with joy, without blaming any body including the Maker. Blame yourself for your miseries.

To the extent is the use of a pond in an all-round flooded place so is the use of all Vedas to a person who knows Brahma. 46.

Brahma knowers have no use for Vedic activities because they have no desires. What is Brahma? See Introduction II.

Your right is to act only but not to its fruits. Action alone is your right, not its fruits, never. Let not the fruits of action be your motive nor let there be attachment to inaction i.e. therefore be not desirous of fruits of action nor have love for inaction. 47.

Mark, advising Arjuna to act without the desire for fruits, Master quietly lays down that he should not discard action lest Arjuna may fall into inaction due to advice. Ishvar [God] alone is the Karmafal-Pradataa i.e. action-fruit-giver. To give or not to give the fruits of actions is within the domain of Ishvar [God] and therefore our duty ends with the action. We should act with total absence of desire for fruits because the result is not in our hands. In the circumstance is it not wise not to worry for the result. Let Him whose pleasure it is to give, worry. Why worry and be unhappy?.

What is Buddhi Yoga? Intellect-Yoga?

Fixed in Buddhi Yoga discarding attachment and becoming even-minded in success and failure, do your Karmas because evenness and equalness [of intellect] is said to be Yoga. 48.

With what attitude we should act? Bhagawaan says jettisoning attachment and remaining fixed in buddhi-yoga, treating alike success and failure, do your actions: Evenness is yoga. Fruit-desired Karma is far inferior to intellect-yoga-karma: Even-intellected Yogi discards both Punya and sins. They attain to changeless supreme state and abode. You will be stable in this even-intellect yoga when you become fixed in Samaadhi being separated and detached from the rites and rituals, enjoyments and paradise preached by Vedas.

Duties for each of the four Varnas i.e. social classes of the society were framed after long trials and errors and these duties cannot be discarded nor dishonestly executed if the society is to be preserved in healthy, wealthy and prosperous state. It has to be progressive and not static. Scriptures preach and prescribe family and social dharma-duties together with non-violence, compassion and mercy. Very same scriptures exhort to wage a ceaseless war against crimes and Adharma. Scriptures have laid down rules and regulations for all conditions in quite a good detail. Modern law-making bodies headed by all shades of politicians are supposed to do in part the work of ancient sages: But the Modern counterpart of the ancient sages is selfish, self-interested to the core, self-centered ego-stuffed and dishonestly intelligent rogues while sages were self-less, egoless godly persons working for the betterment of the human race. Effects are too evident requiring neither proof nor elucidation. The social, moral and legal code laid down by scriptures must be followed and upheld at all costs. Bhagawaan says Svadharma must be followed to its last detail and explains the risks and benefits in failing to follow or following the Svadharma.

Fruit-desired-action is very inferior compared to one done with Intellect yoga. Therefore Oh, Dhananjay! take refuge in intellect yoga: [because] fruit-desirers are miserable misers. [49]:

Superficial reading of Gita will give the impression that Bhagawaan is goading reluctant Arjuna to fight a ghastly war. But no, it is not so. Bhagawaan is trying to convince by every possible reason to fight the righteous war as a matter of personal and social duty. It is Svadharma.

Do not think even for a moment that Bhagawaan is in favor of harshness, cruelty and destruction. He was well aware of the annihilation that would ensue on war. He has tried to avoid war till the last giving one concession after another to Kauravas but to no avail. Then why did he ask Arjuna repeatedly to get up and fight? Shree Krishna lays down very clearly that there should be no crime in the society and so kill at sight every Aatataayin even if he be your relative by birth or by marriage: even if he be your Guru or person worthy of worship. And it was this duty to keep the society clean of crimes that was cast on the warrior class. The present counterpart is Police and the Army. Arjuna was a Kshatriya whose duty it was to cleanse the society of its criminals and he was refusing to perform his duty because relatives and Guru were involved. In chapter 11:32-33. Shree Krishna says, "They are going to die whether you kill them or not: so why not kill as is your duty." Arjuna hears all these arguments silently without stirring as if conveying, 'I accept your philosophy of life but I need nothing, I have no desires: Why should I take the blame and incur the sin?" Bhagawaan realizes this to be the feeling at the base of the silence and promptly proceeds to expound Karma-yoga doctrine beginning with Intellect yoga.

There are two aspects of yoga-system: theoretical and practical. Theoretical is called Saamkhya and practical is called Yoga. Bhagawaan tells, "If you do this act it will not be obstructive to your emancipation on the contrary it will emancipate you, not only this but you are not going to put your feet on the first step of the ladder to emancipation with out this Karma Yoga.

Shree Krishna exhorts unselfish and egoless action in execution of one's Svadharma, one's duties. True: but why should we act if we are to be selfless and indifferent to fruits? What is the motive power for Selfless action?

'From each according to his capacity and to each according to his needs' of communism is a direct corollary of selfless action. Man wants compensation for what he does and not for his needs. He wants the fruits of his labour to remain with him. Self-interest is the guiding force for all human actions. Any social set up which does not take this into account is bound to fail sooner or later. Communism and socialism are failing not because self-interest, the motive power of action is absent but Gita's message is missing from its tenets. Search for persons acting selflessly in society will end in very few discoveries. In capitalism the question is out of question. Proper or improper compensation for work is paid. Both these economic systems have proved their futility in working. Bhagawaan supplies the inspiration and motive force for selfless action. He explains Saamkhya-intellect and yoga-intellect and asks you to surrender to this yoga.

In this [[karma-yoga] man yoked to even-intellect discards both, the fruits of good and evil actions and the ego of acting: therefore be united with Yoga. Intellect-yoga is the skill, proficiency, and dexterity of doing Karmas. 50.

Does this mean that one should have no aims in life. No he should set his goal and then act without worrying for the fruits: leave it to the Almighty whose duty it is to give the fruits. Desire to have fruit is hope and must get it is insistence. Every man is not insistent but he is certainly hoping. Hope should be your servant and not master. It should work for you and not rule you. Do not be the slave of hopes. This should be the royal policy of your life.

Skill will exhibit in all your actions once the desire for the fruits and ego of doing are banished from your intellect. Such a skilled Karma is yoga.

Why this Karma Yoga?

Because knowledgeable persons of even-intellect having abandoned Karma-generated fruits become free from bondage of birth and attain to changeless supreme abode. [a place devoid of sorrows] 51.

You will become indifferent and detached to what you have heard and will hear [Vedic subjects referred to in couplets 41-43] when your intellect swims over the illusion-mud 52.

You will attain to Yoga [even-intellect] only when your intellect deluded by various descriptions [as above] becomes stable and settles steadily in Samaadhi. 53.

From the moment he became silent in couplet 9 Arjuna has not uttered a word till the end of couplet 53. Bhagawaan goes on advancing one argument after another: He explains immortality of the body-dweller: learned lament not for the dead nor for the living: birth and death to be normal natural routine of life beyond our control: misery and happiness produced by contact of organs with object are transient and so should be endured with equipoise because person neutral to misery and happiness is eligible for emancipation: He further argues that considering his warrior-duties it is not proper to retire because there is nothing more beneficial than a Dhaarmic war: it is a gate open to paradise if killed or a kingdom on earth on success: to dispel the fear of sin haunting Arjuna Bhagawaan advises him to fight with the attitude treating misery-happiness, loss-gain and victory-defeat to be equal.

But Arjuna does not make any movement for fighting. Bhagawaan realizes that Arjuna's confusion required a full doze of practical philosophy and he starts the tremendous task of lifting Arjuna to full-fledged Brahma-hood and also unification of two great system of world-views.

What is the resolute intellect and its necessity? It is an intellect divorced from hope and insistence for fruits of actions and yet active in doing actions. Normally intellect would be dead and not active for action in absence of hope and insistence. Under this condition Bhagawaan says act with the duty-bound-intellect and God-surrendered-intellect. If you desire to act selflessly then this resolute and determinate intellect i.e. intellect-yoga is a must. One is likely to say, it is hollow advice: Is it possible to act at all under these conditions? Bhagawaan says, Yes, it is the only way; Surrender your intellect to God and see the result. Gita is sung to explain this secret.

Your hope and insistence for fruits is cut at the root by an unequivocal declaration that only right you have is to act but not to its fruits. Why do you think of fruits to which you have no right. This applies to all creatures. Once you enter the world Bhagawaan gets the Karma done from you willingly, unwillingly or forcibly. You are merely an instrument in the hands of Almighty whether you will it or not.

Bhagawaan says, 'be a yogi and do Karma.'

When Arjuna heard Shree Krishna saying that all Karmas, irrespective of their sinful or Punyaful effects can be performed without having their effects, his curiosity woke up. He becomes eager to know fully about a person who acts in this way.

He looks with eagerness and asks,

Arjun spoke

Oh, Keshava! What is the language of Sthita-Prajya i.e. one with steady-prajyaa and also of one-in- Samaadhi-state ? How does one with steady intellect talk? How sits? Moves how? 54.

In nutshell Arjuna asks, "What is his way of life? How does he behave in such a state?" Arjuna has posed an all-important question and extremely relevant for the present world. Shree Krishna begins to answer from here on.

Can a man act without desire for fruit and ego of action? 'It is almost impossible' was the feeling of Arjuna. So is the question. In the first part of 2nd chapter Arjuna becoming

Pupil asks for a shreya-path, a beneficial path. In answer Bhagawaan explains Saamkhya yoga in the second part: explains Svadharma, faith-in-karma and yoga-intellect in the third Part: and steady-Prajyaa in this last part.

It is when the body dweller is cleansed of all dirt by following Svadharma and Saamkhya-intellect it metamorphoses into Aatmaa and Brahma: Body dweller purified to the nature of Aatmaa that it becomes of steady Prajyaa and is stable in Brahma. It is in the last part that He uses the word Aatmaa and Brahma because body dweller has ceased to be soul and has become Aatmaa by the alchemy of Saamkhya knowledge and Yoga-intellect. Question is how such a person whose body-dweller has metamorphosed into Aatmaa behave in life.?

From here on Shree Krishna describes person of steady Prajyaa i.e. a person who lives as a Jeevan-mukta:

Thinkers and theoreticians like Kant believed that such a person can exist only in theory but not in life: superman of Greeks is a myth in life. It is an unattainable giant leap of philosophy. Gita is a slap on the face of this proposition. The manner, method and the language of the question points that such persons do exist. It is not an imagination. Arjuna does not ask, 'What is the idea of Sthitaprajya' but how does he behave and act? Bhagawaan describes the life style of such a person vividly. Cardinally He lays down that every desire is an impediment in reaching Aatmic happiness. These should be jettisoned tracelessly.

What is the ideal goal of life? What does it mean? This ideal goal is an ideal, which creates an earnest-ness impelling one to go beyond the shackles of physical body to merge in the Maker even if it is going to take life spans of births. It should be an ambition of every individual to achieve this goal, this ideal. Gita teaches how to achieve this ideal goal.

Gita accepts Brahma and Paramaatmaa as absolute reality and the rest as relative reality. It does not say that universe is a nullity but on the contrary accepts very much the existence of souls, creatures and material universe. Gita sets forth the ideal-goal for man to unite and merge in Brahma step by step by individual efforts through many births. Gita does not give you a baggage of emancipation but a baggage of efforts to be put in for achieving the goal.

Sthita-Prajya state means to act outwardly like an ordinary common man and to remain completely detached and peaceful within. It is a difficult state, is it not? Politicians can show love outwardly with poisonous hatred within? Cheats and rascals show love for all but with contrary emotions within. They are never detached. If the above state is possible why not misery-happiness outside with detachment within? It is difficult to achieve Sthitaprajya-life-style out-wardly showing all the signs and symptoms of emotions, worry, misery and happiness but mentally detached. To achieve this state without being hypocrite is a marvelous art. How to achieve it? Bhagawaan Shree Krishna sang the means to achieve it on the battlefield. You can learn it.

Life-style of a Sthitprajya

Shree Krishna spoke

Oh, Arjuna! a person is said to be of steady-intellect when he jettisons all the desires harbored in mind: [his] Self [Aatmaa] remains satisfied with Self [Aatmaa] only, then is called of steady-prajyaa [intellect]. 55.

Such a Muni as one whose mind remains untroubled in midst of miseries: whose longing for happiness has retired and whose raag-passion, fear and anger have perished is said to be of steady-Prajyaa, Sthitprajya. 56.

Passion, fear and anger automatically leave the person who has no desires for sense-pleasures and whose mind is not disturbed by any miseries visiting him. Thus a person freed from differences is Sthitaprajya.

The person who having become loveless [having discarded minness and thineness] in all things and does not rejoice nor hates, neither rejoices nor resents, neither gets delighted nor dejected on attaining good or bad thing, his Prajyaa is steady. 57.

When a person withdraws his senses from the sense-subjects in a manner a tortoise withdraws all his limbs [within his shell], his Prajyaa is in steady state. 58.

Here the phrase used is Sense organs for the sense organs only; it means not for the sense-objects. This means he withdraws senses from the objects. This is Pratyaahaar of yoga-system.

The senses of the body dweller whose sense organs are starved [of sense-subjects as said in the last couplet] retire but not the longing, the taste, the interest. Even this longing retires on the seeing the supreme, on realizing the supreme. 59.

Does the couplet mean starving the senses or the physical body? Use of the word Dehinah i.e. body-dweller clearly points to starving the senses. But why not take both the meanings? Non-feeding with food weakens the physical organs destroying the capacity to enjoy temporarily. They would revive with food. When the organs are starved of their sense-subjects they loose their capacity but the longing remains which vanishes when supreme is experienced because, the ego that 'I am the body' ceases altogether.

Oh, Arjuna! despite all the efforts, these mind-churning sense organs forcibly abduct the mind of a practicing learned person. 60.

Powerful unruly sense organs forcibly abduct the mind. It is common experience that all controls to control senses go out of control when fires of passion are on fire. Years of discipline snaps in a fraction of second. History is littered with such incidents from the beginning till modern times. Raajarshi Vishvaamitra of ancient India is a famous example. Even master yogis are entangled in one miracle or the other and are lost. Organs are powerful bombs that will blast out your years of discipline. Therefore, always be on the guard, be on the vigil every moment.

[Therefore] Controlling all these [sense organs] be united in Me because the intellect of one under whose control the sense organs are becomes of steady-prajyaa. 61. For one whose sense organs are under control, his Prajyaa is steady.

In the following two couplets Shree Krishna explains the result of attachment which is the condition of one who is not united in Bhagawaan and therefore not of steady-prajyaa. Incidentally it also tells how attachment arises and leads to ruination.

When a person contemplates on subjects, attachment therein develops; passion-desires develop from attachment; anger arises from desires [when obstructed in use]; infatuation arises from anger; memory loss from infatuation; intellect perishes with memory-loss; and total ruin from intellect-loss. 62-63.

Person contemplating sense-subjects develops attachment therein; desires arise from attachment; Anger erupts from desires [when obstructed in their fulfillment]; infatuation results from anger; memory-loss is born of infatuation; intellect loss results from memory-loss; and intellect loss results in the ruination of the person.

Dwelling and uniting with Bhagawaan will make it easy to completely control the senses and finally even subtle interest in the senses will vanish on realizing Him.

Having explained the disastrous result of not dwelling in Bhagawaan and musing on the sense-subjects Shree Krishna proceeds to explain the beneficial effects of self-control and abandonment of raag and envy.

But a person in Aatmic State freed from passion and jealousy, love and hate, acquires delightfully purified and satisfied [Chitta] though grazing in the sense-subjects with self-controlled sense-organs. 64.

For the first time Bhagawaan alludes to Aatmaa in clear terms and not body-dweller. He means Body-resident is metamorphosed into Aatmaa. Body-dweller shorn of pairs of opposites becomes Aatmaa. Aatmaa and Aatmaa are distinguished here. Aatmavashyair means self controlled.

All his miseries-pains and sorrows disappear on his Chitta acquiring delightful purity and joy because the intellect of the person with delighted and joyous Chitta quickly becomes steady. 65.

Ununited has no steady-intellect, ununited has no Bhaavanaa i.e. meditation, one who does not meditate has no peace, how can there be happiness to the unpeaceful [one who has no peace]. 66.

The intellect of the sense-bound persons never remains steady and will not have even a desire for steady intellect. How can he have peace in absence of even a desire for steady-intellect? Just as emancipation does not even glance at sinners similarly even by a mistake happiness does not visit him who has no peace. Sense-churned intellect being the sole cause of miseries, best action is to acquire control over organs.

For, when the mind of a persons joins one of the freely grazing organs, that organ abducts his Prajyaa just as wind pulls and tosses a boat in water. 67.

Therefore, oh, mighty-armed! the Prajyaa of one whose organs are for the organs i.e. controlled [by withdrawing them] from their subjects becomes steady. 68.

Senses for the senses means controlled because senses are for the senses and not for the sense-objects and you.

Where it is night for all creatures, there the self-controlled remains awake and wherein all creatures are awake Muni sees night there. [69].

This couplet shows the divergent paths of the self-controlled and the free-lance sensuous persons. Self-controlled sleeps over the sense-subjects while the sensuous one graze the sense-subjects. Nicholson describes a Sufi in 'Mystics of Islam';

"At night prisoners forget their prison: at night kings forget their power. No sorrow, no brooding over gain or loss; no thought of this person or that; this is the state of the Gnostic, even when he is awake."

Though being continuously filled from all sides, the ocean

of stable limits accommodates the inflowing waters of all rivers without crossing the shore-limits. In the same manner one in whom all Karmas i.e. passions and desires enter [without causing agitation], acquires peace, [and] not the desirer of Kaama - passions. 70.

The person of steady Prajyaa is like an ocean. Its limits are constant and stable. It neither over-flows nor diminishes whether rivers flow-in or stop. This is so with persons of steady Prajyaa. Desires may flow in or stop. It does not make a jot of difference. His quietude and equipoise remains constant, steady and stable.

The gentleman who, without ego and pride, abandoning all desires, mineness and thineness moves indifferently, attains peace. 71.

This is the Braahmic state, oh, Arjuna! Once attained, one is never deluded [bewildered, confused, never fascinated]. Resting in this state even at the end time [at the moment of leaving the body] one gets Brahmanirvaana i.e. merges in Brahma, one goes to the root. 72. He is emancipated into Brahma

Under what conditions one will rest in Braahmic State at the time of death is stated later on. For explanation of Brahma, Braahmic state, Aatmaa and Paramaatmaa and three Gunas see Introduction II.

AUM TAT SAT: thus is the 2nd chapter named Saamkhya-yoga in the Shree Krishna-Arjuna conversation on Yoga-Scripture of Brahma-learning in Shreemad Bhagavad Gita Upanishad.

CHAPTER : 3

Karma-Yoga: Selfless Action Yoga

Karma-Yoga in nut-shell

Arjuna misunderstood the whole sermon on knowledge of Saamkhya and selfless action Yoga and asks the question if Knowledge is superior and enough to land in Brahmahood 'Why propose me in this all-out war?'

Bhagawaan realizing Arjuna's dilemma under the misunderstanding of his sermon now explains in detail the knowledge yoga of Saamkhya and the Karma Yoga i.e. Buddhi yoga of yogis.

Man does not attain Naishkarmya state i.e. inactive state by not beginning to do action nor does he attain the accomplishment i.e. knowledge by abandoning actions. [4] Because no body ever remains without doing actions even for a moment as all act helplessly being controlled by three gunas born of Prakruti.[5]. Stupid one who control the organs but muses on the vishays are hypocrites and showy but those detached ones who controlling the organs begin Karma Yoga are superior. Therefore do the actions prescribed by scriptures because it is better to do acts than not to do acts. Without activity even your body will not be maintained. Naishkarmya is a state where karma becomes non-karma incapable of producing karmic bondage.

All acts not done by way of sacrifice bind the person and therefore do actions by way of sacrifice in a detached manner. Yajna is translated as sacrifice. Normally it is associated with religious acts but not always. Broadly speaking it means any act which exhausts itself and gives some thing else in its place. For education we sacrifice time to study and money for coaching. Every effort is a sacrifice in this sense. Every material used up in the process is the sacrifice. In this view every activity is a sacrifice for gaining something. Prajaapati Brahmaa created the peoples by sacrifice and said you increase by this Sacrifice and be that sacrifice the giver of desired fruits. Actions have arisen from Brahmaa. Brahmaa from Akshara and therefore all pervasive Brahma is always present in sacrifice. Passionate and sinful person who does not follow this universal activity is living in vain. Person who is in love with Aatmaa, is contented with Aatmaa and is satisfied with Aatmaa has nothing to do. In this world this person has no purpose to act nor any purpose not to act. He has no self interest to serve. Therefore be detached and carry out duties efficiently because detached person though acting reaches the supreme.

Why should man act when he has no purpose of his own to be served? It is to set the precedent for the people because people follow the path set by such great people. King Janak and other great people in the past acted in the public interest: Bhagawaan says he has no reason to act. He has no duty to fulfill. He has nothing to gain nor nothing remains to be gained which is fit to be gained and still he acts. He says if he does not act all the worlds would perish and people will follow his path and ruin themselves.

Under the conditions Krishna says knowledgeable should perform the same acts without attachment which the ignorant does with attachment. The only difference in modus operandi is that the ignorant does with attachment and knowledgeable does without attachment: One does without desire for the fruits and other does it with the eye on the fruits.

Now Shree Krishna explains the Saamkhya doctrine of inactive Purusha and active Prakruti. Stupid Aatmaa with ego believes that he acts while in fact all the acts are done by the three gunas of Prakruti. But the Tattva knower who knows the difference between Guna, action and Aatmaa i.e. Purusha believes that gunas are acting and reacting with guna and remains detached. Persons fascinated by the gunas of prakruti become attached to gunas and their actions. Knowledgeable persons should not dissuade such fools from the path of activity.

This being the case discard all remorse and fight after surrendering all karmas to me with spiritual chitta and becoming devoid of hopes and mineness. People who follow this path with faith gain emancipation but others who do not will fall from the path of emancipation. Even knowledgeable acts as per his Prakruti i.e. innate nature. How can obstinacy obstruct it?

Every organ has Raag and Dwesh i.e. love and hate for its Vishayas. Never be under their control because the same are the enemies in the path of emancipation. One's own Dharma though less profitable and honorable or improperly performed is superior to alien dharma though more honorable and profitable or efficiently performed. It is better to die in one's dharma, alien dharma is dangerous. Dharma means and includes duties and actions which give peaceful and joyous life.

Arjuna is still perplexed: If Aatmaa does not act and if Prakruti is acting then How is it that he commits sins? By whose inspiration does he commit sins helplessly though he does not desire?

Incarnate replies that they are kaam and Anger generated from Rajo guna. Know these two unsatiating great sinners to be the permanent enemies in the path of emancipation. Knowledge is covered by them. They reside in organs, mind and intellect and covering the knowledge these fascinates and stupefies the soul through organs, mind and intellect. First conquer the organs and then slay these sinners, the destroyers of knowledge and relative knowledge. For the explanation of Prakruti, her three Gunas, Changeless Aatmaa see Introduction II.

NOW WE TURN TO TEXT

Arjuna spoke

Oh, Keshava! why do you plan me in this monstrous, savage and heinous action Oh, Janaardan! if, in your opinion, Buddhi i.e. Intellect is superior to action? 1.

You seem to confuse and delude my intellect by seemingly mixed words and mixed views, therefore tell one thing decisively whereby I attain to Shreya i.e. emancipation. 2.

This chapter is titled Karma-yoga and so it begins with a question why act if knowledge is superior to action.? Let us analyze the situation.

To various problems and queries on Dharma-duties in relation to the war at hand Bhagawaan states that: Body-dweller and body are two different things without naming body-dweller either as a Jeeva i.e. soul or Aatma and describes the body-dweller to be uninjurable by any physical means, is immortal migrating from body to body while bodies are subject to birth, growth, decay and death. Next explaining Saamkhya yoga he says that pleasures and pains are produced by the contact of the sense organs with sense objects which are temporary and transient and therefore should be enjoyed and endured with Titikshaa i.e. with equanimity equalizing happiness and misery, pleasure and pain, gain and loss, victory and defeat. By so treating sin will not be incurred:

After stating the tenets of Saamkhya yoga Bhagawaan tells Buddhi-yoga translated as Intellect Yoga. He advises Arjuna to become gunaless, to be beyond the pairs of opposites, to always remain in stable State i.e. Brahma, to be worriless regarding future and to be Aatmavaan i.e. remain-in-self: and non-desirer of fruits of actions without discarding the actions. Bhagawaan says he alone is the giver of fruits of all actions. One has a right to act only but not to its fruits. He asks to act without desire for its fruits, abandoning attachment and treating equally success and failure. Evenness is yoga. This is intellect-yoga of action. Action done with this intellect does not bind. With the perfection of intellect yoga persons become Sthitaprajnya and dweller is metamorphosed into Aatmaa and realizes Braahmi-state.

Arjuna does not realize the true import of Saamkhya yoga and Buddhi-yoga. He has gathered from the talk to be Aatmavaan by becoming Gunaless as per couplet 45. and that if nothing like doer and done, actor and action remain in Aatmic-form then why act or how to act? He takes it that in karma yoga the intellect underlying the karma is superior to karma fruit and therefore the desire for the fruit should make no difference. Arjuna concludes that Karmic sin does not cling if the vaasanaa- desire and motive at the foundation of karma is selfiess, pure and good. He also equates information to the experience of knowledge.

Bhagawaan states in no uncertain terms that action done with balanced and even-intellect is better than fruit-desired action. Action with even-intellect will not laden one with sin. No, on the contrary it will push you on the spiritual path.

Arjuna seems to be fully confused and says to Shree Krishna, "True, Intellect at the root is the best to act but why should I perform such an outwardly horrendous act.? Is it not possible to progress on the spiritual path without engaging in this act? Is there no other way? If there is then is it necessary to do this act? He further thinks that no action can be done in a gunaless state and he is asked to be gunaless.

Arjuna further feels that on the one hand Bhagawaan prohibits all actions by asking him to become gunaless and purely stationed in Aatmaa and on the other hand exhorts and honors Karma path and plans him to engage in war. He is confused and bewildered to the core because Bhagawaan has praised both equally one by one. Arjuna also seems to have equated Buddhi to knowledge: This situation becomes the starting point of the third chapter:

Arjuna questions why he is asked to engage in all out war if Intellect Yoga is better than action. He is confused and asks Bhagawaan to tell him unequivocally which one of the two is best for him.?

Karma Yoga and Saamkhya Yoga

Bhagawaan realizes massive misunderstanding under which Arjuna was laboring and began explaining Karma yoga and Saamkhya yoga in full.

Shree Bhagawaan spoke

Oh, Sinless and blameless one! In this world I have previously spoken two faiths [attitudes and ways of life]: Knowledge yoga for the Saamkhyas [and] Karma-yoga for the yogis:3.

Shree Krishna says that both the paths are eternal and originate from Him. And begins to deal with Karma yoga from the couplet four onwards.

By not making the beginning of an action, man does not enjoy the state of non-action nor does he attain to knowledge accomplishment by renouncing actions. 4.

No man can become action-free by not doing actions. He also can not achieve Knowledge-siddhi by not doing actions i.e. renouncing doing actions. Krishna says it is impossible from another angle also.

Because no creature can remain even for a moment without doing action. Compelled by the three gunas born of Prakruti, all act helplessly.: 5.

Guna means character or property of nature which are three; Satva, Raja and Tama. Except Aatmaa we are composed of three gunas of Prakruti i.e. nature whose property is ceaseless activity and therefore to say that we can either reject or accept to do karma suggest ignorance. The doing of the prescribed actions depend on the desire of the doer and therefore does it follow that discarding the karma by malice, distress or otherwise, the natural activity of mind or the automatic working foe body organs will cease. By refusing to do actions, do the hearing, tasting and other organs stop their activities? Does the heart stop beating ? Does mind stop thinking? Do hunger and thirst leave you? Do the waking, dream and slumber states disappear? What have you renounced by renouncing if organs do not stop or renounce all these activities? Position is as good as sitting in a car. Though we are stationary in the car, we being subject to car, we also move along with the car. Therefore being under the control of gunas, even a person of action-free-state does bodily activity, specially autonomous ones. For the explanation of three Gunaas of nature i.e. Prakruti and Aatmaa see: Introduction II.

Who is hypocrite?

Those, stupid Aatmaa, [wholly-deluded Aatma] who physically outwardly controls and restrains action-organs but mentally remembers the subjects of organs is said to be hypocrite.6. But, Oh, Arjuna! he who keeping his organs under the control of the mind and remaining unattached begins Karma-yoga with organs, is best remarkable and distinguished.: 7. He excels.

Shree Krishna advises to regulate and control the organs by mind, to remain steady and unattached within and then let the organs do all the activities, no worry at all.

Why act than not to act? Why act by way of sacrifice without attachment?

Carry out scripture-enjoined and allotted acts because action is better than inaction. Even your life-journey will not be accomplished by non-action. Life-maintenance will not be carried out by non-action.:8.

If it is impossible to remain without activity why not act in unison with scriptures? How to carry out Niyat i.e. scripture-enjoined actions?

Karmas not done for sacrifice bind the person in karmic bondage. [therefore], Oh, Arjuna ! do sacrificial actions without attachment :9.

Every act except sacrificial one binds the person in karmic bondage therefore should be done as and by way of sacrifice without attachment.

In the beginning of the Kalpa, Prajaapati [Brahmaa] created the peoples by sacrifice and said 'increase by this sacrifice': let this sacrifice be your Kamadhuka i.e. the giver of your cherished desires and fruits.:10.

For the explanation of Prajaapati Brahmaa, Akshara AUM, Kalpa, deities and time scales in creation: See Introduction II.

Kamadhenu is the cow of Indra who fulfills all the desires of Indra

Satisfy the deities with this [sacrifice]. Those deities will satisfy you. Being satisfied with each other both of you will attain supreme Shreya i.e. emancipation. 11.

Another rendering

Serve the deities with this [sacrifice] and let the deities serve you. Thus serving each other may you attain supreme Shreya.11.

Because the sacrifice-satisfied deities will give you cherished enjoyments. He, who enjoys these gifted enjoyments without offering the same to them in return is verily a thief: 12.

Those saints [good persons] who eat left-overs from sacrifice are released from all sins and evils but those sinners who cook for themselves, eat their sins only. 13. Verily digest their sins only.

Creatures come into being from food, food is produced from rains, rains is produced from sacrifice, Sacrifice comes to be from karma i.e. actions, Karma rises from Brahmaa or Veda, Brahmaa or Veda from Akshara AUM, know thus. Therefore omnipresent Brahma is always present in sacrifice. 14-15.

It is unfortunate that almost all commentators have misread Brahmodbhavam as meaning Brahma-udbhavam. It should be read Brahmaa -Udbhavam. By reading Brahma instead of Brahmaa the next part of the couplet becomes redundant as the last part says Brahma nityam Yajye Pratishtitam. Brahmaa should be taken as origin of Karma and not Brahma: reverse sequence is Karma, Brahmaa, Akshar AUM and Brahma.

Oh, Partha! One who does not follow this set-wheel of the universe, that licentious and sinful person is living in vain. 16.

This is the doctrine of Svadharma in nut shell. That arrogant person who does not carry out his Svadharma and utilizes his time in sensuous activities is wasting his life. He is a burden to the society. Duteous karmas are born with your birth: Why abandon them?

Having advised, "Execute your duties selflessly dedicating to Ishvar'[God] Shree Krishna says no karma remains to be done for a fully emancipated souls i.e. Aatmic persons.

But no action remains to be done for the person who is in love with the Aatmaa only, who is satiated and contented with the Aatmaa and who is satisfied with the Aatmaa only.17.

Aatmic person requires nothing. He is above scriptures. Being at the highest state of existence every thing including scriptures proceed from him. To act or not to act is his sweet will because read the next couplet.

In this world such a person has no purpose to act nor has any purpose not to act nor has he any relation of self-interest with all creatures.18.

He gains nothing by action nor looses anything by not doing action. He has no relation of self interest with any creature. He has selfless relation with all creatures. No sooner one begins to play as Aatmaa, activity or inactivity becomes purposeless for him because he is alpha and omega of every thing.

Therefore always remaining detached, perform your to-be-done-actions very well because detached person attains the supreme state though doing actions.19.

Through [such] actions alone, king Janak and others have achieved supreme siddhi i.e. supreme state. It is fit and proper for you to so act keeping in view the public interest. 20.

King Janak and others attained emancipation not by abandoning actions but by acting in a detached manner. Therefore have faith in detached actions because there will be social gain too. People follow the path treaded by great persons as their actions will create the precedents.

Whatever is done by best persons, other common people do the same. Whatever is justified by them and set as precedent people follow it.21.

Oh, Arjuna! I have not even a smallest duty [to be done] in all the three worlds as well as nothing worth obtaining is unobtained. Even so I engage in actions.[in public interest] 22.

If I were not to engage in actions remaining alert, vigilant and attentive, then Oh, Partha! people would follow my example in every manner in all details, will follow my precedent on all fours. 23.

And if I do not act, all these people will fall [from karma-path] and I will be the creator of hybrids and chaos as well as the destroyer of all these people.:24.

[Therefore] Oh, Bharat! Just as the not-learned, ignorant common man does actions with attachment similarly the learned should do the acts without attachment in public interest, with a desire to benefit the society and for the welfare of the people: 25.

Knowledgeable persons not desiring fruits should act in public interest in the same manner as a fruit desirer acts. This is necessary to protect the public and public interest. It is for the best persons to inspire and activate common man to tread on good path by first themselves walking on it. The torch of Dharma should be kept burning by the elders of the society.

Knowledgeable ones should not create confusion and insipidity in the intellect of the not-learned ignorant persons attached to actions but [on the contrary] acting with detached intellect yoke them to act, set them to work, generate in them a taste for good actions. 26.

Prakruti Acts and not Aatmaa. Aatmaa alleges the activity of Prakruti in Him.

All actions though being done by the gunas of Prakruti, ego-stupefied Aatmaa believes, 'I am the doer': 27.

Shree Krishna states the fundamentals of Saamkhya system by explaining how and why actions bind the ignorant persons? What happens if we carry the burden of another person on our head? Our neck would ache. Exactly this is what happens when the ignorant acts. Every action and every activity is the result and effect of the action and reaction of the three gunas of Prakruti: It is Prakruti and her three gunas that act. All the karmas done by the body and mind are purely the activity of Prakruti and her gunas but what happens? Aatmaa believes that he is doing the acts. This belief is caused by ego. Ego-stupefied intellect makes Aatmaa to believe to be carrying the burden of Prakruti. In fact he is not. But ignorant and fruit-attached person will not understand this and therefore it is not advisable to preach him this initially. For the explanation that the Prakruti and her three Gunas act and not Aatmaa see Introduction II.

But, Oh, Mighty armed! knowers of the division of Gunas, their actions and [Aatmaa,] knowing thus that Gunas react with Gunas i.e. properties of the Prakruti react with each other, are not deluded, are not fascinated. 28

Tattva knowers see that the properties of Prakruti are acting and reacting with each other. They clearly perceive that the activity of gunas is the sole cause of karmas. So they are not in the delusion that they are the actors. They are separate and aloof from Prakruti who acts. Bhagawaan continues elucidating:

Deluded and stupefied by the gunas of the Prakruti one gets attached to the gunas and their activities: Knowledgeable should not dissuade the slow-intellected half-truth knowers from acting: 29.

After having explained the position of Karta and karma, actor and action, doer and deed in the scheme of the universe as per Saamkhya doctrine Shree Krishna extols Arjuna to fight with certain state of chitta and mind.

With chitta fixed-in Aatmaa, renouncing and surrendering all actions to me, becoming free from hopes, mineness-thineness and remorse, fight: 30.

Shree Krishna now unfolds the positive effect of his method of action.

Those persons, who-so-ever with faith becoming unenvious always follow this opinion of mine become free from all actions. 31.

Know that those, who with a faulty understanding do not follow this view of mine have become fools and stupid in knowledge and are ruined [fallen from the path of Kalyaana]: 32.

Even the knowledgeable act as per his Prakruti, constitution and nature and also all creatures act according to their nature: In that what can restraint do? How can one restrain or constrain? 33.

Constraint, restraint, repression and suppression is not useful in the matter of one's nature. It is the conversion that will do the job. Put your energy to a different use.

Every organ has fixed and settled Love and hate, likes and dislikes towards their sense-subjects and objects. Do not come under their sway and control because both are the opponents and enemies of Kalyaana-path: 34.

One's dharma is better then alien one

Better are one's own duties [Svadharma] devoid of merit though ill carried out than the alien dharma [Paradharma] well performed, carried out: Even death is beneficial [Shreya] in execution of one's duties [Svadharma]; Alien duties and Paradharma is dangerous and perilous. 35.

Who compels and propels reluctant Soul to commit sins? Passion-lust and anger are the agents who cover the knowledge and delude the soul.

Arjuna spoke

Oh, Krishna! Then by whose inspiration does this Purusha though reluctant and undesiring commit the sins as if impelled, compelled and propelled.? 36.

Krishna spoke [in answer]. Knowledge is covered by passion-lust and desire.

It is passion-lust, and it is anger both produced by Rajo guna, always unsatiated are the great sinners. Know them to be enemies in this [kalyan path]. 37.

Just as fire is covered by smoke, mirror is covered by dust and fetus by amnion, so is knowledge covered by these [i.e. Passion and anger]. 38.

Oh, Arjuna! This knowledge is enveloped by the unsatiating fire of passion, lust and desire [Kaama] the permanent enemy of the wise and the knowledgeable. 39.

Organs, mind and intellect are said to be its residences [and] covering the knowledge this [passion] fascinates the body-dweller through the agency of these i.e. organs, mind and intellect. 40.

Therefore, Oh, Arjuna! controlling the organs in the first instance slay this sinful destroyer of absolute and relative knowledge [Gyaana-Vigyaana] i.e. wisdom, knowledge and discrimination. 41.

Organs are subtler than body, mind is subtler than organs, Intellect is subtler than mind and extremely beyond intellect is He the Body dweller or. [Aatmaa?] 42. Oh, Mighty-handed! knowing supreme in this manner to be beyond intellect, control the self by Aatmaa and slay this difficult-to conquer Passion-form enemy.43.

AUM TAT SAT: Thus it is the third chapter, named Karma-yoga in Shree Krishna-Arjuna dialogue on Brahma-knowledge yoga-scripture Shreemad-Bhagavad Gita Upanishad.

CHAPTER : 4

Gyaana-Karma-Sanyaas Yoga

As Arjuna keeps mum Bhagawaan continues the sermon

He tells Arjuna that the Saamkhya and karma yoga told now was told by Him to Sun Vivasvaan who related it to Manu who passed it to Ikshvaanku which was orally passed on to sagely kings but slowly perished with the passage of time. Arjuna disbelieved the statement because the birth of Krishna was recent while that of Vivasvaan was much earlier. Bhagawaan tells about the incarnations of Bhagawaan Vishnu and transmigration of souls. He says that, "We have taken many births. I remember them all but not you." He further tells, "Though undiminishing Aatmaa, though Ishvar [God] of all, I manifest by my Maayaa under the shelter of my Prakruti. I manifest in human body whenever Dharma declines and Adharma prospers. I manifest in every Yuga for the protection of Saadhus, the destruction of sinners and for reestablishing Dharma."

Krishna further says that, "My birth and Karmas are divine: one who realizes this is also released from the sansaar."

He further tells that all people follow his path and he worships them in the same manner as they worship him. He reciprocates the worship in the same manner.

He reverts to Vedic rites in a different manner. He says, "In this world the desirers of fruits worship deities because in the world of mortals such worship gives the fruits very soon."

Four Varnas. He explains the theory of four Varnas. Shree Krishna never meant the present day caste-system by birth by the use of the word VARNA. He says, "I have created four Varnas viz. Brahmins, Kshatriyas, Vaishyas and Shudras on the basis of their gunas meaning nature and karmas. Though their creator know me to be their undiminishing non-creator. Karmas do not defile me nor have I desire in the fruits of the karmas and one who knows me thus Tattvically is also not bondaged by karmas. Knowing thus the aspirants of the past have done the acts and advises Arjuna also to act similarly. This is in accordance with Saamkhya system where Prakruti and her three Gunaas act and not Purusha and Aatmaa who imagines that he acts. See Introduction II.

Shree Krishna now explains what is Karma, Akarma i.e. non-karma and Vikarma. He categorically says that every action that elevates one to higher spiritual status is sacrifice: He accepts Vedic rites and rituals, mantras etc. which give worldly and paradisal wealth and happiness as sacrifices. But says that the wealth and happiness produced is temporary. On exhaustion of the momentum of the action one will revert to from where he started. He argues of what good such results are? He points out various means and methods to land you in a state of no return, a state where there is eternal peace. Now let us turn to text:

Shree Bhagawaan Spoke

Formerly I had spoken this imperishable yoga path to Sun Vivasvaan, Vivasvaan told to his son Manu and Manu had told to king Ikshvaanku. 1.

Oh, Parantap! thus continued in line of succession sagely kings knew this [yoga] till it perished from the world with the passage of long time. 2.

Arjuna has not asked any question at the end of third chapter. The fourth chapter begins with a statement to emphasize the antiquity of the yoga. It was told to Vivasvaan who orally passed it on to Manu and Manu to Ikshvaanku and then traditionally to sagely kings. And as the value for the sense-enjoyments increased with passage of time this yoga lost its importance and vanished. What is the value of clothes in a nudist colony? Who will honor a musician in a colony of deaf? What pleasure a fox will derive from the moon-light? Who knows why and how has this love for sense-pleasure increased? But certainly it did increase and the yoga perished.

That very same ancient yoga is spoken by me to you today because you are my devotee and friend. It is really a best secret. It is best mystery and super secret.3.

Krishna says, "Do not doubt my words. I have divulged you this best secret because you are an idol of love, ocean of devotion, life of pure friendship, location of unflinching faith. How can you be disregarded? Before asking you to fight I must dissolve your ignorance."

Arjuna could not swallow this talk of ancient traditional yoga told by Bhagawaan. So he asks a question expressing the doubt.

Arjuna spoke: Your birth is recent and the birth of Vivasvaan Sun is prior in the past. How should I know that you had initially told it? 4.

Arjuna points out a seeming impossibility of the event. How could Krishna with recent birth have told to Vivasvaan of the past?

Krishna explains the seeming impossibility by repeating and reiterating the doctrine of rebirth of individuals and incarnations of God-Vishnu.

Shree Bhagawaan spoke: Many births I have passed through and you too, Oh, Arjuna! I know them all but not you, Oh, Parantap! 5.

Why does God Vishnu incarnate on earth? Bhagawaan Krishna now explains how and the purpose of his incarnation in couplets 6-8.

Even though undiminishing and birthless Aatmaa, even though God [Ishvar] of all creatures, under the shelter of my Prakruti I manifest by my Maya i.e. I incarnate as a human being. 6. Oh, Bharat! whenever dharma declines and whenever Adharma rises, increases, prospers and prevails I manifest my Aatmaa [in human form].7.

I incarnate and manifest in every Yuga for protecting saintly persons [Saadhus], to root out the wicked ones and to reestablish Dharma. 8.

Bhagawaan explains in the bunch of these three Couplets 6-8 how, why and when God Vishnu descends in human form. His motive and purpose is clearly defined. Shree Krishna tells to doubting Arjuna that though he is not subject to birth and death: that though he is the directing controller of all, embracing his nature he incarnates through Maya. Bhagawaan says, "This birth and death of the incarnation does not destroy my indestructibility nor prove that I am the doer. Factually I am formless yet I assume a form and dance on the world stage like a dancer"

Very idea of Paramaatmaa coming in human form is exhilarating. It fills us with joy. Only condition is we should have unbounded and selfless love for him and only then we will enjoy the ever present bliss of his divine love.

Reading these couplets some people argue that why should it become necessary for such an Omnipotent power to come on earth for destroying evil persons and establish dharma? Can he not do without incarnating? Others are complacent that they need not do anything because Bhagawaan will come on earth to destroy the evil-doers and save them. Both should realize that their very view of Almighty's inability or ability makes them weaklings. Dharma does not ask you to be weak. It exhorts you to be strong with firm faith in that Omnipotent power's promise. He comes on earth in human form with the paramount and avowed purpose to embrace his lover-devotees so that they can play with him, chit-chat with him with all their emotions, feelings, love and traits of a human-being at full throttle. One can orally or even mentally shower all praises and respect in abstract to invisible formless Being but try as you may, you can not feel that love in the abstract which you feel for your formful object of love. One can not visualize any thing which has no form and therefore it is difficult to feel love for it. Bhagawaan comes as an incarnate for merry-making with his devotees and as he has descended in human form he destroys wicked people as his side activity or shall we say his hobby. Reestablishing Dharma, making the world-stage safe for his devotees and saintly persons to play their roles unhindered is the side activity of God-incarnate.

Now Shree Krishna tells in nut-shell who can break the shackles of rebirth?

Oh, Arjuna! my birth and karma are divine. One who knows this on principles [Tattvically] has no rebirth on leaving the body [but] attains me. [comes to me]. 9.

The word Evam in this couplet refers to couplets 6-8 which state how, why and when He incarnates and not succeeding couplet as suggested by some interpreters. Couplet ten is an independent one giving an alternative method for attaining Bhagawaan.

Taking my refuge, free from raag i.e. passion, fear and anger, me-minded, me-filled and purified with knowledge-penance, many have attained to my bhaava [nature].10.

What does Manmayaa i.e. me-minded [me-filled] mean? It means persons whose intellect and minds are totally engrossed in the life-stories of Bhagawaan, saints and sages. Bhagawaan-filled state comes by constant musing on qualities and virtues of Bhagawaan, sages and saints. Musing on Bhagawaan will remove your weakness and feebleness. You will cease to be small and inferior. You will be humble but not weak. You will be strong and self-respected yet not arrogant and proud.

It is a doctrine of Yogic psychology that you will become as you muse on. Muse on Bhagawaan and you will become like Bhagawaan.

Mamupaashrita means who has taken my refuge. You and you alone and none-else i.e. to the exclusion of all others i.e. exclusive refuge.

In nut shell one, who is free from fear and anger, love and envy, who is me-filled and me-minded, who has taken my refuge, who is purified by knowledge-penance, has no rebirth.

Such a one attains me. This couplet is a key to salvation. Free from love means free from mineness and thineness and not devoid of love.

Oh, Arjuna! All people follow my path. I worship [Bhaja] them in the same manner in which they worship [Bhaja] me. 11.

Bhaja has no English equivalent as it includes meditation, physical Pujaa, Kirtan, singing songs and Aartis etc. Worship is nearest equivalent.

In 2:47 Shree Krishna said in categorical terms that one has right to act only but not to its fruits and asks one to act selflessly. In this Chapter Bhagawaan emphasizes the same point indirectly with the assurance that he, though under no obligation, suo-moto fulfills the desires with which people worship-bhajes him and act. He reciprocates in the same manner and tenor. Shree Krishna says that by nature man is inclined to worship him "But being ignorant he imputes different deities in me and gives them various names though I am nameless. In all places at all times I am one and the same yet people imagine me in different forms and names and I reciprocate from these forms and names fulfilling their desires." In the light of these two couplets Krishna tells you that devote your whole and undivided attention and energy to action only: And in all readiness he is there to give you fruits commensurate with the nature of the worship. He says,"I present myself to the devotee in the form in which he worships[bhajes]". Bhagawaan assumes the form worshipped by the lover-devotee. Love and worship him in any form of your choice and in any relation either as a lover, master, father, son, even as a lady-love and he will respond in the same manner in measure equal to the intensity of your love and worship.

In this world desirers of the fruits of actions worship deities because in the world of men the fruits of actions is acquired very quickly. 12.

For various fruits people worship me in various ways and

forms laid down in Vedas and Scriptures because such worship fructifies very quickly in the physical world of mortals. Each one gets according to his desire in fulfillment of worship.

Four Varnas created by Bhagawaan on basis of guna-karma

Four Varnas [classes] of people are created by me on the basis of their guna-karma i.e. nature and actions [and] though their creator know me as their undiminishing non-creator. 13.

Four divisions are [1] Brahmin [2] Kshatriya [3] Vaishya and [4] Shudra and respectively form the head, hands, chest and stomach, and the feet of the Viraat Purusha i.e. universal person.

[1] Brahmins: highly intellectual and moral like saints, sages, lawgivers, priests, teachers theoreticians etc.. [2] Kshatriya. kings, military and police force. Their job is to protect the society from external and internal enemies. Military from external foes and police for the internal security. [3] Vaishya: Business, industry and agriculture. They maintain the economy of the society in sound condition. [4] Shudra: Labor class. menial labor.

Hinduism recognizes inherited characters and qualities but that was not the sole criterion for fixing his Dharma i.e. social duties in the social set-up. His fitness for the social duties were recognized and fortified by the education. It is the dictum that "Janmanaa Jaayate Shudro" i.e. man is born Shudra. He has to be educated in the residential schools maintained by sages where education along with religion was imparted on the basis of the child's aptitude making him fit and eligible for social duties giving him livelihood. Natural aptitudes and inclinations fortified with proper education was the basis of the Varna-system created and set up. The present caste-system is the degenerated Varna-system and requires whole-sale and whole some changes incorporating the modern conditions which can be done by creating many sub Varnas within four main ones.

Actions do not affect, [defile coat or react] and bind me. I have no desire for the fruits of actions. Even one who knows me thus also does not get bound or bound by the actions. 14.

Bhagawaan repeats that he is free one. He is neither affected by the actions nor has he longing for the action-fruits. One will not be bound by the karmic bondage if he realizes Bhagawaan thus. Knowing thus the aspirants of the past have performed their karmas i.e. actions. And therefore you too perform actions as were done by the ancestors in the past. 15.

Karma, Vikarma and Akarma

Even Pundits are delusively confused, perplexed, bewildered, and confounded in the matter of what is karma and what is Akarma: action and non-action. Therefore I will tell you clearly what is karma knowing which you will be released from Ashubh i.e. Sansaaric bondage.16.

[One] Should know karma and should also know Vikarma i.e. for-bidden, prohibited and unlawful action and as well as non-action [or inaction] because the direction and the end-result of action is inaccessible, mysterious and incomprehensible. What will be the result is indecipherable. 17.

That one, who perceives and sees non-action feeling in action and action in non-action that person is intelligent, wise and discerning amongst persons. He is yogi though doer of all actions. 18.

That one, whose commencement of all actions is without Kaam-Sankalp i.e. with out passion-desire and whose actions are burnt by knowledge-fire is said to be Pundit by the wise.[Budhah].19.

Etymologically Pundit means person of self-realization

That one remaining always satisfied, renouncing action-fruits and attachment does nothing even though engaged in doing actions. 20.

One, who with Aatmaa renouncing all possessions by chitta and with no hopes, does karmas with body only, does not commit sins. i.e. does not commit sins though doing karmas for maintaining the body. 21.

One who remains satisfied with whatever is obtained by the way of its own accord fortuitously and who is beyond the pairs of opposites and who is without envy and jealousy and is equipoised in success and failures does not get bound even though he acts.22.

[Because] Actions done as a sacrifice by persons devoid of attachment and with chitta steadily fixed in knowledge, vanish together with their fruits. 23

Why? because, Equipment for Homa i.e. sacrifice, sacrificial material, sacrificial fire, sacrificer, sacrifice ritual-activity are all Brahma in the view of Brahmavettaa i.e. Brahma-knower. The fruit to be obtained by Brahma-knower absorbed in Brahma-form is also Brahma. 24.

Gita puts sacrifice on a universal scale. In its view every act done for gaining some thing good is a sacrifice. Vedas have a large number of sacrifices with rites and rituals for earthly gains and not only gaining entrance in paradise but to become Indra also. Gita accepts these sacrifices and says God gives the fruits of these acts but these fruits are temporary and man returns to earth on the exhaustion of the merit by enjoyment in Paradise. He says there are other sacrifices which lead you to Brahmahood. He enlarges the definition beyond the range of ritual sacrifice and applies to every act that leads to Brahmahood.

Every activity landing one in Brahma-Samaadhi is a sacrificial activity. He pinpoints these activities in the couplets that follow. In Krishna's view every selfless action is a sacrifice leading to Brahmahood.

Other [Karma] yogis perform Yajna in the form of worship of deities, still others oblate Yajna with Yajna i.e. sacrifice with sacrifice in Braahmic fire. 25.

Others oblates ears etc. all organs in control-form fire: others yoke word etc. the vishayas i.e. sense subjects in organs etc. i.e. withdraw senses from sense-organs. 26.

Others yoke activities of all organs and of all Praanas in

self-control-form yoga-fire by illuminating them with knowledge. 27.

Others perform money-sacrifice i.e. give money in charity: as well as perform penance-sacrifice [and others] yoga-sacrifice, others observe vows of non-violence and non-jury etc. others do Japa-sacrifice, scripture reading and knowledge sacrifice etc.28.

Others oblate Praan in Apaan, others yoke Apaan in Praan while still other Praanaayaam-practitioners and regular in balanced diet obstructing the flow of Praan-Apaan oblate Praan in Praan. All these are the knowers of Yajna i.e. sacrifice and destroyers of sins by sacrifice. 29-30.

Oh, best Kuru Arjuna! enjoys of the nectar [Amrit] left over of sacrifice go to [Sanaatana] eternal Brahma. And this mortal world is not happiness giver to non-performer of Yajna then how can other world be? 31. Yajnasheshaṁ Tathaamrutam. Manu smruti:3:285.

In this manner many kinds of sacrifices are described by the mouth of Vedas: know that all are performed through actions i.e. Karma-yoga; Knowing thus you will be released, emancipated, freed and liberated. 32.

Knowledge Sacrifice [Yajna] better than Material Sacrifice [Yajna]

Oh, Arjuna! Knowledge sacrifice is superior to and better than sacrifice with physical materials, because Oh, Partha! all actions culminate, merge and end in knowledge. 33.

If you desire to have that knowledge] know it by prostrating at the feet of Knowledgeable and Tattva-knowers and by asking pertinent questions in all humility. They will sermon you that knowledge. 34.

In Hindu tradition a seeker pays humble homage by prostrating at the feet of knowledgeable and Tattva knowers and repeatedly asks the questions in humble tones who sermons according to fitness of the seeker.

Knowledge is not the subject of speech then how can it be sermonized?

Sadguru Shree Sai Baba of Shirdi has interpreted the 3rd part of the couplet quite differently from all the commentators on Gita. Once devotee Chaandorkar was massaging the lotus feet of Sai and was slowly muttering Chapter four of Gita. When he completed 34th couplet, Sai asked, "What are you murmuring, Naanaa! speak loudly, let me hear. Read again very attentively third part 'Updeshyanti Te Jyaanam'. And then Sai further said read, 'Te Ajyaanam' instead of 'Te Jyaanam' and you will have correct meaning. Elucidating Sai said, "Knowledge is not the subject of speech then how can it become the object of sermon? Ignorance becomes the subject of speech while knowledge is beyond speech. Why so? It is because Bhagawaan has said Knowledge is covered by ignorance [ch:5:15] and therefore on the removal of ignorance knowledge will automatically shine. Knowledge is not the subject of acquisition. It is existent eternally. Remove from your mind the illusory universe as a fact and your are nothing but knowledge i.e. Prajyaanam Brahma. Shree Sai Sachcharit by Govind Raghunath Dabholakar. Chapter: 39: 44-70

Can knowledge be the subject of speech? Absolute Brahma is not the subject of knowledge but of experience only. Couplet 38 says knowledge will spring automatically in the heart with the purification of chitta. At the end Shree Krishna does not ask Arjuna ,"Have you acquired knowledge? but asks, 'has your fascination i.e. Moha vanished' " and Arjuna gives clean receipt by saying, "Yes, Moha has vanished" Thus Knowledge can not be sermonized but can.be pointed out by sermonizing on ignorance. Relative knowledge is the product of ignorance and it can the subject of sermon but not absolute knowledge. There is a possibility that during the course of oral transmission Ajyaan may have been replaced by Jyaan or it may have been replaced by misunderstanding what is knowledge, relative knowledge and ignorance.

Knowing which you shall not fall into such Moha i.e. fascination, delusion and confusion again and Oh, Arjuna by which knowledge [you] will see all bhootas within you as well as me. 35.

Bhootas means that which has come into existence and being and not merely living creatures; Bhagawaan says the entire animate and inanimate universe will be seen in Bhagawaan as well as within each of us when knowledge dawns. On Dawning knowledge sinner ceases to be sinner.

You will easily swim over very well all the sins by the knowledgeship even if you are sinner greater than all others.36.

Oh, Arjuna! Knowledge-form fire reduces all actions to ashes just as ignited fire burns out all wood to ashes. 37

Bhagawaan assures that with that knowledge one will crossover the worldly web even if he be the epitome of sins, even if he be the totality of sins personified.

Because in this world there is nothing more purifier and holifier like knowledge. Yoga-purified person acquires that knowledge automatically within the self in due course of time. 38.

Person having faith with controlled organs and always ready [for knowledge] gains knowledge and on obtaining knowledge, immediately attains to supreme peace. 39.

Ignorant, without faith and doubting Aatmaa perish, gets ruined, gets away from kalyaan-path. There is neither this world nor the one beyond nor is there happiness for such doubting and suspicious soul [persons]. 40.

Oh, Dhananjay! Karmas-actions do not bind one with Aatmic knowledge who has renounced all actions through yoga-intellect and whose doubts are destroyed by knowledge.41.

Therefore, oh, Arjuna! on cutting asunder these mental doubts born of ignorance located in your heart by the sword of knowledge of self-realization, and becoming steady resort to yoga of even intellect and get up[to fight].42.

AUM TAT SAT: Thus it is the fourth chapter, named Jyaan-Karma-Sanyaas Yoga in Shree Krishna-Arjuna dialogue on Brahma-knowledge yoga-scripture Shreemad-Bhagavad Gita Upanishad.

CHAPTER : 5

Karmasanyaas Yoga i.e. Action-Renunciation Yoga

After learning Karma, non-karma i.e. selfless action and renunciation of action i.e. inaction Arjuna asks which is better inaction or non-karma i.e. selfless action? Reply is both are kalyaan producers but of the two karma-yoga i.e. selfless action is better than renunciation of action i.e. inaction.

What is renunciation of action? What acts are discarded by an ascetic? An ascetic renounces only action leading to earning? He carries on all the activities which keeps him alive. He does not earn but eats the food given by others. He breathes, eats, excretes etc. these out-ward activities means nothing. He has not stopped mental activities i.e. his fascination, anger, sexual emotions etc. are in tact. He is outwardly fitted as an ascetic but inwardly not different from us. If one has to act why not act fully in the world without desiring fruits of the actions that is selflessly. How this can be done is explained now.

Detached actions purify Chitta-Antahkaran. Persons with purified Antahkaran acquire knowledge by serving knowledgeable Tattva-seers who sermonize them. It is also stated categorically that knowledge is superior to action.

In this chapter Bhagawaan says that Karma-yoga is superior to knowledge yoga though both lead to the same result. End product of both the processes is the same. Renunciation of karma is difficult while karma-yoga following one's nature and make-up is easy to practice. Inactivity is impossible while renunciation of desire for fruits though difficult is not impossible.

Arjuna spoke

Oh, Krishna! you praise renunciation of Karma [action] and then again karma-yoga. Tell me which one of the two is decisively shreya-kalyaan-producing. 1.

Shree Bhagawaan spoke

Renunciation of action and karma-yoga, both are kalyaan-producing but out of them Karma-yoga is special than renunciation. 2.

Karma yoga has a speciality which renunciation has not: how? Oh, mighty-handed! know him, who neither hates-dislikes nor desires i.e. neither loathes nor desires to be always a renouncer i.e. permanent renouncer because free from pairs of opposites, dualities and paradoxes, he, oh, mighty-handed! happily and easily becomes free from Sansaar-shackles, worldly-bondage. 3.

Only children talk that Saamkhya-knowledge and yoga-selfless action are different but not the pundits-learned-wise because one who is well-settled, [well versed, well sheltered, well stabilized] even in one of the two obtains and gains the fruits [results] of both. 4.

The state, position and abode obtained by Saamkhya-yogis-knowledgeable is also obtained by karma-yogis. Person, who sees Knowledge-yoga and karma-yoga as one, really and correctly sees. 5.

But, oh, mighty-handed! It is difficult and painful for a non-karma yogi to attain renunciation and detachment. Again karma-yoga-joined i.e. karma-yogi swiftly and speedily goes to Brahma i.e. quickly attains Brahmahood. 6.

It is difficult and painful to attain renunciation and detachment without purifying chitta by karma-yoga first. It is when chitta is purified that person become Brahma in no time.

Yoga-yoked i.e. Karma-yogi i.e. selfless actor, self realized pure Aatmaa, who has controlled organs and knowing Aatmaa of all bhootas to be his Aatma is not tainted, besmeared and defiled though acting. 7.

Tattva-knower Karma-yogi believes that though acting, he does nothing but only organs are active in their subjects.

Tattva-knower Karma-yogi though seeing, hearing, touching, smelling, eating, walking, sleeping, breathing, speaking, excreting, taking and grasping, closing and opening the eyes, thinking and holding believes that he does nothing but it is the organs that are active in their own subjects: thus he believes. 8-9.

One, who dedicating karmas to Brahma and renouncing attachment does actions, is not smeared with sin like a lotus-leaf remaining unwetted in water. 10. Renouncing attachment, Karma-yogi acts with body, with mind, with intellect or only with organs for the purpose of purifying chitta. 11. United [with karma-yoga] i.e. karma-yogi by discarding fruits of actions obtains Brahma-form supreme peace. Ununited one, being passion-loving becoming attached to fruits gets bounded and bondaged.12.

Equipoised selfless actor obtains well grounded eternal peace by abandoning and discarding attachment to the fruit of actions but selfish actor being desire-driven is attached to fruits and so gets entangled in the web of storage of actions and rebirth.

Self-controlled body-dweller mentally renouncing all actions stays happily in the city of nine-gates neither doing nor getting done [anything]. 13.

Prabhu does not create for the creatures [Loka] Doerness, deeds or actions nor the union of action and its fruit but Prakruti plays and works out. 14. Vibhu takes upon himself neither the sins of anyone nor the good-ones. Knowledge is covered by ignorance and by that all creatures get fascinated, deluded and bewildered. 15.

Gopaalaananda Swami of Swami Naaraayana Sect interprets Prabhu means self-controlled and Vibhu means Aatmaa.

Saamkhya Principle enunciated in couplets 13-14.

Couplets 14-15 reiterate Saamkhya principle where Purusha

does not act. Only Prakruti acts by the presence of Purusha so Prabhu means self controlled and Vibhu means Aatmaa. For Prabhu i.e. the self-controlled there is neither Doerness, nor deeds nor the union of the act and the fruits. He believes that it is Prakruti that acts and not he. Factually Aatmaa does not do good acts or sins but due to ignorance he believes that the acts are his. It is something like king becoming a beggar in the dream and suffering the pangs of begging and hunger. On waking he is king and not beggar. He realizes the falsity of his beggars. So is the with you all. Wake up from the dream and you will find yourself to be Brahma. See Introduction II.

But those, whose ignorance of the self is destroyed by knowledge [of Aatmaa] their knowledge illuminates i.e. reveals that Supreme [Brahma] in the manner of a Sun. 16.

Just as sun makes visible the things so does that knowledge makes visible that supreme Brahma.

Those, whose intellect, self and faith are suffused and infused and entirely devoted to and fully absorbed in that [supreme], becoming free from sins through knowledge go to the state of unrepetition i.e. where there is no repetition of births. He attains nirvana.17.

Pundit has an even eye

Pundit has an even eye i.e. looks with equal eye a learned and humble Brahmin, a cow, an elephant, a bitch and Shavapak i.e. lowly person. 18.

In their eyes there is no difference between them. To him all are equal. Reason is that they have realized the entire Universe as nothing but the vivartic modification of Brahma.

Those, whose mind is stabilized in evenness are stable in Brahma and have conquered this sarga i.e. Maayic world here and now [in living state] only because Brahma is innocent and even. 19.

Brahmanized person of stable intellect and stabilized in Brahma without delusions does not become glad, delighted and joyed on obtaining what is dear and pleasant and does not lament and become sorry, dejected and agonized on getting what is unpleasant and disagreeable. 20.

Brahma-united and yoga-united Aatmaa continuously enjoys that very undiminishing happiness which is enjoyed within self by Aatmaa detached from external sense-subjects like words etc. 21.

Aatmaa united with Brahma and Aatmaa detached from senses enjoy the same undiminishing happiness continuously.

Sensory enjoyments have a beginning and an end so wise do not play in them.

These sensory enjoyments arising out of contacts [between organs and their objects] are the causes of miseries having beginning and end. Therefore, oh, Arjuna! wisely intelligent do not play in them. 22. Refer to Ch:2:14.

Full stop the flood of passion and anger and be a yogi. One who, while in this world before leaving this body is power-full enough and able to endure and estop the flood of Kaama i.e. passion and anger, he alone is yogi [and] he alone is the happy person. 23.

Endure with equipoise the vigorous agitation arising in mind from the passions and angers and you are happy and a karma yogi.

One who is happy within, who rests within, who is Aatmically lighted within, that yogi becoming Brahma-form emancipates into Brahma, becomes one with Brahma.. 24.

Self-mastered sages having sins nullified, doubts destroyed and engrossed in the well-fare of all creatures gains emancipation in Brahma or Braahmic emancipation. 25.

Yati finds Brahma every where

Yatis-knowledgeable yogis, who have conquered chitta, who are free from passion and anger and who have realized Aatmaa, find Brahma every where around them. [another rendering is: find peace every where.].26.

Who is always free? That sage, who making even the Praan-

Apaan roaming within nose i.e. equalizing the breathing for Praan-augmentation and shutting out external sense-contacts and fixing the gaze on the mid-point between the eye-brows, and who has conquered organs, mind and intellect: such a Moksha-seeker sage who is free from desire, fear and anger is always free i.e. emancipated. 27-28.

These two couplets are the prelude to Raaja Yoga which is elucidated in the next chapter.

Knowing me to be the consumer and enjoyer of sacrifice and penance, supreme Ishvar of Sarva-Loka i.e. all creatures of all regions and selfless lover of the entire creation attains peace. 29.

AUM TAT SAT: Thus it is the fifth chapter, named Karma-Sanyaas Yoga in Shree Krishna-Arjuna dialogue on Brahma-knowledge yoga-scripture Shreemad-Bhagavad Gita Upanishad.

CHAPTER:6

Aatma-Sainyam Yoga : Self-Controlled Yoga

Bhagawaan teaches Raaj yoga method to attain the highest state whereby one sees the entire existence as one unitary field of Brahma or Aatmaa. He expounds this yoga for those who have become proficient in Saamkhya and Buddhi yoga. He maintains that nothing done in this yoga is wasted. Once you start it will drag you even against your will to the final destination. Process awaits you to begin if you are Buddhi or Saamkhya yogi..

Who is a yogi and a Sanyaasi?

Shree Bhagawaan spoke:

One who does the worth-doing karmas without taking refuge and asylum in their fruits is a Sanyaasi [renouncer], is a yogi, but not one who does not ignite sacrificial-fires nor an inactive one. 1.

Shree Krishna says in no uncertain words that he alone is a yogi and he alone is a Sanyaasi i.e. a renouncer who does prescribed actions without attachment to their fruits and not one who does not light sacrificial fires nor does not do actions.

Oh, Arjuna! Know that to be yoga which is thus called Sanyaas, renouncement and detachment because no one who has not renounced Sankalps can become a yogi. 2.

Here sankalpa means thoughts and decisions to act and includes the desire of fruits of actions.

For a sage desiring to ride Yoga, the [selfless] action is said to be the means-cause, but for a yoga-rider their cessation i.e. cessation of all Sankalps is said to be the cause and means of kalyaan. 3.

Because when one does not become attached to the sense-subjects nor is attached to the actions then that renouncer of all Sankalps is said to be yoga-rider. 4.

One's Aatmaa should salvage, emancipate and deliver one's Aatmaa and should not lead Aatmaa to degradation because Aatmaa is the brother of the Aatmaa and Aatmaa is the enemy of the Aatmaa.5.

Aatmaa of one whose self is conquered by Aatmaa is the brother of the Aatmaa but Aatmaa of the uncontrolled self acts like an enemy of Aatmaa. 6.

In these two couplets Shree Krishna is talking from the highest level of monism as well as from the Saamkhya point of view. Aatma and Brahma in their nascent state do not possess any of the qualities of the phenomenal universe including living creatures. But it is also true that it suo moto becoming a point called Sadaashiva Point explodes causing a vibrating field and at the point of explosion is called Shabal Brahma i.e. energized Brahma. This explosion creates three gunied Prakruti binding Brahma and reducing him into Aatmaas without actually dividing It. Thus Aatmaa is its own enemy when it vibrates and becomes his friend when it stops vibrating. It is for the Aatmaa to decide and none else. So Krishna says Aatma is its own friend and enemy too. Vibrating Aatmaa produces the entire animate and inanimate universe. It is unfortunate that some commentators have translated Aatmaa in this couplet to mean Mind or Chitta. With due respect to them I would say Shree Krishna knew all these words and if he had wanted to say Mind or Chitta he would have used these words and not Aatmaa. He was well aware of these words and their meaning.

Self-conqueror, who is tranquil and equipoised in heat and cold, happiness and misery, honor and dishonor, fully attains to supreme Aatmaa: becomes supreme Aatmaa. 7.

To the self-controlled every thing is same and of the same value. One who has conquered organs, whose Aatmaa is fully satisfied with knowledge and science i.e. relative knowledge, who is in steady and change-less state and to whom clay, stone and gold are of the same value is a [Brahma]-united yogi, so it is said. 8

He is special and best who has the same even intellect towards selfless benefactor i.e. good-hearted, friend, foe, fit-to-be-hated, brothers, pious and sinners as well as impartial and indifferent mediator 9.

Residence for a yogi and his life style

Staying alone in a secluded place and controlling the self i.e. Chittaatmaa, becoming desireless and non-possessor, yogi should continuously join his chitta in Aatmaa. 10.

Remaining all alone in solitude in an uninhabited area, keeping his Chittaatmaa i.e. chitta under control, freeing from desires and longing from possessions, let the yogi constantly concentrate on his Aatmaa i.e. chitta on Aatmaa.

Asan, Seat and practice of Yoga

In a clean and holy place one should fix his seat which is neither too high nor too low consisting of Kush-hay, deer-skin and clean cloth [cotton] placed one above the other. 11.

Sitting on that seat, concentrating the mind, and stopping the activities of chitta and organs, should practice yoga for purifying the self, self-purification. [*Aatma- Vishuddhaye.*] 12.

Keeping steady and still the trunk, the neck and the head erect in a straight vertical line, fixing his look at the tip of the nose without looking in other directions: 13.

And Becoming fixed in a vow of celibacy, becoming free from fear, becoming quiet Aatmaa, and controlling the mind, with Me-suffused-chitta and Me-suffused, be united in Me. 14.

Always uniting his chitta in this manner a yogi of controlled mind attains to Moksha-form supreme peace which is in My Form. 15.

Food and sleep

This yoga is not for over-eater i.e. a glutton, nor is for an over-faster i.e. eats too less, oh, Arjuna! It is not for over-sleeper nor for under-sleeper: 16. This misery destroying yoga is achieved by those whose food, behavior and life-style is proper, suitable, and health-conducive, whose actions are fit and proper, sleep and waking are moderate and proper. 17.

When completely controlled chitta steadies well in self-Aatmaa then a person freed from all passions and desires is yoga-united, thus it is said. 18

Controlled Chitta is steady and quietly flows in Aatma and experiences limitless Bliss. The flame of a wick-lamp located in a breezeless place does not flicker. This is the simile given to the controlled chitta of a yogi joined in the meditation of Aatmaa. 19.

The controlled chitta of a yogi meditating on Aatmaa is compared with the unflickering wick-lamp in a place having no air currents. Chitta is steady and quietly flows in Aatmaa.

Know that state as yoga wherein chitta obstructed by yoga practice quietens and subsides, wherein self realizing Aatmaa satisfies in the Aatmaa.20

One experiences that limitless happiness which is beyond the cognizance and grasp of organs but cognizable by intellect: wherein once thus fixed, yogi does not move out from this final Tattva i.e. Brahma. 21.

Remember that once you have attained the state of Brahma you never loose it under any circumstance. From here on one plays as a Brahma in Brahma for Brahma though his outward form is of a being in the phenomenal world.

And yogi does not believe any other gain greater than this gain and the yogi fixed in this state does not move i.e. is not perturbed by any calamity however great. 22.

Know this state free from misery-form sansaar as yoga: This yoga is decisively fit to be achieved with unagitated chitta. 23.

Shree Krishna now explains the process for achieving this Yoga

After abandoning all passions-Vaasanaas-desires born of

Sankalps [mental activities] without leaving a trace, after fully controlling the entire group of organs from all sides with the mind, 24. and with firm and patient intellect fixed in the self-Aatmaa quieten the mind slowly and gradually step by step without pondering on any thing else, 25. and withdrawing this unsteady, flickering and restless mind from wherever it wanders, fix it in the Aatmaa; 26.

Condition of a yogi in Braahmic-embrace

Because that sinless yogi free from Rajo guna with limitlessly peaceful mind who has become Brahma-form obtains best happiness.27. Sinless yogi with Aatmaa always united in this manner, happily experiences the supreme happiness of Brahma-contact, Braahmic-embrace. 28.

Yoga-united Aatmaa having even-sight for all and every thing sees [the same] Aatmaa located in all and sees all bhootas in his Aatmaa.29.

To him, who sees Me every where and sees all [bhootas] in Me I do not disappear from his presence nor does he disappear from My presence.30.

Aatmaa is the sole substance constituting the entire universe and creation. For one who realizes this situation, Creator and created do not disappear from each other's presence as nothing else is there besides Aatma.

That yogi, who, being established in such oneness-unity, worships Me as located in all bhootas [as Aatmaa] acts in Me even though he behaves in all manners. 31.

Shree Bhagawaan says one who is stabilized in the unity of the universe in its multiplicity and worships Me as present in the entire creation lives in Me, no matter, how he behaves. Such a yogi is beyond the laws governing the universe, he is always located within Me, within Brahma.

Therefore, oh, Arjuna! a yogi who sees everywhere evenly, happiness or even misery evenly by his own illustration, that yogi is opined to be best. 32.

By the illustration of Aatmaa a yogi sees evenly

everywhere, he sees happiness and even misery of all to be even. A yogi being Aatmaa-form sees every where Aatmaa only. For him there is neither misery nor happiness. He sees the same Aatmaa everywhere and therefore every thing is even and equal without any difference or distinction.

Arjuna spoke

[About unsteady mind] Oh, Madhusudan! You have told this yoga of even-intellect, but I do not see its steady-state i.e. steady-state of long duration because of actively unsteady mind, because of the restless and fickle mind. 33. I believe mind to be as difficult to obstruct and control as it is to obstruct and control the wind Because, Oh, Krishna! this mind is strong and firm. Organ-agitating mind is restless and unsteady. 34.

Shree Bhagawaan spoke: No doubt, oh, Mighty-handed! it is difficult to obstruct the restless mind but oh, Arjuna! it can be obstructed by practice and detachment [renunciation]. 35.

It is, no doubt, difficult to control and checkmate the mind because it is restless, strong and obstinate but it is amenable to obstruction and control by practice and detachment to worldly objects. Renunciation, detachment and practice are the corner stones of yoga achievement. No body should labor under false notion that yoga does not require efforts. It does.

It is my opinion that this yoga is difficult to be attained by one who is not self-controlled but it is possible to be accomplished by the self controlled by striving with proper means and technic. 36.

Destiny of a fallen yogi i.e. a yogi moving away from yoga or death.

Arjuna spoke: Possessed of faith and lacking self-control, not achieving yoga- accomplishment due to mind slipping away from yoga, to what way and destiny oh, Krishna! does he go? 37.

Oh, mighty-handed [Krishna]! Does he or does he not, becoming dislodged and aimless being deluded away from the Brahma-path and fallen from both, yoga and sense-enjoyments perish like a lone exhausted cloud.38.

Oh, Krishna! you are fit and enlightened enough to tracelessly destroy this doubt of mine because it is not possible to get any one else to pierce this doubt. 39.

Arjuna poses a question what is the destiny of a person possessed of faith but who does not achieve yoga success as he stops the practice due to mind moving away from yoga or by death? suppose you have faith in yoga and you take to yoga practice and before you achieve the perfection you stop yoga practice for any reason. What will happen to you? You have become aimless. You have lost the path to Brahma and also the happiness of sense-enjoyments. Will you perish like a lonely cloud ?Is your effort lost for ever? Answer is No: You do not. Your effort is not lost. Couplets 40-45 tell us the destiny of one who takes to yoga and leaves it unaccomplished due to any reason.

Fallen yogi goes to meritorious region, enjoys there for a long time and then takes birth to carry on yoga practice.

Shree Bhagawaan spoke: Oh, Partha! his destruction [or ruin] does not take place in this world nor in the next because, oh, son! doer of kalyaanic actions [emancipative actions] does not go to any evil destiny, any evil state. 40.

Person fallen-from-yoga goes to the region of meritorious people [Punya-Krutaam] and staying there for very long time takes a birth in the house of the pious, holy and wealthy house. 41. Or, is born in the family of knowledgeable yogis and in this world the birth of this kind is really extremely difficult to get. 42.

Oh, Son of Kuru! There that person gains the even-intellect Sanskaaras i.e. impressions [acquired in] from previous birth and by their influence he tries again to achieve success in yoga. 43.

Such a fallen yogi though not self-controlled is dragged towards yoga by reason of previous practice because even the inquisitive of yoga [karma-yoga] crosses over Shabda-

Brahma. [then what to say of such a fallen yogi?] 44.

Does Shabda Brahma mean the words of Vedas and rituals enjoined for fruitive actions or does it mean beyond the vibrations of Brahma i.e. kinetic Brahma? It seems beyond the state of vibrations because Shabda Brahma is used for the initial vibratory state of Brahma. This means he attains Brahmahood.

Yoga fallen yogi takes his birth in a suitable family and by the force of the Sanskaaras carried forward from the previous births carries on his yoga practice further. The effects of efforts made are not lost but are suspended temporarily. They wake up in the next birth and drags one to travel on the path to emancipation.

Reason to become a yogi

Becoming cleansed of all sins and accomplished with continuous and assiduous striving of many births that yogi attains supreme destiny, supreme state i.e. Brahmi-state.45.

Yogi is superior to penance-doer and even to knowledgeable, Yogi is superior to selfish-karma doer so is the opinion. Therefore, oh, Arjuna! be a yogi. 46.

Who is best yogi? Of all the yogis, one who having faith worships [bhajes] Me with inner-Aatmaa merged in Me is in my opinion best yogi attuned-in-Me. 47.

AUM TAT SAT: Thus it is the sixth chapter named self-control Yoga in Shree Krishna-Arjuna dialogue on Brahma-knowledge yoga-scripture Shreemad-Bhagavad Gita Upanishad.

CHAPER : 7

Jyaana-Vijyaana Yoga Knowledge and Relative-Knowledge Yoga

Now Bhagawaan describes the composition of the universe and living beings. Out of millions and millions few thousands become accomplished and of such millions of accomplished ones rarely one knows Me Tattvically i.e. in Tattva and essence. Bhagawaan describes these Tattvas? He says, "My nature i.e. Prakruti is divided into eight Tattvas viz. Earth, Liquid, Fire, Vaayu i.e. Gases, Space, Mind, Intellect i.e. Mahat and Ego. Apart from this inanimate Prakruti I have another Animate Prakruti called Soul by which this universe is upheld. All creatures are the products of these two Prakrutis and therefore I am the creator as well as destroyer of the universe. There is no Tattva other and greater than me." He is the only constituent in every thing. Every thing is the product of three gunas of his Maya which is difficult to cross over. For full elucidation see Introduction II.

Taking His shelter those who try to be free from the cycle of birth-death should know completely Brahma, Adhyaatma, Adhibhoota, Adhidaiva, Adhiyajya and Karma: Now let us turn to text.

Three conditions precedent to know Bhagawaan fully.

Shree Krishna spoke

Hear, oh, Partha! understand that, you will know me wholly and entirely without even a shadow of doubt by attaching mind in Me, having refuge in Me and united in yoga. 1.

Bhagawaan lays down three condition to know him as he is without any doubt: [a] Mind riveted in Bhagawaan,

[b]: refuge in him and [c]: united in yoga. Hear now, how these conditions operate to impart you that knowledge and its experience.

I will tell you that knowledge together with its Vijyaan i.e. knowledge relating to universe leaving nothing unsaid knowing which there remains nothing else to be known in this world. 2.

Jyaan and Vijyaan

Jyaan means experience of not only Aatmaa but Aatmaa as Brahma: realization that Aatma is Brahma and finally Brahma is universe. Vijyaan means information of the universe, its constitution etc. excluding Brahma and Aatmaa. Vijyaan means knowledge of Maya and her products. Vijyaan is made up of Vi and Jyaan: Vi is the short form of Viruddha meaning opposite, so Vijyaan means opposite of knowledge. Brahma and Aatmaa is knowledge and its opposite is Maya and her product universe. We are dealing with Saamkhya system where Prakruti is the constructor of the universe. Brahma and Aatmaa is only an activator. To use the scientific term Brahma and Aatmaa is merely a catalytic agent in the process of universe production.

From among thousands of men, hardly one strives to achieve perfection and accomplishment: even from these striving Siddhas [accomplished ones] scarcely one knows me Tattvically i.e. by Tattvas and in essence. 3.

What are the Tattvas and essences by which one is to know Him is enumerated in couplets 4-5.

Bhoomi, Aap, Agni, Vaayu, Kham as well as Mind, Buddhi and Ego, thus is the eight-fold division of this prakruti of Mine.4.

Usual rendering in English of this couplet reads, "Earth, Water, Fire, Air, Ether, Mind, Intellect, and Ego; this is the eight-fold infra-inferior-inanimate Prakruti of Mine: see chapters: 13:5 and 15:16. First five are the five great elements of Saamkhya physics and the remaining three are the physical components of the mental complex. Therefore the correct rendition would be: "Sky and Space, Gases and Electromagnetic and other Forces, Heat and light, Liquids, and Solids, Mind, Intellect and Ego is the eight-fold inanimate-infra Prakruti of mine." 4.

For understanding these eight Prakrutis see Introduction II.

This [eight-fold Prakruti] is infra-inferior one: but another one apart from it, oh, mighty-handed! know my supra-superior Jeeva-bhoot [soul] Prakruti by which this universe is taken upon and upheld. 5.

Nothing beyond and outside of Bhagawaan

All creatures are produced from these two Prakrutis, know thus, [therefore], I am the creative cause of the universe as well as I am the cause of its dissolution: 6

Both the Prakrutis being of Bhagawaan he is, in effect the creator and destroyer of this entire universe.

Oh, Dhananjay! there is nothing beyond and outside of Me. This whole [universe] is strung in Me like jewels on a thread [in a necklace]. 7.

I am savor [Rasa] in liquids, oh, Kaunteya! I am the Prabhaa-light in the Sun and the Moon, I am Pranava i.e. AUM in all Vedas, the Shabda i.e. Word in the sky and manliness-manhood and valor in men. 8.

For the meaning of AUM and the word 'Word' see Introduction II.

I am the sweet and holy smell in solids: brilliance and heat in fire: the life in all creatures and I am the penance of the Tapasvi i.e. Penance-doer. 9.

Oh, Partha! know me to be the eternal seed of all bhootas i.e. all creatures [or all that exists in the phenomenal universe]. I am the intellect of the intelligent and the splendor of the splendorous or the power of the powerful.10.

Oh, best Bharat! I am the power and strength devoid of Kaama-passion and raag of the strong and powerful: and I am the passion not contrary to Dharma-duties .11.

Dharma-Viruddha means not-opposed-to-dharma or Dharma-approved

And whatever Saatvik, Rajasic and Taamsic Bhaavas i.e. feelings and substances are, know them all to be from me. They are [imagined] in me but I am not in them. 12.

Who crosses over Maya and who does not

Fascinated and stupefied by Bhaavas i.e. the feelings and substances composed of these three gunas i.e. waves, the whole universe does not know me who am beyond the three gunas i.e.. waves and undiminishing [= Avyayasya] 13.

Because this Daivi i.e. divine three-gunied i.e. three waved Maya of Mine is difficult to subdue and overcome. But those who take shelter and refuge in Me alone swim-over this Maayic field. 14.

Evil-doers, stupid and lowly persons of demonic nature whose knowledge is abducted by Maya do not come to my refuge.15.

Kinds of persons who Bhajes Bhagawaan?

Oh, best of the Bharat-descendants! distressed and miserable, inquisitive i.e. spiritual seeker, worldly-objects-seeker and knowledgeable, these are the four kinds of meritorious persons who bhajes me, worship me.16.

Of them, always united knowledgeable devotee of exclusive devotion is special and best because I am extremely dear to knowledgeable and he is extremely dear to me. 17.

Certainly all these devotees are magnanimous and of high quality but the knowledgeable is my very Aatmaa. So is my opinion because that united-Aatmaa is stationed in the best state which is Me. or his Aatmaa is located and united with Me as his final destination. 18.

Knowledgeable, realizing at the end of many births that 'All this is Vaasudeva' comes to my refuge: Such a mahatma is difficult to come across. 19.

Who worships other deities and why? What is the net result?

Those whose knowledge is dulled and lost by passions and controlled by their nature take refuge of other deities following their rules, rites and rituals.20.

In whatever form a devotee desires to worship with faith and devotion, I make that faith firm and steady in that form [in that deity] 21.

And united with that faith he does Aaraadhanaa i.e. worships of that deity and gains from him his desires which are prescribed by Me only. 22.

Each deity is endowed by Bhagawaan with powers to give certain things for enjoyments i.e. Bhogas. They, on their worship will grant you those Bhogas. Thus the same are in effect given as already prescribed by Bhagawaan. Powers are delegated and can be withdrawn by Bhagawaan.

But that fruit gained by these short-sighted with small intellect is of perishable nature because deity-worshippers go to deity but my devotees come to Me and attain Me only. 23

Belief of deluded persons regarding Bhagawaan

Not knowing my best undiminishing supreme state, unintelligent ones believe Me who am unmanifested to be an embodied person. 24.

Covered and veiled by my Yoga-Maya I do not become visible to all: This stupid world does not know Me as undiminishing and birthless. 25.

Oh, Arjuna! I know all creatures that existed in the past, those existing now and those to come in the future, but none know Me.26.

Who firmly worships Bhagawaan?

Oh, Bharat-descendant foe-conqueror! All creatures in this creation are extremely bewildered being deluded by the pairs of opposites generated by desires, envies and hates. 27.

But those pious people [Punya shaali] whose sins have

perished becoming free from dualities i.e. pairs of opposites worship Me firmly with firm conviction. 28.

Those who try to be free from old-age and death by taking refuge in Me know wholly and completely Brahma, Adhyaatma and Karma. 29.

Those, who know Me together with Adhibhoota, Adhidaiva and Adhiyajya, they with chitta united in Me know only Me at the time of death. 30. They attain Brahma.

The technical terms used in these two couplets forms the basis of the next chapter.

AUM TAT SAT: Thus it is the seventh chapter, named jyaan-vijyaana Yoga in Shree Krishna-Arjuna dialogue on Brahma-knowledge yoga-scripture Shreemad-Bhagavad Gita Upanishad.

CHAPTER : 8

Akshara Brahma Yoga

Imperishable Brahma Yoga

The chapter is titled Akshara Brahma yoga: Akshara means that which does not perish. It means Brahma is imperishable. Imperishable Brahma is supreme. In couplets 29-30 of chapter seven Shree Bhagawaan introduced Brahma, Adhyaatma, Karma, Adhibhoota and Adhiyajna. In this chapter Arjuna asks as to what does these terms mean? and Bhagawaan answers the same. The nature of Brahma is called Adhyaatma. Activity is karma: Perishable ones are called Adhibhoota. Purusha is Adhidaiva; Bhagawaan is Adhiyajya in all bodies. AUM is AUM-Brahma. It deals in nut shell the time scales of creation and destruction of worlds and who and how one attains the highest.

Arjuna spoke: What is that Brahma? What is Adhyaatma? What is karma? Oh, Purushottama! and what is Adhibhoota and what is called Adhidaiva? 1.

Who is Adhiyajna here and how [it stays] in this body? Oh, Madhusudan! How can it be known by the self-controlled one at the time of departure, at the moment of death? 2.

Arjuna asks about Brahma, Adhyaatma, Karma, Adhibhoota and Adhidaiva and Adhiyajna. Shree Krishna now answers the same.

Shree Bhagawaan spoke

Imperishable Brahma is supreme. His Svabhaava i.e. nature is called Adhyaatma and the activity creating universe of bhootas and creatures maintaining and dissolving the universe is called Karma. 3.

Transient and perishable Bhaavas i.e. things are Adhibhoota, and Purusha is Adhidaiva. Oh, best of the embodied ones! and in this body I am the Adhiyajna. 4.

Couplets 3 and 4 defines the terms used in couplets 1 and 2.

[a] Brahma is supreme and imperishable; [b] Adhyaatma means the properties and qualities of Brahma; [c] Activity creating and destroying universe and the bhootas is called Karma; [d] Adhibhoota means transient and perishing universe and all its contents; [e] Adhidaiva means Purusha, and [f] Adhiyajna means Ishvar.

Gita teaches us to merge in Brahma. This chapter says Brahma is supreme and imperishable. Brahma is the goal. Therefore it is very important to know what is Brahma and its nature.? For understanding these terms scientifically see Introduction II.

Pure monism, the finest experienced philosophical flower of Sanaatan Dharma of Hinduism declares that nothing exist save and except Brahma-stuff in its unaltered-unchanged-nascent-original form and the universe never existed and does not exist. Whatever solidity comes to be seen or experienced is nothing but an illusion, merely an appearance without substance depending only on senses. Even science admits that in ultimate analysis the smallest known particles are nothing but waves. Science as of late has started referring to it as living Void. Remember that Brahma is the root substance ever existing.

Who merges in Brahma?

And a person who leaves the body remembering Me only at the last moment, enters my nature, merges in Me, in that, there is no doubt. 5.

Basis of rebirth in a specie

Remembering whatever bhaava at the last moment, when one leaves the body, he goes to that bhaava [he remains in that bhaava after death] because he was always engrossed in that Bhava, in that thought. 6.

In chapter 2:72. it is said that resting in Brahma State even at the end time [at the time of leaving the body] one gets Brahma-nirvana i.e. merges in Brahma. One goes to the root. Here the same thing is repeated in different words with the condition that you will leave the body with that Bhava-thought with which you are always engrossed. And therefore next couplet gives you that advice.

Therefore remember Me at all times and fight. With mind and intellect thus surrendered to Me, you will doubtlessly attain Me.7.

Supreme divine Purusha and how to merge in Him

Oh, Paartha! one musing i.e. concentrating with non-wandering chitta united with yoga practice attains supreme divine Purusha.8.

Shree Krishna describes supreme divine Purusha and how to attain Him. Supreme divine Purusha and Brahma means one and the same thing or Being. Brahma is the term of Vedas and Purushottam i.e. Best-Purusha is the term employed in Saamkhya system. Mark the description is the same.

Person united with Bhakti and yoga power who remembering the supreme Divine Purusha [who is] omniscient, beginningless, the ruler of all, smaller than the smallest atomic-particle, of inconceivable form, Sun-colored i.e. of the sun-brilliance and beyond the Tama-darkness-ignorance, carefully and steadily fixes his Praan with the unmoving and steady mind in the mid-point between the eye-brows at the time of departure [at the death-time] attains to him i.e. that supreme Divine Purusha. 9-10.

At the time of departure, one united with Bhakti who carefully and steadily fixes his Praanas in the mid-point between the eye-brows by yoga-power and with steady mind remembers- meditates on that one who is omniscient, beginningless, the ruler of all, smaller than the smallest atomic-particle, of inconceivable form, sun-colored and beyond the darkness-ignorance, attains to that supreme-divine purusha.

Mid-point between the eye-brows is the seat of the Aajyaa Chakra and meditation on it leads through various stages to Brahmahood.

Akshara i.e., imperishable. Who attains it?

I tell you briefly that state which the Veda-learned call Akshara i.e. imperishable [Brahma] and wherein enter the striving Yati free from passion and desiring which state [one] observes celibacy. 11.

Whoever stabilized in yoga-contemplation of Aatmaa controlling all doors i.e. organs and imprisoning mind in the heart, and uttering AUM, the one word-Brahma and simultaneously remembering Me fixes his Praan in Moordhani and discards the body and goes: he attains supreme destiny i.e. Brahma. 12-13.

Moordhani means Brahmarandhra i.e. thousand-petalled lotus in the cranium or the space six inches in front of the forehead. AUM is of singular significance for Hindus. Why? See Introduction II.

Oh, Paartha! one who continuously and exclusively remembers Me with his chitta, I am always easy to reach to such a Me-united yogi. 14.

Bhagawaan is easy to be reached by one who continuously and exclusively remembers him. Bhagawaan requires exclusive remembrance. It should be single-pointed to Bhagawaan. Your remembrance should not be divided between him and some body else or something else.

Supremely accomplished Mahaatmaas having attained supreme destiny i.e. Me do not come to take a transitory rebirth, the place of miseries and sorrow. 15.

Arjuna! All the worlds inclusive of Brahmaa are givers of rebirth, but Oh, Kunti-son! Me-attained have no rebirth. The rebirth of those who have attained Me does not take place. 16.

Who are knowers of time?

People who know the day of Brahmaa to be of the length

equal to one thousand units each of four Yugas and night also of equal duration are the knowers of day-night time. 17.

At the dawning of the day all beings get created from the unmanifest and at the night fall they merge and dissolve in the unmanifest.18.

Oh, Arjuna! that very same multitude of bhootas i.e. creatures come into being again and again helplessly merging at the coming of the night and coming into being at day-break. 19.

Supreme Abode of Bhagawaan

But above and beyond that unmanifest, there exist yet another eternal unmanifest bhaava i.e. substance and Being which does not perish on the destruction of bhootas [creature]. 20.

That unmanifest is Akshara i.e. imperishable, it is thus said, and the same is also called supreme destiny. Why? because, attaining which [people] do not come back: that is my supreme abode.21.

Oh, Paartha! That supreme Purusha within whom bhootas are located and by whom this whole is pervaded can be gained only by exclusive devotion. 22.

Akshara and supreme are the adjectives of Purusha as the final source and is a synonym for Brahma. For creation cycles and their time-scale see Introduction:chapter II.

Time of death and destiny

Now, I will tell you, oh, best Bhaarat! those times at which yogis who have left the bodies will return and will not return i.e. gets a rebirth or is emancipated. 23.

Knower of Brahma who have gone [left the body] on the path under the influence of god of light, fire, day, bright-half of the month and six months of the sun's travel in the northern zodiac attain and unite with Brahma. 24.

Yogi who leaves the body during the influence of god of Dhuma-darkness, fog, night, dark-half of the month and six months of the sun's travel in the southern zodiac goes to the light region of the moon and returns on exhaustion of his meritorious deeds[by enjoying there]. 25.

Because, light and dark [white and black] these two are believed to be the destinies in this universe. There is no return by going on one while you return by going on the other.26.

Oh, Paartha! any yogi knowing these two paths is not deluded and bewildered. Therefore, oh, Arjuna! be yoga-united at all times.27.

Yogi, who knows this [secret] decisively crosses over [discards] all the fruits arising from and as described in performing penance, Yajna, and giving to charities, as well as Vedic studies and attains eternal supreme state. 28.

AUM TAT SAT: Thus it is the eight chapter, named Akshara Brahma Yoga in Shree Krishna-Arjuna dialogue on Brahma-knowledge yoga-scripture Shreemad-Bhagavad Gita Upanishad.

CHAPTER : 9

Raaj-Vidyaa Raaja-Guhya Yoga: Royal-Learning and Royal-Secret yoga

The entire universe is permeated and pervaded by the unmanifest form of Bhagawaan. All Tattvas and creatures are in Him but not He in them and factually speaking they are not in Him.

How is this possible? It only means that this universe is merely false show. Brahma substance vibrates setting forth three kinds of waves in various ranges. These waves create the illusion of time, space and forms. Combination of forms create complex forms of elements. Some waves act as souls. These two sets of forms combine to form living world but these are only waves of the vibrating Brahma just like the waves of the waters of the sea and not separate products. Waves are continuous. Each wave is not separated from the rest. Similarly Brahma is continuous. It never snaps into parts though in wave form. It is merely an appearance.

Let us turn to text

Remember that in this chapter Krishna talks from the point of view of Brahma. Krishna is Vishnu incarnate and thus is with all that is Brahma in tact.

Bhagawaan spoke

But, now, I tell you this faultless and extremely secret knowledge together with relative knowledge i.e. knowledge of the universe knowing which you will become free from Ashubh i.e. non- good meaning this sansaar. 1.

Jyaan-Vijyaan means Brahma and Non-Brahma: universe and creatures are non-Brahma. Brahma is beyond description.

This knowledge is the Raaja Vidyaa i.e. Royal learning and king of all secrets, best of the best, extremely holy, pure, and direct-fruit-giver, undiminishing, Dhaarmic and easy to practice.2.

Oh, Foe Oppressor! persons who have no faith and trust in this Dharma, do not attain Me but roam in the mortal world. 3.

This whole universe is pervaded and permeated by Me by my unmanifested form. All bhootas [animate and inanimate] are in Me but I am not in them. 4.

This means that bhootas exist as supported by Him but He exists independently of them: He does not require their support to exist.

And again it can be said that all bhootas are not in Me: but look and behold at my Yogic glory and powers! my Aatmaa though creator of bhootas and upholder of bhootas, is not in them. 5.

This shows transcendental nature of Brahma in accordance with Saamkhya view.

Just as every-where-roaming great Vaayu is always located in the sky, similarly all bhootas abide in Me.6.

Creation and merger of all living beings

At the end of every Kalpa, oh, Kunti-son! all living beings attain to and merge in my prakruti and in the beginning of the Kalpa, I create them again. 7.

Resorting to and making use of my Prakruti I create again and again this multitudes of living beings who, being subject to the power of my prakruti, are helpless [in the matter].8.

But, these karmas [creation etc.] do not bind Me because, oh, Dhananjay! I remain detached in them like an indifferent and uninterested person.9.

Prakruti creates under the direction and control of Bhagawaan.

Under my stewardship [direction, supervision and control] Prakruti produces moving and non-moving [animate and inanimate universe] and for this reason, oh, Kunti-son! the universe goes on changing ceaselessly. 10.

Who are stupid and condemn Bhagawaan and who are not?

Being unaware and not knowing my supreme nature as the Sovereign Ishvar of bhootas and seeing me sheltered and embodied in human form, stupid persons despise and condemn me. 11.

Those of reverse-intellect [fools] are refuged and sheltered in the bewitching fiendish and demonic nature. Their hopes and aspirations are vain, their actions are vain, their knowledge is vain and devoid of discrimination. 12.

But the mahatmas being sheltered in my divine nature, oh, Partha! and knowing Me to be undiminishing and unwasting source of bhootas, [bhajes] worship Me exclusively with mind.13.

Some, firmly resolved, constantly doing my Kirtan, striving and bowing me repeatedly and always yoga-united do my Upaasana with Bhakti-devotion. 14.

Others do my Upaasana with knowledge-sacrifice taking Me as one with universe or as separate and distinct whose face is every where i.e. immanent or transcendent with universal face. 15.

Now Bhagawaan describes how he is universal face

I am Kratu i.e. Shraut-sacrifice, I am Smarta-sacrifice, I am Swadhaa i.e. food offered to ancestor manes, I am the medicines and foods, I am Mantra, I am Ghee, I am fire, I am the act of offering. 16.

I am the feeder-protector and fruit-giver father, mother and grand-father of this universe and I am also the thing worth knowing, holy AUM, Rig, Saama and Yajur Veda too. 17.

I am the goal and final destination, the upholding sustainer, Prabhu i.e. master of all, witness, the abode, the refuge, selfless benefactor, creator, destroyer, resting place and dissolution place, I am the undiminishing seed i.e. uncaused cause. 18.

SAT and ASAT i.e. Is and Is not

Oh, Arjuna! I radiate heat [Tapaami], I gather water as clouds and rain them, I am the nectar i.e. life and death, I am SAT and also ASAT i.e. I am 'Is' and also 'Isnot'.19.

SAT means absolute reality. ASAT means universe which is relative reality. Supreme is both. It is a Being when manifested and non-Being in the unmanifested state. Naasaadiya Sukta begins, *Naasadaaseenno Saddaseetta Daantam:* Rig-Veda 10:129:1.

Vedic rites and Rituals sing the glory of three Gunas and gives only coming and going to Paradise.

Three Veda-knowers, taking Soma-juice and being freed from sins performing Veda-prescribed sacrifices pray for going to paradise; attaining Indra-region i.e. Paradise as a fruit of the Punya [sacrifice] enjoy divine enjoyments of deities in paradise.20.

On exhaustion of their Punyas by enjoying in vast world of paradise, they return to the mortal world. In this way enjoyment-seekers by resorting to [taking shelter under] Vedic Dharma earn only coming and going i.e. rounds of rebirth. 21.

Bhagawaan personally carry on the Yoga-Kshema of his meditator.

Those people who worship Me by meditating on Me exclusively I personally carry on the Yoga-Kshema of such always-united-with-me persons.22.

Yoga-Kshema means giving what they have not and protecting what they have.

Relation of Bhagawaan with other Deities

Oh, Kunti-son! those devotees, who worship other deities with faith, they worship me only though improperly and in ignorance.23.

As every deity is another form of Brahma whatever form is worshipped with faith, only Brahma is worshipped in incognito. Bhagawaan says also because:

I am the enjoyer of all sacrifices and Prabhu i.e. master also i.e. fruit-giver also but they do not know me by Tattvas [in essence] and so they fall [in the cycle].24.

Deities-worshippers go to Deities, worshippers of Pitris i.e. ancestor manes go the ancestors' mane region, worshippers of low spirits and ghost goblins go to them and those who worship Me come to Me only. 25.

Bhagawaan accepts anything offered with devotion

Whoever gives with devotion a leaf, flower, fruit or even water that offering made with devotional heart by striving Aatmaa, I accept. 26.

[Therefore], whatever you do, whatever you eat, whatever you offer in oblation, whatever you give [in charity] whatever penance you perform, oh, Arjuna! dedicate and surrender all that to Me. 27.

Thus [doing] you will be emancipated from the bondage of the good and bad fruit-giving karmas — deeds. With freed Aatma united with renunciation-yoga, you will attain Me. 28.

Relation of Bhagawaan with a Bhakt, a devotee

I am equal and even to all creatures: none is hateful to me nor dear to me but those who worship [bhajes] me with Bhakti-devotion, they are in Me and I am also in them. 29.

Even if a person of most vile conduct [a most heinous sinner] bhajes-worships me with exclusive devotion he is worthy to be opined as Saadhu because he is of correct resolve.30.

And so he soon becomes Dharmaatmaa [dhaarmic Aatmaa or pious Aatmaa] and attains to eternal peace. Oh, Kunti-son! Know it for certain that my devotee never perishes. 31.

Because, oh, Partha! even they, who take refuge and asylum in me, though born of sinful womb, or be a woman, a Vaishya or a Shudra, attain to supreme destiny i.e. final goal Brahma. 32.

If this be so then what to say of meritorious, Brahmins

and sagely kings? Certainly they will. Therefore, having obtained this transient, unhappy and miserable world, Bhaja Me, worship Me. 33.

Royal technique to attain Bhagawaan

Be Me-minded, be my devotee, be my worshipper, bow to Me. In this manner uniting Aatmaa and becoming Me-goaled you will attain Me only. 34.

AUM TAT SAT: Thus it is the ninth chapter, named Raj-Vidyaa Raaj-Guhya yoga kingly- Learning and kingly-Secret yoga in Shree Krishna-Arjuna dialogue on Brahma-knowledge yoga-scripture Shreemad-Bhagavad Gita Upanishad.

CHAPTER : 10

Vibhooti Yoga

Deities and sages do not know Me because I am the initial cause of them all. Every thought, feeling and emotion come to be because of Brahma only. Brahma is the beginning, middle and the end of every thing. He is the alpha to omega. Brahma is the efficient and material cause of everything that was, is and will be the animate and inanimate universe. This idea is elaborated in the chapter.

Shree Bhagawaan spoke

Oh, mighty-handed Arjuna! hear again, my dear, my supreme and final words which I tell you with a desire to benefit [you]. 1.

Neither the society of deities nor the great sages know my origin because in all respects, I am the origin of Deities and great sages. 2.

Prabhav means majesty as well as origin. Couplet is true with either meaning. We do not know his origin nor its constitution. None know my source because I am the cause of everything. I am their birth-place. Brahma is taken as the axiomatic base of the entire existence. It is unknowable unknown but experienceable and on experience one is lost in it. On coming out of the experience tongue is sealed within the zipped lips. None of the existing religions except Hinduism, Tarot and Taoism have scaled this height of experience. All are grabbing the entity Vivartically appearing form it. It is called Ishvar, God etc. This Ishvar creates souls and the material universe and then souls and the matter combine to from the creatures. We do not know when the first life began in the universe and in what form.

Who is released from sins?

One who knows Me as beginningless, birthless and Great Ishvar of the worlds, he, of all people being non-stupid is released from all sins.3.

Every thing arise from Bhagawaan

Intellect, knowledge, free-from-bewilderment i.e. non-delusion, forgiveness, truth [Satya], control of organs, control of mind, happiness, distress-misery, birth-death, fear-fearlessness.4. And non-injury [non-violence], equanimity and evenness [balanced mind], contentment, penance and austerity, Alms-charity, fame and infamy: All these various kinds of Bhaavas, emotions, properties and qualities of creatures arise and proceed from Me only: are brought into being by and from Me only. 5.

Seven sages, earlier four [Sanank etc.], and [fourteen] Manus: All of them having faith and love in Me are created from My sankalpa i.e. My thought and all these people in the world are from them.6.

Seven Sages: Marichi, Angiraa, Atri, Pulastya, Pulah, Kratu and Vashistha, all these seven are the created by the mind of Brahmaa.

Earlier Four: Sanaka, Sanandana, Sanatana, and Sanatkumar.

Fourteen Manus: During one day of Brahma fourteen Manus come on the stage of the world and vanish; Svaayambhuva, Svaarochish, Uttama, Taamas, Raivata, Chaakshusha, Vaivasvat, Saavarni, Daksha-saavarni, Brahmasaavarni, Dharmasaavarni, Rudrasaavarni, Devasaa-varni, and Indrasaavarni.

One who knows in essence and Tattvically these Vibhootis and yoga of mine, that person unites with Me in stable yoga, there is no doubt in that. 7.

I am the original [creating] cause of all, because of Me every thing goes on. With this understanding pundits and knowledgeable bhajes i.e. worship Me in deep devotion. 8.

With their chitta in Me, uniting their Praan-breathing in Me, enlightening each other by the knowledge of Brahma, always talking of Me they remain contented and joyous [in Me].9.

To whom Bhagawaan gives intellect-yoga?

To those who are continuously united with Me and [bhajes] worship Me with love, to them I give the intellect-yoga by which they come to Me. 10. By reason of compassion and stationing in their self as Aatmaa, I destroy their darkness born of ignorance by the bright lamp of knowledge. 11.

Arjuna spoke

You are supreme Brahma, supreme abode, supreme holifier and purifier. All sages, Devarishi Naarad, Aasit muni, Deval, and Vyaasa also call you eternal divine, Purusha, birthless and omnipresent first Deva [first cause] as well as even you, yourself say so.12-13.

Oh, Keshava! I believe, whatever you say to be true because, oh, Bhagawaan! neither the deities nor the demons know your personality, know all your manifest and unmanifest states. 14.

You, yourself alone know yourself by Aatmaa, Oh, creator of the [bhootas] creatures, Ishvar of Bhootas, Deva of Devas, oh, Purushottam, oh, Master of the universe! 15.

Therefore You, alone are fit to tell your divine personalities completely [manifestations fully] by which personalities you stay-remain pervading all these worlds. 16.

Again, oh, Yogin! How am I to know you by musing on you as well as oh, Bhagawaan! in what different Bhaavas and manifestations you are proper to be mused and meditated by me.!7.

Oh, Janaardan! Tell me again in detail your Yogic powers, abilities and manifestations because even hearing your nectary words, I still remain unsatiated 18.

Bhagawaan describes his chief Vibhootis

Shree Bhagawaan spoke: Shree speaks as Vishnu the creative form of Brahma:

So be it! I will tell you my chief and main personalities and manifestations because, oh, best Kuru! there is no end of extensiveness, there is no limit of spreading. 19.

Oh, Gudaakesha! As Aatmaa, I am located in the Hridaya i.e. heart of all creatures and I am also the beginning, middle and the end of all creatures. 20.

I am Vishnu amongst Aadityaas: I am the rays-radiating sun amongst the luminous objects: I am Mareechi amongst Vaayuas and the moon amongst the constellations. 21.

I am Saam Veda amongst Vedas; I am Indra amongst Deities; I am the mind amongst the organs; I am the active-energy in creatures. 22.

I am Shankar amongst [eleven] Rudras; I am the master of the wealth [kuber] amongst Yakshas and demons; and I am the fire [Agni] amongst [eight] Vasus; and I am the Sumeru amongst mountain-peaks. 23.

Oh, Partha! know me to be Brihaspati the chief amongst priests; I am Skanda [Karttikeya swami] amongst commander-generals; and I am the ocean amongst the water-bodies.24.

I am sage Bhrigu amongst [Maharishis] great sages; I am the one syllable AUM in language and speech, and Japa-sacrifice in all sacrifices and Himaalayan amongst immovable.25.

[I am] Pipul-Ashvastha tree [Ficus Religiosa] amongst all trees, Naarad amongst all Deitic sages [Devarishi], Chitraratha amongst the Gandharvas and Kapil Muni among the Siddhas i.e. accomplished ones, realized ones. 26.

Amongst the horses know me to be Uchchaishravaa named horse born of nectar, and Airaavat elephant amongst elephants and king amongst people. 27.

I am the Vajra amongst the weapons: I am Kaamdhenu [desire fulfilling cow] amongst the cows: and I am the progeny-producing kandarpa [sex-deity]: and Vaasuki serpent amongst serpents. 28.

I am Anant Cobra amongst cobras: and I am the deity Varuna amongst water-dwellers: And Ayarmaa ancestor amongst ancestors: I am Yama amongst those who maintain law and order. 29.

I am Prahlaad amongst demons: I am the calculable time amongst the time-calculators and lion amongst the animals and the son of Vainteya i.e. eagle amongst the birds. 30.

Amongst the purifiers and holifiers I am the Vaayu-air, I am Rama amongst weapon wielders, and amongst Pisces I am the Makar - alligator and the Ganges amongst the flowing rivers. 31.

Oh, Arjuna! I am the beginning, middle and the end of all the worlds: amongst all the learnings I am the Adhyaatma-learning i.e. learning relating to Aatmaa: amongst the arguing debaters I am the essence of the logical argument. 32.

Amongst the alphabets I am the letter A and of the compounded words, I am the compound-Samaas: I am the unending time: I am upholder and maintainer of all and whose face is every where. [Vishvatomukham]. 33.

I am the all-devourer death: I am the cause of the things that will come to be in future and I am the fame, opulence, speech, memory, erudition, courage, patience, and forgiveness amongst the feminines.34.

As well as I am Brihatsaama amongst the hymns: Gaayatri meter amongst meters: Margashirsha amongst months: spring amongst the seasons. 35.

I am the gambling amongst the cheats and the rogues: I am the splendor of the splendorous: I am the victory: I am the decision and the Saattviness amongst the sattviss. [persons having the satvic Bhava. 36.

I am Krishna amongst the Yaadavas, Dhananjay Arjuna amongst the Pandavas, Veda Vyaasa amongst munis-sages, and Ushana Poet amongst the poets. 37.

I am punishing power of the punishers, I am the Niti i.e.

policy and strategy of the victory-seekers, I am the silence of the secrets and knowledge of the knowledgeable. 38.

And Oh, Arjuna! the seed of all Bhootas, that also is Me, because whatever animate and inanimate bhootas are there, they can not exist without Me. 39.

Oh, Parantap! there is no end of my divine manifestations: I have enumerated these Vibhootis by way of illustrations only 40.

Know that whoever and whatever is found with Aishvarya, power, or opulence, all that is produced from a degree of my Tejo-splendor light. 41.

Oh, Arjuna! What is the purpose to know all this? I am upholding this entire universe with a degree or fragment of myself. 42.

AUM TAT SAT: Thus it is the tenth chapter, named Raaj-Vidyaa Raaj-Guhya yoga kingly- Learning and kingly-Secret yoga in Shree Krishna-Arjuna dialogue on Brahma-knowledge yoga-scripture Shreemad-Bhagavad Gita Upanishad.

CHAPTER : 11

Vishvaroopa Darshana : Sight of Ishavar's Universal Form

At the request of Arjuna, Shree Krishna gives the vision of his universal form as a Living Being:

Arjuna spoke

You told me the supreme secret of Aatmic-knowledge to grace me: by these words my delusion-fascination has vanished, is destroyed. My deluding bewilderment has disappeared. 1.

Oh, lotus-petal-eyed! I heard from you in detail that the creation and destruction of bhootas is from you only and also heard your undiminishing Mahaatmya.2.

You are, Oh, Parameshvar! certainly as you have described yourself: Oh, Purushottam! I desire to see that Aishvaryaful form of yours. 3.

Oh, Prabhu! if you believe that it is possible for me to behold [and withstand] the sight of that form then oh, Yogeshvar! give me the view and sight of that undiminishing Aatmic form of yours: that divine universal form of yours. 4.

Shree Bhagawaan spoke

Oh, Partha! behold and look at my thousands of divine forms of many kinds and of many colors and shapes. 5.

Oh, Bharat! see [in me] Aadityaas [i.e. suns], eight Vasus, eleven Rudras, two Ashvini kumars, and forty-nine Vaayus as well as see many marvelous wonders not seen previously. 6.

Oh, Gudaakesha! now see the entire animate and inanimate universe in one part of my body and also whatever you desire to see. 7.

Krishna says that our universe is only a very minute part of Brahma. He does not say whether there are other universes or not neither does he deny their possibility.

One cannot see with physical eyes Yogaishvarya of Bhagawaan: Only divine eyes can see.

You are incapable to see me with your physical eyes [therefore] I give you divine eyes, [with that] you see my Yogaishvarya i.e. affluence of my yoga: my various manifestations by yoga. 8.

Sanjay describes to the king Dhritraashtra the divine form which Shree Krishna showed to Arjuna who saw it with the divine eyes.

Sanjay spoke

Describes Aishvaryaful divine form of Bhagawaan. He describes what Arjuna saw and spoke.

Oh, king [Dhritraashtra]! so saying great Yogeshvar Hari showed to Partha Aishvaryaful divine form. 9.

That form having many faces and eyes, many wonderful forms, many divine ornaments and brandishing many divine weapons 10.

Is wearing divine garland Umber i.e. vestment anointed with divine perfumes-fragrances: Is full of all the wonders: Is infinite Deva with universal face 11.

Vishvatomukham means having universe as his face or having face every where. Wherever you turn there is the face of this Deva.

If there arises simultaneously in the sky thousands of suns, that combined luminosity may perhaps be like the luminosity of that Mahaa Aatmaa i.e. Paramaatmaa. 12.

At that time Arjuna saw the entire universe of many-fold divisions and of various forms stationed in one part of that body of God of gods. i.e. God-Vishnu. 13.

Thereafter amazed, astonished and with hairs raised on end that Dhananjay bowing that Deva with his head began to say with folded hands. 14.

Sanjay describes what Arjuna spoke

Arjuna spoke

Oh, Deva! I see in your body all devas [gods], multitudes of various bhootas [creatures], Brahmaa seated in lotus posture, Shankar, all sages and divine serpents. 15.

Oh, Ishvar of the universe! Oh, Universe-form Ishvar! Of infinite forms having many stomachs, hands, faces, and eyes I see you every where: also I see neither your end, nor middle nor your beginning. 16.

Crowned, holding mace and Chakra i.e. disc-missile, mass of luminosity shining from all sides, impossible to look at that dazzling brilliance like that of the sun and flaming fire at white heat and unprovable I see you every where. 17.

Ishvar is not the subject of proof and so is called unprovable

You are supreme and imperishable worthy to be known, you are the supreme refuge, support and substratum of this universe. You are the protector of eternal dharma: You are eternal and undiminishing Purusha, [such] is my opinion. 18.

I see you without beginning, middle or end, having infinite strength and numberless hands, having sun-moon as eyes, with face of flaming fire, and heating this universe by your own heat. 19.

Oh, Mahaatmaa! The space between paradise and earth as well as all the directions are fully filled by you only: seeing this wonderfully fierce form, all the three worlds are highly distressed. 20.

These multitudes of devas are entering in you, some frightened ones are praying you with folded hands, Groups of Maharishis and Siddhas saying 'Svasti' i.e. let there be kalyaan' are adoring you with hymns of praise. 21.

Rudras, Aadityaas, Vasus, amenable and boon-giving deities, Vishvadeva, Ashvini kumars, Vaayus, Hot-food-eating paternal manes, Gandharvas, Yakshas, demons and multitude of Siddhas: all of them are gazing at you with wonder and awe. 22.

Oh, mighty handed! seeing this extensive form of yours having many faces and eyes, many hands, thighs and legs, many bellies and extremely terrible canines and molars: I and all people are being distressed. 23.

Seeing this sky-touching form of yours, many colored and luminous, with gaping open mouths and glowing huge eyes, oh, Vishnu! with frightened inner Aatma i.e. completely frightened mentally I am unable to keep peace and patience. 24.

The whole frame of Arjuna is shaken with fear seeing this terrible and fierce form of Bhagawaan pervading not only space between earth and paradise but the entire space. We know nothing about Bhagawaan and little about universe. We think of Bhagawaan and universe separately but not Bhagawaan as universe. Arjuna is terrified seeing this form of Bhagawaan as universe.

Oh, Ishvar of devas! seeing your faces with terrible canines and molars and blazing like the fires of the times of the universe-dissolution, I am unable to decipher the directions and I do not have happiness, be pleased oh, Jaggannivaas! 25.

Jaggannivaas means one wherein the universe is contained and resides. Bhagawaan is the only one wherein resides the universe.

Those sons of Dhritraashtra along with multitudes of kings, Bhishma, Drona, that Karna, and even those on our side along with chief warriors: [26]

All these are gushing into your terrible mouths having crushing molars and pointed canines and some appear clutched between teeth with heads smashed to powdery mass. 27.

Just as the water-currents of many rivers flow towards the ocean similarly all these heroic persons of the human world are entering into your blazing mouths. 28.

Just as insects plunge with high speed in the blazing fire to die [only] similarly even these people also rush with speed in your mouths for their death-destruction only.29.

Oh, Vishnu! you are licking all the worlds from all sides while gulping them with your blazing mouths and your radiant white heat filling the universe with its light heats it.30.

Tell me, who are you with this fierce form? Oh, Devesha! My namaskaar to you, be pleased, I desire to know you, Initial one, Primal One, because [I] do not know all these activities of yours. 31.

Shree Bhagawaan Replies

Destroyer of the worlds, I am extremely terrible and expanded time [Doom-Time] and at this time I have become ready and active to destroy these people. All those warriors in both the armies will not remain [alive] even without you i.e. even if you do not kill. 32.

Therefore, get up, [and] gain glory by conquering the enemies and enjoy the thriving and prosperous kingdom. All these are already killed by me in advance, oh, Arjuna! be only an agent and an instrument [of mine]. 33.

You slay Drona and Bhishma as well as Jaydrath and Karna and also other heroic warriors who are already killed by me; do not be afraid and worried, fight. Doubtlessly you will conquer the foes in the war.34.

Shree Krishna Bhagawaan tells Arjuna that He was the dooms time and at the time He was engaged in killing the warriors of both the armies. Doom time had already decided their doom and so already killed by dooms times. Killed by Me means not physical killing by Bhagawaan but doomed to die.

Sanjay spoke to Dhritraashtra

Hearing those words of Keshava [Krishna] Arjuna tremblingly bowed with folded hands and again bowing began to tell falteringly with fear and emotionally choked voice to Krishna.35.

Sanjay relates

Arjuna spoke

Oh, Hrishikesha! [meaning Internal knower and controller of organs] By singing your glory-songs, universe rejoices and becomes joyous with love. Frightened demons run helter-skelter in all the directions and all the multitudes of Siddhas are bowing in reverence: this is fit and proper. 36.

Oh, Mahaatmaa! and why should they not bow you, the initial creator and greater than even Brahmaa ? because oh, infinite one! oh, Devesha! Oh, Resting place of the universe! You are supreme and undiminishing beyond whatever 'SAT-ASAT 'i.e. 'IS-ISNOT" is there. 37.

You are Eternal Purusha, the initial Deva: you are the supreme resting place [final sanctuary] of this universe, as well as omniscient and worthy to be known and supreme abode: Oh, Of-Infinite-forms! this universe is pervaded and permeated by you, is completely filled by you. 38.

You are Vaayu, Yama [lord of death], Fire-deity, Varuna i.e. water-deity, Moon-deity, Prajaapati Brahmaa and even great grand Sire: thousands of times bowing to you, and again and again and again repeatedly bowing to you. 39.

Oh, Aatmaa-of-all! Obeisance to you in front and in the rear: Obeisance to you from all sides, Oh, infinitely powerful and immeasurably mighty! You have stay-remained permeating and pervading the whole universe and so you are all form. 40.

Believing you to be a comrade and a friend and not knowing this greatness of thine, Hey, Krishna! Hey, Yaadava! Hey, friend! etc.' whatever, I might have said either in love, fun, jest, or pride, 41.

And again Oh, Achyuta! whatever insults I might have flung either in joke or otherwise during picnics, lying, seating and eating either when alone or in a company: for all these offensive faults I pray you to forgive and pardon me, Oh, Unprovable!. 42.

Oh, of unmatched Personality! You are the father of this entire movable and immovable universe and best Guru and worshipable: none is equal to you in all the three worlds then how can there be a greater one? 43.

Therefore prostrating before you in bowing, I pray you to be pleased oh, praise-worthy Ishvar! Oh, Deva! You are fit to endure them in the manner as by father to the son, friend to a friend and a lover to a beloved one.44.

I am delighted seeing your previously unseen-form and my mind is distressed with fear, therefore Oh, Devesha! oh, the resting place-of-the-universe! be pleased, Oh, Devesha! give me the sight and view of that other form. 45.

Oh, Thousand-handed, Oh, Universe-form! I desire to see you in that four-handed form having crown [on the head] holding mace and Chakra in the hands, therefore, be of that form, so assume that form.46.

Sanjay states to Dhritrashtra what Shree Krishna tells;

Krishna spoke

Oh, Arjuna! Being pleased I have shown you with my Yogic powers this luminous, initial, infinite and supreme universal form which form, none save you, has seen previously. 47.

Oh, Best-of-Kurus! In this world of human beings, it is not possible for any one except you to see me in this [universal] form either by sacrifice or by Vedic-studies or by alms-charity or by meritorious deeds [Punyas] or even by severe penance. 48.

Seeing this terrible form of mine, let you not be distressed nor be confused stupidly but becoming fearless and delighted in mind see again my that very [four-handed] form. 49.

Saying thus to Arjuna Vaasudeva Bhagawaan showed again his four-handed form and again becoming gracefully sober-bodied Mahaatmaa Keshava gave solace to frightened Arjuna. 50.

Arjuna spoke

Oh, Janaardan! Seeing this your sober human form now I

have regained composure of my mind. 51.

Shree Krishna spoke

It is extremely difficult to see this [universal] form seen by you. Even devas always desire to see this form. 52.

Neither by Vedas nor by penance nor by Alm-charity nor even by sacrifice am I possible to be seen in the form you have seen Me. 53.

But oh, Parantap! in this [universal] form I can be attained, realized and known in Tattvas by exclusive devotion i.e. Bhakti. 54.

That devotee of mine who is free from attachment, acts for Me only, whose everything is Me and is without enmity towards all creatures: he attains Me oh, Arjuna! 55.

AUM TAT SAT: Thus it is the eleventh chapter, named sight of Universal form in Shree Krishna-Arjuna dialogue on Brahma-knowledge yoga-scripture Shreemad-Bhagavad Gita Upanishad.

CHAPTER : 12

Bhakti Yoga : Devotion-Yoga

Here Bhagawaan states that it is difficult to meditate on the formless form than the formful one. He describes various methods to worship Him and how to act and finally describes the signs and symptoms of the devotee who is dear to Him.

Arjuna spoke

Ever-united thus, devotees who worship [upaasanafies] you in your manifest form and those who worship you in your imperishable unmanifest form, of them who are superior Yoga proficient? 1.

Shree Bhagawaan spoke

Ever united in Me and riveting their mind in me, those, who worship [upaasanaafy] me with supreme faith are yoga-proficient: this is my opinion. 2.

This couplet tells about the worship of the manifested form

Those others, who worship and upaasanaafy my imperishable, cannot-be-pointed-out, unmanifested, omnipresent, unthinkable, immutable, immovable and eternal form. 3.

And having under his control the entire body of organs, and an equal eye everywhere and sees everything without distinction and engaged in the welfare of all, attains me only. 4.

[but] Greater is the affliction and travail to them whose chitta is attached in unmanifest form i.e. the form-less form of Brahma, because the unmanifest as a goal is acquired with distress and difficulty by the embodied ones. 5.

It is difficult for the mind to grasp and comprehend the form-less form. The reason is the mind is never formless and acquires the form of the object it grasps. To grasp the formless mind itself must become formless which is difficult and requires Yoga practice of years. Brahma remains in two forms: formless and formful. Formful is me, you, God and universe: God incarnates for the purposes detailed previously. It is easy to love and worship this human form but it is difficult leaning towards impossibility to love and worship the formless form of Brahma.

But those totally-Me-proned [Matparah], surrendering all actions and their fruits unto Me worship [upaasanaafies] by exclusively meditating on Me: 6.

Oh, Partha! To them with chitta concentrated on Me, I soon become the deliverer from the world-ocean of death. 7.

In couplets 6 and 7 Shree tells us the effect of worshipping the formful Bhagawaan whether human incarnated or not.

Fix mind in Me and stabilize intellect in Me, by so doing you will reside in Me only: there is no doubt in it. 8.

Oh, Dhananjay! If you are unable to steadily rivet the mind in Me, then desire to obtain Me by the technic of practice [Abhyaas-yoga].9.

To fix mind in any thing is a question of practice including the fixing of the mind in Bhagawaan. Shree Krishna tells Arjuna to do that only.

If you are unable to fix even by practice [or unable even to practice] then be the doer of acts only for Me: Even doing acts for Me you shall attain siddhi i.e. attain Me 10.

If you are unable to do even this much, then becoming self-controlled and taking the refuge of my Karma-yoga [intellect yoga] discard and renounce the fruits of all actions. 11.

Because knowledge is more beneficial than practice, meditation is better than knowledge, Renouncement of fruits of actions is better than meditation because [there is] immediate peace on renouncement. 12.

In the following seven couplets Shree Bhagawaan tells what kinds of devotees are dear to him.

One with compassion and without malice towards all creatures, without mineness-thineness: who is friend of all, egoless and prideless, equipoised in misery and happiness, forgiver-pardoner, 13,

And always-satisfied, self-controlled, of-firm-resolve, with mind and intellect surrendered unto Me, yogi who is my devotee: such a one is dear to Me.14.

By whom people are not distressed, who himself is not distressed by the people, and who is free from delight, anger, fear, agitation, anxiety and agony, that one is dear to Me. 15.

Without desire and expectations, holy-pure and clean, skilled and dexterous, unconcerned and indifferent, freed from miseries and renouncer of all beginnings, that one is dear to Me. 16.

That one who neither delights nor envies in getting or not getting things, neither laments nor yearns, who is renouncer of shubha-Ashubh i.e. good and bad, that devotee is dear to Me.17.

Who remains equally same to friend and foe, as well as in honor and dishonor, and remains same in heat and cold, happiness and misery, is free from attachment. 18.

And To whom praise and slander is same, is speech-silent, remains satisfied with whatever comes fortuitously, is without mineness-feeling in the home [residential house], such a devotional person is dear to Me. 19.

Devotees with faith and Me as their aim, goal and destiny, who observe and make use of this dhaarmic nectar as told, they are extremely dear to Me. 20.

AUM TAT SAT : Thus it is the twelfth chapter, named Bhakti Yoga i.e., devotion Yoga in Shree Krishna-Arjuna dialogue on Brahma-knowledge yoga-scripture Shreemad-Bhagavad Gita Upanishad.

CHAPTER : 13

Kshetra and Kshetragya Yogas : Field and Field-knower

In seventh chapter Shree Krishna described eight inanimate and one animate Prakrutis of Bhagawaan constituting the universe and the creatures. In this chapter he describes the gross and subtle composition of living creatures constituted by these two Prakruties and how they carry on their activities.

Human body is the field

One who knows the field is the field-knower. Bhagawaan is the field-knower in all the fields. Knowledge of the difference between the field and the field-knower is the real knowledge. Human activity is carried on by the combination of various components gross and subtle.

Shree tells that which is worth-knowing by knowing which one is emancipated. It is beginning less supreme Brahma which cannot be called either Sat or Asat i.e. Is or Isnot. The chapter describes How He is permeating and pervading the entire universe including living beings. Purusha and Prakruti of Saamkhya Yoga.

Arjuna spoke

Prakruti and Purusha, the field and the field-knower, knowledge and the object of knowledge, these I desire to know, oh, Keshava! 0.

This verse is not found in many editions: So it is numbered zero. With the addition of this verse total verses of Gita would be 701 otherwise it would be 700.

Field and field-knower

Bhagawaan spoke

This body, oh, Arjuna! is called the field and one who knows this field is field-knower, so say the tattva-knowers.1.

Know Me, oh, Bharat! also to be the field-knower in all fields. The knowledge of field and the field-knower is alone the knowledge so is my opinion. 2.

What that field is, as it is, to what changes and alterations it is liable to and from what it is [produced] and who that field-knower is and what glories and powers it has: Hear all that from Me in brief.3.

Sages have sung it in diverse ways in different hymns and also in well-reasoned Brahma-Sutras and other writings. 4.

Five Mahabhootas, ego, intellect, unmanifest-Mahaa Maya as well as ten organs, mind and five senses of the sense-organs, 5.

And Desire, envy, happiness, misery, the physical body, Chetana i.e. life-force, patience: This is the field with the above modifications and activities, I have told you in brief. 6.

Shree Bhagawaan now proceeds to tell the instruments of knowledge and ignorance in couplets 7-11.

Free from pride i.e. humility, free from hypocrisy i.e. sincere, non-violence and non-injury, tolerance and forbearance, straightforward in mind and speech, service to guru, purity of mind and speech, mental steadfastness and self-control, 7.

And Detachment from the sense-objects, absence of ego, and to repeatedly think and muse on the faults and defects of birth, old-age, disease; death and misery, 8.

Detachment from wife [husband], sons, house etc. absence of I-ness, always even and equipoised chitta in the gaining of desirable and undesirable,9.

And Unadulterated i.e. chaste devotion by exclusive meditation on Me, residence in lonely and solitary place, no taste and liking for the association of [passionate] people, 10.

And Permanency of Aatmic-knowledge, to have the correct insight of the meaning of Tattva-knowledge i.e. to realize the meaning of Tattva-knowledge, these are the instruments of knowledge and those opposite to them are of ignorance, so it is said. 11.

Now I will tell you that which is worth and fit to be known by knowing which, one is emancipated: that is beginningless supreme Brahma which can not be called SAT nor ASAT: i.e. IS or ISNOT. 12.

Is or Isnot means existent or non-existent: being or non-being. For further explanation of SAT and ASAT see Introduction II.

[Brahma] has hands and legs everywhere, has eyes, heads and faces on all sides, has ears every where [because] he is pervading-permeating all the worlds.13.

As he is pervading and permeating every thing in the universe he necessarily is in all beings and so he is described here as having hands, feet, heads, faces and ears every where and in all sides: He is all-beings.

Though seemingly appears as all organs with their faculties, He is without all organs, is unattached though upholds and maintains all, and he is gunaless though enjoyer of gunas i.e. the worldly objects. 14.

That [Brahma] is outside and inside all movable and immovable beings [bhootas], but can not be known due to its subtleness, is faraway and also at the end of nearness i.e. touching and within you. 15.

Though undivided and continuous, Brahma appears to be stationed as divided in all beings [bhootas], Know it to be the supporter and sustainer, swallower-destroyer and the creator [of all]. 16.

That [Brahma] is light and luster-jyoti of luminous bodies and is said to be beyond the darkness [of Maya], is knowledge, is subject to be known and knowable by knowledge and is present in the hearts of all. 17.

Thus the field, knowledge and that-to-be-known are

told in nut-shell: Knowing that my devotee attains to my nature. 18

Couplet 18 lays down the conditions for attaining the nature of Brahma i.e. attaining Brahmahood. One should know Field, knowledge, Brahma to be known by knowledge: How, why and by what process Brahma appears as inanimate and animate universe is not told but in nut shell we are told that Brahma appears as all and yet all are not in him. For explanation see Introduction II.

Now Shree Bhagawaan introduces Purusha and Prakruti of Saamkhya expounded by Kapil Muni.

Cause for good or bad rebirth

Know also Prakruti and Purusha to be beginningless and [sixteen] alterations as well as gunas [satva, rajas and tamas] to be produced from Prakruti. 19.

Prakruti is said to be the [material] cause of effects and in the activity of karan i.e. causes while Purusha is said to be the cause in the enjoyment of happiness and miseries. 20.

Because Purusha stationed and attached to Prakruti enjoys the gunas produced from Prakruti and its association with the gunas is the cause for the good and bad births: cause of birth of this Purusha [soul] in good and bad species. 21.

Gunas of the Prakruti are the prime creators and components of every thing in the universe. Nothing is without the combination of these three gunas. Three gunas are the constituents of Prakruti and they go jointly in the composition of everything in the universe. Our body with all its energies is the product of three gunas of Prakruti: Purusha as a soul in association with gunas enjoys them and roams in the good and bad bodies produced from prakruti via gunas.

Position of Purusha vis-a-vis the body and who is not born again?.

In this body Purusha is separate and beyond. He is a witness, consenter or permission-giver, maintainer, enjoyer, as well as is called Maheshvar and Paramaatmaa. 22.

This couplet describes Purusha in different states by harmoniously construing and unifying the views of Vedas-Upanishad and Saamkhya. Saamkhya views Purusha as separate and beyond Prakruti. Prakruti by mere presence of Purusha undergoes various alterations producing the physical universe right from intellect to atoms and human bodies for the use and enjoyment of Purusha. In our normal conditions we are souls enjoying the world of senses. On the path of saadhana from the enjoyer state we pass on where we find ourselves as witness, then finally as Paramaatmaa and sustainer of all. Remember this couplet merely enumerates the various stages of Purusha in human body in his progress from worst soul to best Purusha i.e. Purushottam or Paramaatmaa.

One who knows Purusha and Prakruti with her gunas in this manner that one is not born again though acting in all manners. 23.

Some see [realize] this Aatmaa in the self by meditation on the self, others by Saamkhya yoga [knowledge path], and rest by Karma-yoga [selfless actions]. 24.

Others, not knowing in this manner, worship it [upaasanaafy] on hearing from others [from guru etc.]: and even they being devoted to hearing swim over the death. 25.

Combination of soul and physical body create a living being.

Whatever and whoever movable and immovable beings are created Oh, Bharatrishabh! know them to be from the association of field and field-knower.26.

Who sees really and who does not?

One who sees one and the same imperishable Parameshvar equally in all perishing creatures [bhootas], he really sees. 27.

Because that seer of the same Ishvar equally present everywhere in all bhootas does not kill the self [Aatmaa] and so attains the supreme destiny i.e. Brahmahood. 28.

Again, one who sees [knows] that in every way the actions are performed by Prakruti as well as sees Aatmaa to be non-doer or non-actor, he [really] sees. 29.

When one sees all different creatures [bhootas] located in the same Aatmaa, and sees this spread-out from that one, then he attains Brahma. 30.

This is the real state of emancipation: It is a state where you, the universe and creatures are indistinguishably one with Brahma though every thing remains in tact as before.

Aatmaa and Paramaatmaa unaffected

Oh, Arjuna! Being beginningless and gunaless i.e. attributeless this undiminishing Paramaatmaa though stationed in the body does nothing nor is affected, [nor is coated, defiled, tainted]. 31.

Lipyate is translated as affected but can also be translated as coated, defiled, tainted.

Just as Sky, being subtle, is not affected though pervading everywhere, similarly Aatmaa though stationed in all bodies is not affected. 32.

Oh, Arjuna! Just as one sun illuminates this entire world similarly field-knower illuminates the entire field. 33.

Thus one, who knows by the knowledge-eye the difference between the field and the field-knower is emancipated from the Prakruti-bhootas, and he attains the supreme i.e. Brahma. 34.

AUM TAT SAT : Thus it is the thirteenth chapter, named division of Field and Field knower in Shree Krishna-Arjuna dialogue on Brahma-knowledge yoga-scripture Shreemad-Bhagavad Gita Upanishad.

CHAPTER : 14

Three Divisions of Gunas i.e. Waves

Here Bhagawaan states how the three gunas of Prakruti make the beginning of the universe. Mahat is the first reaction-product of the three gunas. This is called buddhi i.e. intellect in Saamkhya and Chitta in Yoga. Mahat is composed of Satvaguna with the very slight admixture of Rajo guna for the activation of Satva and Tamo guna for stability of the reaction. Mahat is also called Mahat-Brahma. For further explanation refer to Introduction II.

Bhagawaan says, "Mahat Brahma is my womb and I place in it the fetus from which all bhootas [i.e. animate and inanimate universe] are created. Mahat Brahma is the place of origin of all forms [murtayaa] and I am the seed-giver father of all. Three gunas i.e. waves of three wave-lengths in all ranges generated from Prakruti bind the undiminishing body dweller in the body. How the gunas bind the body dweller and who is called gunaatit i.e. guna-transcended is the subject matter of the rest of the chapter.

Bhagawaan spoke

Who is not reborn?

I tell you again the supreme knowledge best amongst knowledges knowing which all munis becoming free [from sansaar] have attained supreme siddhi i.e. emancipation i.e., Kaivalya. 1.

Those, who have attained to My nature by having taken refuge in Me and employing this knowledge are not born at the creation of the world [sarga] nor are distressed during its dissolution.2.

Creation

Who binds the body-dweller?

Oh, Arjuna! Mahat Brahma is my womb, I put embryo-fetus in it: from it all bhootas [creatures] come into being. 3. In Saamkhya system of cosmology Mahat is the first product of the three gunas of Prakruti in the creation of the universe: To employ the Vedic terminology it is the first product of Shabal Brahma: this is the reason it is termed Mahat-Brahma here. First vivartic product of vibrating Brahma.

Oh, Arjuna! Whatever forms [bodies] are created in all wombs, Mahat Brahma is their womb and I am the seed-giver Father. 4. Satva [i.e. Short wave], Rajas [i.e. Medium wave] and Tamas, [i.e. long wave] these three gunas [waves] born of Prakruti, Oh, Mahabaho! bind the undiminishing body-dweller in the body. 5.

Work of Gunas in body: Work of waves in body and psyche

[Satva Guna i.e. Short wave] Oh, sinless Arjuna! Of them Sattva [guna] because of purity is illuminator, miseryless and health-giving, It binds [body-dweller] by attachment in happiness and knowledge.6. [Rajo Guna i.e. Medium wave] Know Rajo guna to be fascination-form [raag-form] arising from thirst-yearning and association, oh, Kaunteya! it binds the body-dweller by the association with the karmas i.e. by attachment in karmas. 7. [Tamo Guna i.e. Long wave] And Oh, Bharat! know tamo guna giving birth to ignorance to be deluding bewitcher of all body dwellers: [and] binds them by indolence, idleness and sleep. 8. Pramaad is also translated as heedlessness, negligence or sloth in other translations.

Oh, Bharat! Sattva [guna] unites, joins and attaches one to happiness, Rajas to actions and activity, and Tamo [guna] covering the knowledge yokes one to indolence etc. i.e. idleness and sleep. 9.

Effect of ruling Guna

Oh, Bharat! Sattva guna increases by suppressing Rajas and Tamas: Rajas guna increases by suppressing Sattva and Tamas: and Tamas increases suppressing Sattva and Rajas.10. Satva Guna. When light, knowledge etc. i.e. happiness is generated in all the doors [i.e. in all the organs and mental complex] of the body then know that Satva guna has increased. 11. Rajo Guna Oh, Arjuna! Greed, activity and the beginning of actions, way-wardness meaning mental restlessness, and yearnings and hankerings, all these are generated with the increase of Rajo Guna. 12.Tamo Guna. Oh, Kuru-son! non-light i.e. darkness, inactivity, Pramaada i.e. indolence, heedlessness, negligence and Moha, all these are generated with the increase of Tamo guna. 13.

Effect of Gunas on death

Satva Guna

Again if the embodied one dies during the [state of] increased Sattva guna then he goes to holy and divine worlds of the knower of the best. 14.Rajo Guna. He is born amongst people attached to actions if he dies during the dominance of Rajo guna. Tamo Guna. He is born stupid, dumb and in lower species if he dies during Tamo guna predominance. 15.

Fruits of Gunas

Satva

The fruits of the Satvic actions is said to be satvic and good: Rajas. The fruit of Rajas is misery and Tamas. The fruit of tamas is ignorance. 16.Knowledge is produced from Satva guna, greed from Rajas and Pramaad i.e. indolence, Moha i.e. fascination and ignorance from Tamas Guna. 17.Those settled in Satva go to upper region, those settled in Rajas go to middle region and Tamsic-persons settled in low inclinations go to lower region. 18.

Upper region means regions where meritorious souls stay: Middle region means human-world of meritorious people and lower region includes world of debased people and all creatures excluding humans.

Who attains Brahmahood?

When the Drashtaa i.e. Seer does not see doer-actor other than gunas and knows the one who is beyond Gunas, he attains My nature i.e. attains Brahmahood. 19. Gunebhyah Param Vetti can also be translated as 'knows himself to be beyond gunas' Because one has not only to realize that gunas are actors but that he is beyond gunas for the purpose of attaining Brahmahood. One cannot know Brahma who is beyond gunas unless one himself realizes that he too is beyond gunas. This rendering is fortified by the next couplet which describes the effect of going beyond three gunas.

Body-dweller going beyond i.e. transcending the body-producing these three gunas becomes free from the miseries of birth, death and old age and gains the nectar i.e. emancipation. 20.

Arjuna now asks

Oh, Prabho! what are the signs-symptoms and what is the behaviour and conduct of one who has transcended the three gunas and how does he transcend the three gunas? 21

How does one become Gunatit and then how does he live and behave?

Shree Bhagawaan spoke

Oh, Pandava! One who does not hate, envy and disdain Prakaasha i.e. light and Knowledge, activity and Moha i.e. fascination and delusion as and when the same arise nor does he desire and yearn them on their retirement i.e. cessation. 22. And Who like an unconcerned and indifferent one is not perturbed and moved by gunas and knowing that only gunas are acting and reacting with each other remains stable and is not agitated. 23. And Stable [in Aatmaa], takes misery-happiness alike; takes earth, stone and gold of equal value, is Dheera i.e. steadfast, confident, calm and resolved and treats non-dear and dear alike and with firm chitta treats praise and slander alike. 24. And Who remains equipoised in honour and dishonour, remains alike to friends and foes, who has renounced all beginnings, such a one is called guna-transcended: One who has transcended gunas. 25.

One who is with all the qualities mentioned in couplets from 22-25 is gunaatit i.e. guna-transcended.

One who serves Me with unadulterated Bhakti i.e. exclusive devotion, he is also fit to become Brahma by crossing over these gunas. 26. Because I am personified form of Brahma who is nectar and undiminishing, eternal, dharma, one-only and bliss. 27.

This is controversial couplet

Is Krishna the personified Brahma? Krishna is taken as an incarnate of Vishnu who is the product of Brahma and therefore Krishna is incarnate Vishnu with all the qualities and properties of Brahma in tact in Him i.e. He can exhibit all the properties of Brahma at his sweet will. He is the real image of the qualitied Brahma and virtual image of qualitiless too.

AUM TAT SAT : Thus it is the fourteenth chapter, named Three divisions of Gunas in Shree Krishna-Arjuna dialogue on Brahma-knowledge yoga-scripture Shreemad-Bhagavad Gita Upanishad.

CHAPTER : 15

Purushottam Yoga

Purusha as souls are many and the best of them is called Purushottama i.e. best Purusha: How is He best? because he is all in all: everything is in him and he permeates every thing. Here the universe together with living beings are compared to an Ashvattha tree which starts growing from above and spreads downwards: animate and inanimate universe are its downward spreading branches and meters are its leaves. These are the products of three gunas i.e. three kinds of waves and karmic bondage are the roots that provide the sap to the universe for its continuance. It describes the state of the person who has cut the roots and he goes to that place which is not lighted by the sun, moon or the fire.

Bhagawaan says that His minute and eternal fragment is roaming as a soul in the mortal world and attracts five organs and mind. The soul leaves the body with all these and enters another body. He enjoys the vishayas through sense-organs.

Universe and Sansaar compared to Pipal Tree

Bhagawaan Spoke

Pipal Tree [*Ficus Religiosa*] with roots above and branches below and whose leaves are Vedas [Vedic hymns], they say, is undiminishing. One who knows this he is Veda-expert. He knows the secrets of Vedas. 1

Nourished by gunas, the branches with new and tender shoots of vishayas [senses] spread below and above: In the world of human beings it has spread the complex root system causing karmas and bondage. 2.

Its form [as it is] as said above is not seen and perceived

here nor its end nor beginning nor its substratum and foundation: [therefore] search for that state going where one does not return [in sansaar] by cutting this Pipal having vaasanaa-form roots with weapon in the form of firm detachment. 3. and after resolving that "I have taken refuge of that first Purusha from whom this purani i.e. ancient activity is born", 4.

Supreme Abode of Bhagawaan and how to reach there

One, who is free from pride and Moha i.e. fascination and delusion, who has conquered the faults and defaults of association [attachment], who is free from dualities and pairs of opposites viz. Happiness-misery, heat-cold etc. whose passions have vanished, who is always engrossed in Aatmic rumination: such a wise and unbewildered one goes to undiminishing state i.e. Brahma. 5.

That [supreme state] is lighted neither by the sun nor by the moon nor by the fire. Going there no one returns. That one is my supreme abode. 6. That abode of mine is supreme going where no one returns.

In effect it is a state where sun, moon or fire do not exist because it is state from which every thing takes birth. That state is certainly luminous but the luminosity is not of this universe. It is a state wherein the point in the lap of the moon in AUM arises. We experience it when we attain Brahmahood.

What and Who is soul? It carries Mind and five sense organs with it wherever it goes.

It is an eternal fragment of mine alone that has become soul in the world of souls and attracts to itself mind together with five sense organ-energies from the Prakruti. 7.

When Ishvar i.e. the knower of the body takes upon the body or even when he leaves the body, It takes them i.e. mind with five senses with him just as the current of air carries away the fragrance from the fragrant object. 8.

How soul enjoys the world?

This [soul] taking the shelter of i.e. by the use of ears,

eyes, skin, tongue and nose as well as the mind enjoys the sense-objects and sense-subjects. 9.

Who sees the soul?

How Bhagawaan upholds the worldly activity?

Deluded stupid ones do not see [the soul] when he is leaving the body, or stationed [in the body] or even when enjoying the products of the gunas [i.e. the sense-objects]. Those with knowledge-eyes see the soul. 10.

'See it' means experience it as an identity separate and distinct from the physical body.

Striving yogis see it stationed within themselves but the ignorant ones with impure chitta do not see it despite the efforts.11.

That light-luminosity in the sun which illuminates the entire universe [i.e. the solar system] and that which is in the moon and which is in the fire know that light-luminosity to be Mine only. 12.

Entering the [gaama] earth, I take upon and uphold all the bhootas by my power-energy and becoming sappy moon, I nourish all [aushadhi] the plants i.e. Plant kingdom. 13.

Rasaatmak means composed of sap meaning sappy. Aushadhi usually means medicinal plants but here it seems it is used in the generic sense meaning the entire plant kingdom.

Becoming Vaishvaanara by uniting with Praan and Apaan and stationing in the body of creatures I digest four types of foods. 14.

Vaishvaanara is the personification of digestive-fire: Ingoing and out going life currents in combination digest the four kinds of foods. It is Bhagawaan who becomes Vaishvaanara i.e. digestive fire which is termed Vaishvaanara. Four kinds of foods:[1] to be chewed, [2] to be swallowed, [3] to be licked, and [4] to be sucked.

Where is Bhagawaan is located in body?

I am stationed in the hearts of all. Memory, knowledge as

well as removal of doubt and false knowledge are from Me only i.e. proceed from Me only. I am the only one fit to be known by all Vedas. I am the author of Vedanta and the knower of the Vedas too. 15.

Kshara and Akshara Purusha. Paramaatmaa = Purushottama

Kshara i.e. perishable and Akshara i.e. imperishable, these are the two Purushas in this word: All bhootas are perishable and [Kutastha] Permanent or immutable is called Akshara i.e. imperishable. 16.

What is the meaning of Kutastha here? It means Dehi i.e. body dweller. Dehi exercises authority over the whole body. Dehi is called Purusha in Saamkhya. Purusha is used for Purushottam, for Aatma pervading the physical bodies and as soul of the creatures exercising the power over physical bodies to enjoy. It may also mean Maya which is concomitant with Purusha or Brahma.

But best Purusha is another one called Paramaatmaa i.e. supreme Aatmaa: That undiminishing Ishvar pervading the three worlds maintains-sustains [all]. 17.

Because I am beyond the Kshara i.e. perishable and superior even to Akshara i.e. Purusha as a soul: therefore I am well known as Purushottam i.e. best Purusha in Vedas and in the world. 18.

Oh, Bharat! whoever non-stupid knows me as Purushottam in this manner, that all-knower worships [bhajes] Me with his whole heart and emotions. 19.

Sarva Bhaaven is rendered with whole heart and emotions: English has no exact equivalent for Bhaava.

The description of Brahma, Purusha and Aatmaa in all the three forms i.e. Kshara, Akshar and Avyaya will be found in Upanishadas. Of them Kshara-Purusha creates the srushti. All alterations are created in it. It is resulting and manifest, second is Akshara Purusha is the creator like a pot-maker, inner-knower, unaltering controller-director and manifest.

Third undiminishing and unaltering Purusha is beyond the cause-effect, Asanga and unmanifest. Kshara Purusha is located here as the srushti while Akshara and undiminishing Purusha are staying secretly.

Oh, sinless Bharat! thus I have told you this extremely secret and mystic science by knowing which one becomes knowledgeable and Krutkrutya i.e. fulfilled. 20.

AUM TAT SAT: Thus it is the fifteenth chapter, named Purushottam Yoga in Shree Krishna-Arjuna dialogue on Brahma-knowledge yoga-scripture Shreemad-Bhagavad Gita Upanishad.

CHAPTER : 16

Daivaasura Sampat Vibhaaga Yoga = Division of Divine and Demonic Wealth

Shree Krishna enumerates divine and demonic wealth i.e. virtues and vices.

Bhagawaan spoke : Divine wealth i.e., virtues

Fearlessness, highest purity of mental complex i.e. ego-chitta-mind-intellect-complex, jyaanyoga vyavasthitah i.e. stability in Saamkhya-knowledge and selfless action, alms, charity and donations, Self-control and sacrifice, scripture-study and penance, simplicity and straightforwardness, 1. Non-violence or non-injury, truthfulness, anger-free, renouncement or renunciation, peace and tranquillity, aversion to defame others, compassion-mercy on all creatures, freedom from greed, tenderness and gentleness, Hrim i.e. shame in bad-actions, absence of vain and useless activity. 2. Oh, Bharat! Teja i.e. vigor, awe-inspiring, forgiveness-pardoning, Dhruti i.e. fortitude, patience and courage, Inner and outer purity, Adroha i.e. freedom from ill-will and malice, free from arrogance born of pride, these are the signs of person born with divine wealth. 3.

First three couplets describe the virtues of a person born with divinity and thus indirectly tells us what are the actions and deeds that can be called virtues. These virtuous acts not only help one to attain peace and emancipation but benefit all concerned in the society.

Please also note that Hreem is a powerful Beejaa Mantra of Gayatri Mantra: R pronounced as in Rum is also fire-seed: H is space seed: Hreem is thus Maya Seed and its Anushthaan will bestow all sorts of Miracle powers. This is the reason why the constant recitation of Rama, Rahim and Rha bestows all sorts of miracle powers.

Now Bhagawaan enumerates the signs of demonic wealth in couplet four

Demonic wealth i.e., vices. 1

Oh, Paartha! Hypocrisy, ostentation and pretentiousness, arrogance and pride, as well as anger, harsh-speech and ignorance; these are the signs of persons born with demonic wealth. 4.

Divine wealth i.e. virtues is believed to be for the emancipation and demonic i.e. vices for bondage. Worry not, Oh, Partha! you are born with divine-wealth i.e. virtues. 5.

Oh, Arjuna! In this world there are two categories of beings:

Divine or Deva and demons or wicked: Daivic and demonic: virtuous and wicked: I told you Daivic in detail now hear demonic ones from me. 6.

Behaviour of Demonic i.e. wicked people

Demonic and wicked people do not know what is the proper activity and inactivity [i.e. what to do and what not to do and how to do them,] have neither purity nor correct conduct, nor truthfulness. 7.

They say universe is without support, is factual reality and without Ishvar and is created not by cause-effect chain but purely by the union of the two sexes, what else? 8. Firmly attached to this view these lost souls of insignificant intellect and doers of horrible deeds come into being not for the betterment of the world but for its destruction.9. Harboring insatiable passions and desires, full of hypocrisy, arrogance, pride and conceit, these people of wicked resolves act delusively holding fast to their false views. 10. And These corrupted souls remain active in their false resolves and bring misery not only to themselves but to human society as a whole. 11.

Taking the shelter of numberless anxieties lasting till death they remain absorbed in the enjoyment of kaam-passion-sex being convinced that it is the only supreme [happiness]. 12. And Bound and entangled in the snare of hopes by hundreds and given to passion, lust and anger, they try to amass money by injustice i.e. unlawfully for the passion and sense gratification.13. I have acquired and gained this to-day, [and hereafter] will fulfill this [manorath] aspiration. I have this much wealth and will have this much more again. 13. I have slain this enemy and will kill others too. I am Ishvar, I am the enjoyer, I am siddha, strong and happy. 14. I am very wealthy and of great and big family, who else is like me? [I] will perform sacrifices, will give alms and donate in charities, will rejoice [in merry-making], thus they are deluded by ignorance. 15. Perplexed and bewildered by many chittas i.e. variegated thoughts and purposes harboured in chitta, entangled in the net-work of Moha i.e. fascinations, extremely attached to sense-gratification, these people fall in the terrible hell.16. Self-conceited and obstinate, rude and puffed up with the arrogance of wealth, reputation and honor, [they] perform sacrifice with hypocrisy for name and show only regardless of rites and rituals. 17. Puffed with ego, power, pride, passion, lust and anger, they are deriders, despisers, slanderers and scorners of Me who am stationed in their bodies and of others. 18.

What does Bhagawaan do with them?

I repeatedly hurl these vile, wicked and despising persons of cruel deeds in the satanic wombs in this world. i.e. lower species. 19. Oh, Kaunteya! coming to satanic wombs birth after birth, and not attaining Me these stupid people slowly sink to the lowest abominable regions. 20.

Passion, anger and greed are gates to hell

Passion, anger and greed, these three gates to hell are the destroyers of the self, therefore discard these three.21. Oh, Arjuna! Person freed from these three gates to hell strives for the kalyaan-good of his self-Aatmaa and so goes to supreme destiny i.e. Brahma. 22.

Scriptures are the authorities for all activities

Persons who abandoning scriptural means and methods behaving as guided by the Kaam and passions do not acquire siddhis nor happiness nor attains to the supreme state. 23. Therefore, in deciding about duties and non-duties, actions and non-actions, let scriptures be the authority for you. Knowing what the scriptural rules state, carry out your task accordingly. 24

Shree asks Arjuna to observe scriptures to the last detail and at the same time maintains to relinquish individual Dharma in favour of social dharma if it becomes necessary for the good of the society. One will find various instances where Shree has acted that way. He has discarded individual vow in favour of social dharma i.e. duty.

AUM TAT SAT: Thus it is the sixteenth chapter, named Divine and Demonic Wealth in Shree Krishna-Arjuna dialogue on Brahma-knowledge yoga-scripture Shreemad-Bhagavad Gita Upanishad.

CHAPTER : 17

Shraddhaatraya Vibhaaga Yoga i.e. Three Categories of Faith

Here Bhagawaan tells us how three gunas i.e. three waves of Prakruti constitute the human nature and its activities. He tells what are the Satvic, Rajasic and Tamasic activities and what are their results. Faith, Deity worshipped, food, penance, Charity and gifts, Japa i.e. continuous chanting of one name or mantra etc. are divided on the basis of the three gunas i.e. short, medium and long waves constituting the individual. In the last chapter Shree has advised Arjuna to act in accordance with scriptural rules. So naturally question is what if one acts disregarding the rules but with faith.

Arjuna spoke

Those who [Yajanta] worship with faith disregarding the scriptural rules, Oh, Krishna! What is their state and condition? Is it Saatvic, Raajsic or Taamsic? 1.

Arjuna asks a very important question. A person may not know the scriptures and therefore his worship may not be in consonance with the scriptural rules, regulations and injunctions and possibly against it but he worships with faith that he is doing correctly. What is the state of such a person? Krishna answers.

Bhagawaan spoke

On Faith: Three kinds of Faith

Produced according to the innate nature of the embodied ones the faith is of three kinds; Saatvic, Rajasic and Taamasic: hear it. 2.

Oh, Bharat! the faith of all creatures is in accordance with the degree of purity of their nature: Every person is faith dominated: As is his faith so he certainly is. 3.

Who worships whom?

Sattvic people worship devas-deities and gods, Raajasic ones [worship] Yakshas and rakshaansi i.e. demi-gods and protectors and Taamsic people worship spirits, ghost and Goblins groups. 4.

In all most all translations either in Indian languages or in English Yaksha rakshaansi is translated as Demi-gods and demons: Rakshaansi means one who protects i.e. protector. It is rakshaansi and not Raakshasaani. Demons does not fit in with Rajas guna but with dominant Tamas Guna. Propelled by the power of passion, lust and raag and welded to ego and hypocrisy, they practice [Ghor] terribly fierce penance not approved by scripture. 5 and Oppressively torture the group of bhootas constituting the body and molest Me too residing within their inner body i.e. self. Know them to be of demonic and wicked conviction and resolve. 6.

On food, sacrifices, penances and charitable donations

The food that becomes dear to all is also of three types. So are the sacrifices, penances and charitable donations. Hear their differences. 7.

Foods. Three types, categories

Satvic food

The foods that promote and augment life-span, Satva i.e. satvic intellect, strength, health and well being, happiness, joy and love, and which are savory, juicy, soft, oily, nourishing and agreeable [not causing allergy] are dear to saatvic persons. 8.

Raajsic food

The foods that are bitter, sour, saltish, very hot, pungent, spicy, rooksha i.e. hard and dry, creating burning, are dear to Raajas persons. They are the producers of disease, misery and grief. 9.

Taamsic food

That food which is improperly cooked, spoiled, insipid, taste-less, putrefying, bad smelling, stale, left-overs and impure is dear to Tamas people. 10.

Sacrifices

Three categories

Saatvic. Sacrifice that is performed in accordance with scriptures by persons not desiring the fruits thereof with the conviction that it must be performed: it is Saatvic. 11.

Raajsic. But oh, Arjuna! That which is performed keeping the mind on its fruits and in hypocrisy for show only, know that sacrifice to be Raajasic. 12.

Taamsic. The sacrifice performed without rites and rituals, without food-serving, without the mantras, without the Dakshina i.e. fees, and without faith is called Taamas [sacrifice]. 13.

Asrushtaannam is also interpreted as not producing food: Adakshinam is also interpreted as giving up something dear e.g. some bad habit anything substantial or not. Chhandogya upanishad 3:17." Austerity-penance, Uprightness, non-injury and truthfulness are said to be the gifts to be offered in Sacrifice.

Penances of body, speech and mind

After describing the Satvic, Raajasic and Taamasic sacrifices Bhagawaan now describes what are the penances of the body, speech and mind and when the same are Satvic, Raajsic and Taamsic.

Body Penances

The worship of and the homage to Gods, deities, twice-born Brahmins, Guru and the wise, purity, straightforwardness, non-violence and celibacy are said to be the body-penances [austerities] i.e. penances of the body. 14

Speech penances

The sentences i.e. words uttered which are truthful, pleasant dear and non-offending, beneficial and helpful, and Swaadhyaaya-practice i.e. regular study of scriptures are said to be the penance of the speech. 15. The Words must be truth, dear, sweet and beneficial to others.

What is Satya i.e. truth and its effect

Let us study it from our scriptures. Patanjal Yoga Sutra 2:36: says the effect of truth realization.37: *Satyapratishtaayaam Kriyaafalaashrayatvam //36//* Translation: Action becomes the shelter of the fruit on the firm fixation of the Truth.

Here action means thought, speech and action. A person who is firmly located in truth, his words will never utter a lie. False hood vanishes from their dictionary because he is the custodian of as-it-is knowledge. His words are unfailing. The fruits follow his speech. His words yield fruits and produce results. His thoughts and word fructify in physical existence. The words do not require any effort on his part to give fruits. Merely his words are enough to generate all the wealth of the world but they desire nothing for themselves. Loin-cloth is his riches and directions are his royal robes. If he blesses someone by saying, 'be happy; be rich; be a spiritual soul' then that happens without further action on the part of the yogi. Such is the power of their thoughts and words.

But remember their thoughts and the words are non-injurious. No body can become a Satya-sankalpa [whose thoughts materialize in physical existence] with lies and evil thoughts filling his mind. By the towering strength of truth-observance his inner organs become so clear and pure that through his speech only such talk comes forth which are going to happen but they hardly talk.

What is truth?

As-it-is knowledge of a thing is truth. To bring it in the use of the body is the truth of the body. To utter it by words is the truth of the speech. To bring it in the mind is the truth of the mind. Whatever must be done as enjoined by morals or law at a particular time by a particular man is truth for him i.e. duty is the truth; Ahinsaa is truth in all the tenses; and therefore whatever is correctly done to perpetrate Ahinsaa is truth. Hinsaa i.e. injuring is always Asatya. Shree Veda-Vyaasa defines SatyaTruth, 'the action of mind and speech according to the fact-as it-is' i.e. to speak by words and think by mind just as it is seen or heard or inferred.

Manu Bhagawaan says, *'Satyam Bruyaat Priyam Bruyaanna Bruyaata Satyamapriyam /'* meaning speak the truth, speak sweet, do not speak the truth that is not sweet i.e. speak the sweet truth but not which is bitter. Speak a truth that is pleasing and agreeable; never utter a truth which is even likely to hurt and injure some body. Avoid bitterness in talk and action.

To tell exactly as is heard or seen is called truth. To say Brahma is truth is truth. SarvaVedanta Siddhanta Sarasangraha.117-118.Swami Shankar.

For a yogi the highest form of truth is discriminative knowledge making the distinction between Aatmaa and non-Aatmaa: chetan-animate and inanimate-inert: pure-impure: holy and unholy: Permanent and the transient. Strictly speaking Social conduct and relations is not the subject only of speech but of duty-dharma too and for this reason truth and vow means and includes that every person to fully understand and performs his duties towards every creature wherever he is and whenever he acts.

Truth is only a transformed Ahinsaa. Social intercourse and dealing of truth does not take place only through speech as normally understood by common man but through the performance of one's duty because duty is nothing but truth. He alone is a truthful who performs his duty as-it-is in a given set of circumstances as prescribed by scriptures, morals and the Law of the land. This is well illustrated by the story of King Harishchandra who was the king of Ayodhyaa in 8th generation prior to Bhagawaan Rama. He was the great- great-great grand father of Rama but by the cruelty of destiny he had to leave his kingdom and his wife took service as a maid-servant along with her son and himself became the slave of the custodian of a cremation ground in another city. It was his duty to collect tax for cremating a corpse there. By evil stroke of destiny his son died of Serpent-bite and his penniless wife Taaraamati brought the corpse of the son Rohit for cremating. For the king Harishchandra it was a painful duty, as in duty-bound to ask the tax from his penniless wife. He kept aside his love for both and did not budge from his demand. He said, "Either pay the tax or take away the corpse." consider his condition. The corpse of his son was lying there for cremation but for want of money to pay the tax he was not allowing the cremation. He would have paid if he had the cash but his salary was daily food. He could have allowed the cremation without the tax but he was true to his duty and the master. This was the acid test of his truthfulness. He proved to be pure Gold and his name is immortal in Hindu culture. Every Hindu child in India is taught this story and is exhorted to tell the truth. Whether they tell the truth all the time or not is a different matter.

Some times even discerning persons thoughtlessly utter words which would hurt the ego of others with disastrous results. It is useful to take note of a small eye-opening incident of Mahaabhaarata. In Vaarnaavrata the capital town of the kingdom of Pandavaas, Mayadaanava had built a wonderful palace with places where water would be seen flowing in place of land and vice-versa. On the completion of Raajasuya sacrifice performed by king Yudhishtira, his cousin brother Duryodhana, the king of Hastinapura was out to see the palace and seeing him faltering from place to place Draupadi, the queen of Paandavaas said smilingly in a jest, 'Blind's son is also blind" Mahaabhaarat: Sabhaa Parva: 30:24. The father was certainly blind but not the son Duryodhana. Queen's utterance was patently false which injuriously hurt the feelings of Duryodhana and inflamed his ego and we know its consequence. An all out disastrous war killing all but five Pandavaas and Bhagawaan Shree Krishna out of 2.5 millions warriors assembled on the battlefield of Kurukshetra to fight against each other. Gita is sermon to fight this very war.

Above are the defining rules for a person who wants to be yogi in pursuit of Brahmahood. What about man in worldly life? Is he allowed some latitude in this matter? Keeping in mind various conditions, Bhagawaan Shree Krishna expounds, 'What is truth under varying conditions' in Mahaabhaarat: Karna Parva: 69: fully dealt in Introduction I.

Let us consider one incident in which Yudhisthira utters a lie on the advice of Krishna. Drona fights with all his might: Duryodhana believes that Pandavaas will retreat and run away but Karna is not under any illusion and says to Duryodhana. Pandavaas such as who have suffered poisoning them, effort to burn them and dyuta-gambling games etc. the affliction and much more than that who had suffered the Forest staying; will not forget the pangs: so they will prefer to die in the war than to accept defeat from those who showered these afflictions. Drona: 22:20.

Pandava army is terrified and distressed by the terrible fight of Drona and it was feared that if it continued like that half the army of Pandavaas would be destroyed. Under these conditions Krishna advises Yudhisthira that to tell the story of the death of son Ashvatthaamaa before Drona would not be a lie. Krishna says, "Hey, Yudhisthira! save us from Drona. At this juncture falsehood is superior to truth. If have to speak a lie for protecting life then one is not afflicted with sin of speaking a lie." Drona:22:47

Bhima kills elephant Ashvatthaamaa. Yudhisthira says, 'Ashvatthaamaa Hatah' loudly and adds in low tone, 'Hatah Kunjarah' and immediately the chariot of Yudhisthira which was four finger- breadth above the ground touched the ground.

Before this the chariot of Yudhisthira was remaining four fingers above the ground but from that moment on the horses of his chariot began to touch the ground. Drona 190:56.

Is Shree Krishna correct? Here we realize the power of truth: so a lie even if it be for protecting life remains a lie: but in life-destroying circumstances absolute truth is not useful so Krishna advises that for protecting life there is no sin committed in telling a lie. What Shree Krishna says is the truth of war policy to maintain and uphold Dharma and peace of the society but not absolute and pure truth. A Dharma which gives victory to Adharma ceases to be dharma and becomes out right Adharma. He asks to tell a lie to destroy a person who is helping wicked people to win the war. If one has to tell a lie to destroy a wicked person committing crimes he must tell a lie and the lie will truth under the conditions.

Whenever Arjuna fights mildly Krishna does not remain without inspiring Arjuna. When Arjuna is found to be lacking in enthusiasm in fighting with Ashvatthaamaa He says, "Do not be indifferent to the valor of Ashvatthaamaa thinking him to be guru-son. This is not the time to be indifferent. It is time for fighting. The only way is to fight with strength and ability. Karna 16:36.

Krishna's yard-stick for measuring truth and falsehood based on all pervasive Dharma are different from yoga system: These are dealt in Introduction I.

Krishna keeps in view the all pervasive meaning of Dharma and any dharma in conflict with that meaning is unacceptable to Krishna. It was not within the power of Pandavaas to conquer Bhishma or Drona. This was Dharma war and if Pandavaas lose this war it would be the defeat of Dharma and victory of Adharma. Krishna gives his consent and often actively assist in some Adhaarmic acts of killing Dhaarmic persons like Bhishma etc. so that Adharma may not succeed on extensive scale. Krishna says for the purpose of maintaining dharma kill even a dhaarmic person if he takes the side of Adharma.

In the matter of truth this much should be certainly kept in mind in initial stages: not to utter a lie or bitter and unpleasant truth: should not indulge in talks whereby unnecessary envy, malice and animosity will be generated between the persons: Should not back-bite: Do not give a promise which you cannot keep or do not intend to keep. Take every possible care to keep the promise if you make a one. It is a sin to lie and must not be uttered. If the bitter truth is uttered regarding any one there is a possibility of resentment, anger and revenge. You will not be benefited but are purchasing the possibility of future injury.

Now let us understand Swaadhyaaya

What is Swaadhyaaya?

Meaning as per Patanjal Yoga Sutra 2:44 is: 44: *Svaadhyaayaadishtadevataa Samprayogah //44//*

Translation

Family deity or the deity of one's choice is realized by the scripture-study and mantra Japa.

Ishta devataa normally means the family presiding deity because one and the same deity is usually worshipped in a family from generation to generation unless by a change in faith a different deity is installed in the family; therefore Ishta-devataa also means a deity of one's desire and choice. One who is engaged in Svaadhaaya have the sight of[sees]deities, sages and the accomplished yogis and they help in the yoga-path, so says Maharshi Vyaasa. Bhojavrutti says that by the maturing of the Swaadhyaaya of chanting-Japa of deity's mantra the deity physically comes in the presence of the devotee.

Mental Penances

Mental pleasantness, serenity, gentleness-tranquillity, silence, self-control, Bhava sanshuddhi i.e. purity of heart, feelings and emotions: these are said to be the penance of the mind. 16.

Saatvic Penance

These three kinds of penances performed with extreme faith by persons not desiring their fruits and Aatmaa-united are said to be Saatvic. 17.

One will find Krishna advising Dharma to Pandavaas at every step in their difficulties: Krishna finds Yudhisthir in sorrows even after acquiring kingdom and immeasurable wealth: Krishna advises: The evenness of Satva, Rajas and Tamas is the mark of well balanced mind. Two alphabets is the form of death and three alphabets is the form of eternal Brahma: Mama i.e. mineness is death and Na Mama i.e. not-mine i.e. renunciation of mineness is eternal Brahma. Aashvameghic 13:. At the root of all worldly actions is desire Kaamanaa. The obstruction of this Kaamanaa i.e. desire is Dharma which is the root of emancipation. We have to fight with our own mind where nothing is useful except our own will power.

Raajsic Penance

That penance which is performed in hypocrisy only for praise, honor and adoration, is unsteady and transient [in this world] and is said to be Raajasic [penance]. 18.

Taamsic Penance

That penance performed in obstinate stupidity causing pain to himself or for causing ruinous injury to others is said to be Taamas [penance]. 19.

Dana i.e. Charitable gifts

Saatvic Dana

Thing given in charity as a matter of duty at a proper time and place to a worthy person who cannot return the obligation that Dana is said to be saatvic. 20.

Raajsic Dana

That Dana which is given with a desire for the return, or with a desire for its fruits, and again causing distress is said to be Raajas Dana. 21.

Taamsic Dana

And that Dana which is made at an improper place and time to unfit person without respect and in contempt is said to be Taamsic. 22.

The word used is Pariklishtam: with Klesha i.e. either grudgingly or in tone causing distress to the receiver or those who are present. Given in manner which causes distress to the giver or receiver or to those present or all of them.

Why AUM TAT SAT is uttered by Brahma believers at the beginning of every activity?

AUM TAT SAT thus in three ways Brahma is indicated and remembered. By it in the beginning were created the Brahmaa [Brahmins ?], Vedas and sacrifices. 23.

In most of the commentaries Braahmanaah has been understood as the Brahmin class of Hindu community. Brahmaa is more appropriate meaning because Brahmaa is the author of Vedas and of Sacrifices: he created the rest of the universe by sacrifices as per chapter 3.

AUM. Therefore Brahma-believers carry out the acts of sacrifice, Dana, and penance as prescribed and enjoined always with the prior utterance of AUM. 24. and Tat,

TAT. and pronouncing Tat [meaning Brahma is all in all] Emancipation-desirers carry on the various acts of sacrifices and penances and also the acts of Dana [alms and charities] without desiring for their fruits. 25. and SAT

SAT. The word SAT is utilized to mean reality i.e. 'IS'ness and goodness, and oh, Partha! the word 'Sat' is also used for praiseworthy acts and deeds. 26.

The firmness and the faith in the acts of sacrifice, penance and Dana is called SAT: And the acts to carry out the above is also called SAT. 27.

Brahma-believers begin all their activity uttering loudly or mentally AUM TAT SAT. The purpose of utterance is explained in the above couplets.

What is ASAT?

Oh, Arjuna! oblated substance, Dana given, penance performed and whatever done [for the above purposes] without faith is called 'ASAT': It counts for nothing here and on death. 28.

AUM TAT SAT: Thus it is the seventeenth chapter, named Three divisions of Faith in Shree Krishna-Arjuna dialogue on Brahma-knowledge yoga-scripture Shreemad-Bhagavad Gita Upanishad.

CHAPTER : 18

Moksha-Sanyaas Yoga i.e. Emancipation-Renunciation Yoga

It is the concluding chapter recapitulating in nut-shell the fruitive actions and selfless action: renunciation and detachment: Action, inaction and non-action, How best to do actions so that they do not bind. What is the nature and duty of Brahmin, Kshatriya, Vaishya and Shudra i.e. Learned-law giver, fighter-warrior-protector, agriculture-manufacturer-trader and finally laborer. It lays down that performing one's duty selflessly whether paying or not though inferior to others' is emancipative but alien dharma is dangerous. It says death in execution of one's dharma is superior to better-performed alien dharma.

In the final round of the sermon Bhagawaan pronounces the royal road to emancipation. He says to Arjuna, "Discard and throw away all Dharmas, come to me as thy sole refuge, I will emancipate you from all sins, don't worry." Arjuna was afraid of committing sins and their effects. Bhagawaan assures him of salvation from all sins if he goes to Him as his sole refuge renouncing all Dharmas without buts and ifs.

Let us turn to the text of Gita

Arjuna spoke

Oh, Mighty-handed! Oh, Hrishikesha [inner-knower]! Oh, Keshi-killer! I desire to know separately and distinctly the principles and essence of Sanyaas and Tyaaga. 1.

Shree Bhagawaan spoke : What is Sanyaas?

Renunciation or not-doing of fruit-desired actions is known

to be Sanyaas by pundits: Learned-wise [Shrewd] one calls the abandonment of fruits of all actions to be Tyaaga.2. Some intellectuals say thus that actions being faulty and evil are fit to be abandoned and the rest say that the acts of sacrifice, Daan and penance are not fit to be abandoned. 3.

What is Tyaaga?

Oh, Bharatasattam ! hear my decision and judgment in the matter of Tyaaga, oh, tiger man! that Tyaaga is said to be of three types. 4. Abandonment of fruits is Tyaaga.

What acts should not be discarded ? but should be performed with detachment to its fruits.

Acts of sacrifice, alms and charitable donations as well as penances are not fit to be discarded but should be done: [because] Sacrifice, alms and charitable donations as well as penances are purifiers and holifiers of even the shrewd and intelligent. 5.

But these acts and other duteous acts should be done as a matter of duty renouncing attachment and their fruits: oh, Paartha! such is my decisive best opinion and judgment 6.

Taamas Tyaaga. It is not fit and proper to discard and abandon the scripture-prescribed acts. Their renouncement in Moha, fascination and ignorance is said to be Taamas [Tyaaga]. 7.

Raajas Tyaaga. He, whoever, believing actions to be misery abandons action for fear of bodily distress, does not get the fruits of that Raajas-Tyaaga even on doing it. 8.

Saatvic Tyaaga. Oh, Arjuna! Those prescribed acts done with the belief that they ought to be performed and are done discarding the attachment and desire for the fruit, that Tyaaga is opined to be Saatvic. 9.

Who is a real Tyaagi?

Learned and wise [Tyaagi] abandoner united with Satva guna, free from doubts, does not hate nor disdain misery-producing acts and does not become attached to happiness producing acts. 10.

Because it is not possible for the embodied one to abandon all actions without leaving a trace, therefore one who is the renouncer of fruits of actions, he alone is Tyaagi, so it is said. 11.

Three kinds of fruits of actions for the non-renouncer

Ishta, Anishta and Mishra i.e. desirable, undesirable and mixed, are the three types of fruits of the acts that accrue to the non-renouncer of fruits after death but never to the Sanyaasi i.e. who renounces the fruits of the actions. 12. Ishta, Anishta and mixed can also be rendered as good, bad and mixed or agreeable, disagreeable and mixed, or pleasant, unpleasant and mixed, or acceptable, unacceptable and mixed, or likable, unlikable and mixed. But desirable etc. is more apt.

Five causes working in the execution of every Act

Oh, mighty-handed! Hear from Me the five causes as per Saamkhya [system] working in the execution of every act. 13.

Adhishtaana, Kartaa i.e. Doer, Karan, Various activities and Daiva is the fifth. 14.

Adhishtaana means time-space and every thing else other than you out side your body.

Kartaa means body dweller i.e. Purusha as soul

Karan means inner organs ego, chitta, mind and intellect: and five sense organs and five action organs.

Activities i.e. coming, going, doing, thinking, etc. etc.

Daiva: the unseen destiny karmas which bring all these together.

Whatever actions prescribed or otherwise [right or wrong] a person begins with mind, speech and body: these five are their causes. 15.

Such being the case i.e. despite the presence of five causes the person of untrained intellect sees Aatmaa as the doer: that [Durmati] perverse-intellected does not see. 16.

In Saamkhya doctrine Purusha is always inactive and Prakruti is active: Purusha alleges the activity of Prakruti in himself and vicariously enjoys the world.

Under what kind of mental state one is not bound by his actions. couplet:17.

One who has no ego of 'I am the doer' and whose intellect is unaffected i.e. remains unaffected [by action] neither destroys nor is bound even if he destroys all these people or [worlds]. 17.

This state is the state of Brahma or Paramaatmaa who can do no wrong. Shree Krishna has said, 'I am not the doer nor do the karmas affect me.'

Who inspires the action?

Knower, Knowledge and the Object-to-be-known are the three inspirers of karma-action and doer, organs and the activity these three constitute the action-group i.e. group by which karma activity is carried out. 18.

Three types of Knowers, Karmas and Doers

Knowledge, Karma and Doer each is of three types by reason of different gunas [waves] composing it as per the gunas of Saamkhya system, hear them also as they are. 19.

Three types of knowledge: Saatvic, Raajsic and Taamsic

Saatvic. Know that knowledge to be Saatvic by which one sees undiminishing, only one and the same undivided Being in all separate bhootas i.e. creatures. 20.

Raajsic. The knowledge which knows various kinds of many entities in all bhootas to be separate and distinct: know that knowledge to be Raajsic. 21.

Raajasic knowledge does not recognize the unity of Aatmaa in all beings: It considers that each has an entity which is distinct and separate from the rest. These people recognize soul but not Aatmaa.

Taamsic. And that [knowledge] which is fascinated in and clings completely to a single thing i.e. body believing it to be all-in-all without concern for cause or reason, and which misses the real essence and is meager: such knowledge is Taamsic. 22.

Three types of acts: Saatvic, Raajasic and Taamsic

Saatvic. That prescribed act-karma done without love or hate, without attachment and ego by a non-desirer of fruits: that is called Saatvic act: 23.

Saatvic acts are good and beneficial to all.

Raajsic. But those acts done by the fruit-desirer or with ego and pride and with great labour and effort: that is called Raajasic. 24.

Taamsic. Those acts-karmas which are begun without any regard to or thinking about the consequences and results, loss, injury and violence [to others or himself] and of one's strength and capacity: that is called Taamsic. 25.

Three types of doers or actors: Saatvic, Raajsic and Taamsic

Saatvic. A doer who is free from attachment, speaks not with ego and pride, unperturbed and unaffected in success and failure: has patience, courage, firmness and enthusiasm is said to be Saatvic. 26.

Raajsic. A doer who is [Raagi] fascinated and passionate, craver of the fruits of actions, greedy, violent-injury-inflictor, impure, unholy and affected by joy and sorrow is said to be Raajsic. 27.

Taamsic. A doer who is Ayuktah i.e. ununited and not-single minded, Praakruta i.e. rustic and uncultured, Stabdha i.e. stubborn and without humility, rogue and deceitful, ungrateful, woe-begone, despondent and idle and procrastinator is said to be Taamsic. 28.

Three types of Intellect and Dhruti

Oh, Arjuna! Hear separately without any thing being left the three categories of Intellect and Dhruti i.e. Steadiness and will in consequence of [three] Gunas. 29.

Saatvic. The intellect which knows in essence and Tattva activity and retirement from activity, actions to be done and not to be done, what to-be-feared and not-to-be-feared, bondage and emancipation, that is Saatvic. 30.

Raajsic. Oh, Partha! that intellect which knows Dharma and Non-dharma as they really are and What must be done and what must not be done not as they really are, is said to be Raajsic. 31.

In these matters of dharma and Adharma the intellect holds erroneous, mistaken and incorrect views.

Taamsic. Oh, Arjuna! The intellect wrapped by Tamo guna i.e. ignorance believes Adharma to be dharma and every subject and thing in a wrong and reverse way, that intellect is Taamasic.32.

Saatvic Dhruti. Oh, Partha! the unadulterated Dhruti i.e. patience and steadiness acquired through yoga technic of contemplation by which one carries on the activities of mind, Praan and organs, that Dhruti is Saatvic. 33.

Raajsic Dhruti. Again, Oh, Partha! that patience and steadiness by which a person with attachment and a desire for the fruits of actions firmly holds dharma, passions i.e. sense-pleasures and wealth, that Dhruti is said to be Raajasic. 34.

Taamsic Dhruti. Oh, Partha! that patience by which the person of wicked intellect does not abandon sleep, dreaming, fear, sorrow, grief and remorse as well as self-conceit and arrogance, that Dhruti is called Taamsic. 35.

Three kinds of Happiness

Oh, Best Bharat! hear from Me the categories of happiness wherein one plays by practice and ends the miseries. 36.

Saatvic. The [happiness] which is born of Aatmic-intellect [Aatmic-knowledge] which is initially [felt] like poison but nectar-like in the end-result, that happiness is said to be Saatvic. 37.

Raajsic. The happiness [generated] from the contact of the sense-organs with the sense-objects in nectar-like in the beginning but poison-like in the end-result, that is called Raajsic. 38.

Taamsic. The happiness generated from sleep, idleness and arrogance and which stupefies and deludes the self during the enjoyment and in the end-result, That is said to be Taamsic. 39.

This happiness is stupefying and deluding from the beginning till the end i.e. all along.

Nothing is free from three gunas of Prakruti

There exist nothing either on the earth or in the paradise or amongst the gods-deities and also any other thing free from these three gunas born of Prakruti. 40.

Shree Krishna emphatically states that the entire animate and inanimate universe is the product of three gunas of prakruti only i.e. Short, Medium and Long waves of Prakruti..

He repeats and reiterates that three gunas i.e. short, medium and long waves of Vibrating Brahma i.e., Prakruti are the sole causes of the universe and the activity of all beings. Every thing is composed by the combination of these three waves in varying proportions in various ranges. Waves project the illusion of space and solidity whirling in it in a chronology which we call time-regularity.

The acts of Four Varnas differ: Why?

Oh, Parantap Arjuna! The acts of Brahmins, Kshatriya, Vaishya and Shudra are different and separate because of the qualities born of the innate nature. [of their innate nature born of Gunas i.e. waves. 41.

Of Brahmins. Serenity, self-control, Penance, forgiveness and forbearance, Uprightness, knowledge, Vijyaan-science, faith and trust in almighty, these are the natural karmas-acts of the Brahmins, or the acts of the Brahmins born of innate nature.42.

Of Kshatriyas. Bravery and heroism, Teja i.e. spiritedness

and power, courage and patience, shrewdness and resourcefulness, not-to-retire from battle, Daan i.e. alms-giving and charitable donations, and Ishvar-bhaava i.e. are the natural karmas and acts of Kshatriya 43.

Ishvarbhava: to exercise authority over the subjects and protect the subjects and selflessly work for them.

Of Vaishyas. Agriculture, dairy-farming and cow-protection, commerce and industry are the natural acts of the Vaishyas;

Of Shudras. While service and labour are the natural acts of Shudras. 44.

Who gains Siddhi i.e., Supreme State?

Person engrossed in his natural acts gains supreme siddhi i.e. supreme state: Now hear, in what manner, one having faith in one's karmas-acts of own Dharma gains siddhi. 45.

By Abhyarching Him i.e. worshipping Him from whom bhootas-creatures arise, by whom this whole is pervaded and permeated with one's nature-born acts person gains siddhis i.e. supreme state. 46.

Who does not earn sin by acting? One's own Dharma i.e. one's nature-born acts though devoid of benefits is superior to alien dharma i.e. others' natural acts though done well because doing acts prescribed by one's innate nature, man does not earn sins. 47.

Oh, Kaunteya! one should not abandon one's natural acts though faulty and defective because all beginnings [act-karmas] are enveloped by faults and defects as fire by smoke. 48.

Every act whether prescribed or not has some fault and defect. There is no action that is faultless and therefore one should do acts dictated by his own innate nature.

Extreme Limit of Taatvic knowledge

One whose intellect is unattached everywhere, has realized Aatmaa, and is devoid of desires attains Supreme

Naishkarmya siddhi through Sanyaas i.e. supreme inactivity through the renunciation of fruits. 49. Therefore, Oh, Arjuna! know from Me in nutshell the manner in which that siddhi-attained person gains Brahma which gain is the extreme-end faith of knowledge [Tattvic-knowledge] i.e. extreme limit of Taatvic knowledge. 50.

Who is eligible for Brahmahood?

United with very pure intellect, having controlled the self with courage and patience, discarding the word etc. the vishays, and discarding the Raag-Dwesh i.e. love and envy, 51 and dweller in solitude and lonely place, Moderate-abstemious eater, regulator of speech, mind and body, always devoted to and engaged in meditation, and settled in detachment, 52 and Discarding ego-pride, power and strength [show of strength], arrogance, passion, anger and hoarding, without mineness-thineness and tranquil person is believed to be eligible for attaining Brahmahood. 53.

Who gains supreme Bhakti of Bhagawaan and with what result?

Brahma-realized delighted Aatmaa neither grieves nor desires, [neither worries nor craves] being even to all creatures [being of the same attitude to wards all creatures] gains my supreme Bhakti i.e. devotion. 54.

By and with Bhakti-devotion, he knows me well Tattvically [in essence and by Tattvas] what and who I am as I am and on knowing Me in Tattva and in essence merges in Me immediately thereafter. 55.

Result of action with total refuge in Bhagawaan. Result on not heeding to this advice.

Even one, who always remaining in my refuge does all acts attains to eternal undiminishing state by my grace. 56. Therefore mentally surrendering all acts to Me, Matparah i.e. Me-goaled and Me-suffused, taking refuge of Buddhi-yoga i.e. yoga-of-even intellect, be always of Me-chitta. 57.

Concentrating thus your chitta in Me and with my grace, you shall cross and swim over all difficulties and obstacles but if you do not listen [heed to my advice] out of ego and pride you shall perish: you shall fall from the path of kalyaan. 58.

Man is bound by his nature

Under the shelter of ego, if you believe 'I shall not fight' then vain and futile is your resolve because [your] innate nature shall impel, propel and compel [you to fight]: 59.

Oh, Arjuna! being bound hand and foot by acts born of your nature You will helplessly do and carry out the very karmas-acts which you do not desire to do out of Moha i.e. fascination and delusion. 60. Because, Oh, Arjuna! Ishvar-Paramaatmaa resides in the region of the heart of all creatures and by his Maayaa moves, revolves and swirls all creatures as mounted on a machine. 61.

The nature of Arjuna was Kshatriya Dharma and it is this dharma that will forcibly activate Arjuna to rise against Adharma and fight. He would be helpless against the urge of this dharma. Bhagawaan says to Arjuna, "You shall not be able to resist the urge to fight because of your warrior nature of fighting against all evils and therefore get up and fight in consonance with your inborn and nurtured nature. It is not your desire that will compel you to act but your nature that will. Your nature will prevail over desire."

Sovereign Advice to go in the shelter and refuge of Bhagawaan

Oh, Bharat! go under his [Parameshvar's] shelter and refuge with all your Bhaavas i.e. with all your heart and soul [because] by his grace [you] shall attain eternal place and state of supreme peace. 62.

I have told you thus this knowledge, secret of all secrets, act as you please after considering it fully from all angles 63.

Bhagawaan says clearly that in matter of actions choice rests with the actor. He does not order nor force them to act.

But as is his duty he lays down thread bare before us the circumstances and conditions governing the actions. It is then the duty of the actor to coolly consider the facts from all angles including the scriptures and decide his course of action under the circumstances and act with firm resolve without worrying for the out come of the action leaving it to Almighty to see to it. Our duty ends with the action and the duty of Ishvar to give fruits begins. Why should we worry about his duties? Remember we may fail in our duties but He never fails in his duties nor does his laws forgive our failures.

Hear, again my supreme words, secret of secrets, I tell you these beneficial words because you are firmly dear to me. 64.

Finally Advises A very simple rule of Action in couplets 65-66.

Oh, Arjuna! be of Me-suffused mind, be my worshipper, be my Bhakt i.e. devotee and do prostration before Me: [doing thus] you will attain only Me. I tell you this truth on oath as you are dear to Me. 65.

Discard and throw away all Dharmas, all duteous-acts and come and take refuge and asylum in Me alone. I will free you from all sins: worry not. 66.

Having expounded the entire realm of Dharma and actions to maintain Dharma and how to carry them out so that they may not bind, Shree Bhagawaan thought that it may be difficult for some people to digest what was expounded so he laid down a very simple rule of action: He says, "Do not bother about dharma and non-dharma just do one thing. Come to my refuge: Take shelter in Me alone. Fully and completely surrender to Me without ifs and buts and act in whatever manner you like whether good or bad or mixed: I will salvage you from all sins." Remember it is difficult to go under his shelter in toto. It cannot become a fact unless you totally rub out your ego, your I-ness in toto. Try it and you will soon find yourself telling 'I did this and that.' The moment the thought of I-ness stirs you are out of his refuge, his shelter. You cease to have been surrendered. Seemingly simple rule is most difficult to be observed but there is no harm in trying it. Do not loose heart and stop. Renew your resolve every time you fail and some day you will find that you have really surrendered for all times thereafter.

You should never tell this [knowledge] to one without penance: and to a non-devotee neither to one who does not desire to hear nor serve and to one who slanders me. 67.

One, who will expound and sermonize this supreme secret to my devotees that one gaining supreme devotion in me will, no doubt, attain me. 68.

None amongst men on earth is a doer of more dear things than this one and none is going to be more dear to Me than him. 69.

And one who will study this dhaarmic discourse of ours then I am being worshipped through that knowledge-sacrifice: that is my opinion and belief. 70.

Again one who will hear with faith and without scorning [view] this, even he becoming free from sins shall attain the best region of meritorious people. 71.

Krishna does not ask whether Arjuna acquired knowledge but asks whether his Moha has perished or not? Why? Because Knowledge cannot be sermonized.

I hope, Oh, Partha! you must have heard this with single-pointed chitta [mind]? have you not? Oh, Dhananjay! I hope that your ignorance-generated Moha [delusion and illusion] must have perished. has it not? 72.

Arjuna spoke

Oh, Achyuta, Krishna! By your grace my Moha i.e. delusion and illusion has perished: I have regained my previous state of understanding: I have come to self: I am steady with doubts gone and will act as you direct i.e. will put your words into action. 73.

Arjuna gives a receipt that his Moha has vanished and has regained his composure. He does not say that he got Knowledge..

Sanjay spoke at the conclusion of the dialogue

Thus I have heard this wonderful and hair-thrilling discourse of Vaasudeva [Shree Krishna] and Mahaatmaa Arjuna. 74.

By the favour and grace of Shree Vyaasa I have directly heard this supreme secret of yoga as told by Yogeshvar Shree Krishna himself. 75.

Oh, King! I become delighted repeatedly by remembering again and again this wonderful and Punyaful dialogue of Shree Keshava and Arjuna. 76.

And Oh, King! recalling to memory again and again that wonderful universal form of Shree Hari, I become highly surprised and become delighted repeatedly. 77.

Where there is Yogeshvar Shree Krishna and where there is archer Arjuna, only there is wealth, victory, Bhooti i.e. divine powers and glories as well as stable Niti i.e. correct code of conduct: thus is my understanding. 78.

AUM TAT SAT: Thus it is the eighteenth chapter, named Moksha-Sanyaas Yoga i.e. Emancipation-detachment yoga in Shree Krishna-Arjuna dialogue on Brahma-knowledge yoga-scripture Shreemad-Bhagavad Gita Upanishad.

NOTE: NORMAL EFFECTS OF THE SERMONS

Gita is a sermon to fight tooth and nail against Adharma. The relationship of elders, gurus, relatives, kith and kin should be jettisoned in toto in fighting against Adharma. If these people are the criminals, culprits and offenders fight them to the finish. Question of mercy is out of question if peace and prosperity of all concerned and the society is to be maintained. Arjuna suffered from this Moha. His very relatives were the criminals and his gurus and grandfather were on the side of the relatives ready to sacrifice their lives for these criminals. Arjuna shudders to kill these horde of relatives out of compassion and for the fear of committing sin by killing them. Gita is told to dispel this Moha. At the end of the sermon in couplet 18:73 Arjuna does say in reply that his Moha had vanished and he would do as directed by Krishna. But Is it possible to rub out Moha so easily by hearing a sermon once or twice? No: It requires repetition, insistence and Practice. Arjuna's love for Grand father Bhishma and elders had not diminished much less perished. It was covered by advice in the manner of live coal by ash.

This can be judged from his mild fighting with Bhishma during war and Krishna breaking his vow not to take to arms. *Ayudhyamanh Sangraame Nyastashasro Ahamekatah:* Udyog 7:17. One not taking part in the war and secondly with a decision not to take weapon. He jumps twice from the chariot and runs to kill Bhishma as a protest against Arjuna's mild fighting with Bhishma. It is like this:

Paandu army shows extreme heroism on the battle field and Duryodhan complains to Bhishma who replies: *"Ajeyaah Pandvaaa Yudhhe Devairapi Savaasavaih: Yattum Shakyam Mayaa Kartum:* Pandavas can not be won in war even by devas even so I will do what I can do." Bhishma 58: 42. Bhishma shows fierce heroism and ferociously assaults Paandu army which was retreating helter-skelter in the face of Krishna and Arjuna. Arjuna is waging the war for victory and blazon heroism even so he is not fighting with all his heart and mind. Krishna realizes that Moha has not yet fully vanished and for the first time He becomes active as warrior and tells Arjuna, "Hey, Paartha! The time which we had desired has come". Bhishma 59:42. Krishna further says, "Oh, tiger-man! You strike now, otherwise becoming subject to Moha, you will not be able to do anything." Bhishma: 59:43.

It seems dejection and despair of Arjuna is not dispelled even after hearing Gita. Information on Knowledge is not important in life: Bhagawaan is important: Bhagawaan himself may sermon knowledge but its capacity is limited. Bhagawaan may sermon but the importance is teaching duties by and through action: This stage of Krishna becoming active in war teaches the second stage after Gita sermon. Krishna is angry because Arjuna is unable to put in practice the knowledge even after hearing it from Him. Krishna realizes that Arjuna is under the illusion that 'even on the battle field the Gaurava i.e. greatness, fame and dignity of Bhishma should be protected:' Bhishma 59:73. He does not know his duty as a Kshatriya. All His talks on duty and non-duty has gone in vain. Arjuna carries on as before even after these words. Krishna realizes that his sermon had no meaning. Army was speedily retreating and Saatyaki was explaining not to run away. Seeing this Krishna looses his temper and tells Saatyaki in anger: 'Let them who are running run away and let them who are steady but desire to run away, run away: Bhishma 56:84. Now I alone am sufficient. I am enough for them all." It should be remembered that Krishna is well known as an eternal Dharma-protector. In this war he has promised that he will not take up arms as his personal dharma. But seeing Arjuna fighting mildly His anger left the limit. He throws away the reins of the horses:

Mahatma Vaasudeva threw away the reins of the horses, and taking the Chakra, sharp like thousand Vajras and hot like the sun in his hand jumped from the chariot and advanced towards Bhishma. Bhishma 59:89.

This is a rare scene of Mahaabhaarat war. Moment before fierce war was raging. Bhishma was annihilating the Pandava army which was retreating. Now Krishna is rushing towards Bhishma with a Chakra in his hand. There is not an iota of doubt in any body's mind as to who Krishna is? Bhishma is not deluded but making the sound of his bowstring prays in roaring words: "Hey, Devesh! Hey, Jagannivaasa! Hey Yaadava! Hey, Chakrapaani!, I bow to you, You are the master of the world, throwing me off the chariot, kill me. Killed by you, Oh, Krishna I will have Shreya in this as well as in the next world." Bhishma 59:97-98.

Imagine this entire scenario. Arjuna was mildly fighting against the ferocious attacks of Bhishma. His army was running away. At this Krishna's anger knows no bound. Arjuna realizes that Krishna has discarded his vow and was running with the Chakra in his hand. It is a complex situation. Krishna is dharma-protector and so he in fighting without weapons on the side of Dharma but for the protection of Dharma he is not afraid to discard his individual dharma . The protection of dharma and destruction of Adharma in Bharat is the main theme of this war. Not to take upon weapons is the individual dharma of Krishna as it was his promise and vow. Krishna takes weapon in breach of his individual dharma but for protecting the Dharma of whole Bhaaratvarsha. If Krishna kills Bhishma it was the moment of greatness for Bhishma. Pandava would win but at the insolvency of their well known valor in the peoples' court and that too at the expense of Krishna's individual Dharma. In a moment Arjuna realizes the perilous situation and runs after Krishna and catches hold of Krishna's legs. Krishna is in anger. Arjuna is unable to estop Krishna and is dragged ten paces like a fallen tree in a typhoon when he is able to stop and tells Krishna, "Quieten your wrath I will fulfill my vow to kill Bhishma." Bhishma 59:101.

How perfect must have been the desire of Krishna to protect the Dharma which impelled Him to discard his individual Dharma? And how intense must have been the desire of Arjuna to protect the individual Dharma of Krishna that he prefers to be dragged for ten paces like a tree in a typhoon. Arjuna tried to protect the individual Dharma of Krishna and save all from the infamy of their bankruptcy of valour.

Arjuna is not out of dejection which peeps out at every opportunity: At the condolence meeting on the death of Arjuna's son Iraavan by Naagkanyaa Ulupi, Arjuna tells Krishna, " Oh Best man! this abominable act is being done for wealth. Hate to that wealth for which the Jyaati destruction is being carried on. It is better to die wealthless. Wealth is no better than Jyaati destruction. By destroying the Jyaati group, Oh, Krishna! What are we going to acquire? Here the dejection is not for the death of his son but for the Jyaati-destruction. Bhishma 96:5-6.

War proceeds. Bhishma is numerically reducing the army of Paandu day by day and Krishna's surprise was that yet Arjuna was fighting mildly. Krishna had said only two days back: 'hey, lion- man! You strike if you are not subject to Moha'. Arjuna had reiterated his vow only two days back. Again Bhishma is fighting with increased vigor under the pressure of Duryodhana's censuring allegations. Even then Arjuna is going mildly as usual. Krishna again tells Arjuna, 'Hey, lion-man Strike here and now'. Arjuna tearing away his hypocrisy says: which one is the good Karma [Sukrut] of the two: to gain the kingdom more censurable than hell by killing people not fit to be killed or to suffer by remaining in Jungle and then quietly adds 'Take the horses where Bhishma is and I will do as you order.' Bhishma 106:38-39.

Despite this assurance Krishna sees that Arjuna is carrying on mild war. Once again Krishna discarding the reins runs raising his arms as weapons. Atmosphere is tense with the impression that now Bhishma will be finished. Bhishma welcoming the situation prays: "Hey, Saatvashreshta! In this great war killing me to day throw me on the ground: My shreya will happen if I am killed by you, Hey, Deva!." Bhishma 106:65.

The same condition is repeated as in the first instance and now Arjuna says, "By the vow of Weapons, truth and Satkarma I assure you that the burden of killing Grandfather is on me." Bhishma 106:73.

On the ninth day of the battle Arjuna fights with all his might but Bhishma is not killed. All meet at the night in the camp and Krishna tells Yudhishtir taunting Arjuna that, "You order me once and see, 'I will kill heroic Bhishma in the face of Kauravas If Arjuna is not desirous of killing [Bhishma].' " Bhishma 107: 29. Krishna now openly told the assembly which he was till then telling Arjuna alone that Arjuna is not desirous of killing Bhishma.

Krishna further says, "Your Brother is my friend, relative and pupil. I will give for him even my flesh if it need be.

Bhishma 107:33. In the same breath he further tells, "If Arjuna cannot do what he ought to do then I must complete that work, there is no doubt." Bhishma 107:37

Bhishma has already decided to die on the tenth day and shows the way to kill him. This condition again puts family loving Arjuna in a despair state. How can he kill him in whose lap he had played as a grandchild? and Arjuna speaks decisively these words, "Let him destroy my army but I will not fight with that one with mighty mind whether there is my victory or death," and then quietly adds, *"Katham Vaa Krishna Manyase.* Or What do you think, Krishna?" Bhishma 107:95. You will remember till this time Krishna has not talked in terms of authority but now he tells. "You have already taken a vow to kill Bhishma and now I will see how you do not kill. You are stable in Kshaatra dharma. There is no alternative but to kill." Bhishma 107:96.

This shows that Bhagawaan gets the things done even forcibly if you have decided it once and if it is in the interest of the world as a whole.

The mild manner in which Arjuna fought with his Grand father Bhishma and Guru people tells us in no uncertain terms that to mentally discard the worldly love for objects and relatives and be detached is extremely difficult and needs tenacious efforts. It needs constant struggle and vigil. It is for this reason we are asked to join Sat-Sangs and read repeatedly the scriptures till we are irretrievably detached mentally from the love for the worldly objects. Best method is, 'Unconditionally Surrender to Him whole heartedly.' This is the easiest solution for all who desire to live as Jeevan- Mukta without much effort with the greatest advantage that It is free from every danger.

AUM TAT SAT.

INDEX

S